D1564613

GUODIAN

GUODIAN

The Newly Discovered Seeds
of Chinese Religious
and Political Philosophy

KENNETH W. HOLLOWAY

OXFORD
UNIVERSITY PRESS
2009

OXFORD

UNIVERSITY PRESS

Oxford University Press, Inc., publishes works that further
Oxford University's objective of excellence
in research, scholarship, and education.

Oxford New York
Auckland Cape Town Dar es Salaam Hong Kong Karachi
Kuala Lumpur Madrid Melbourne Mexico City Nairobi
New Delhi Shanghai Taipei Toronto

With offices in
Argentina Austria Brazil Chile Czech Republic France Greece
Guatemala Hungary Italy Japan Poland Portugal Singapore
South Korea Switzerland Thailand Turkey Ukraine Vietnam

Copyright © 2009 by Oxford University Press, Inc.

Published by Oxford University Press, Inc.
198 Madison Avenue, New York, New York 10016
www.oup.com

Oxford is a registered trademark of Oxford University Press

Library of Congress Cataloging-in-Publication Data
Holloway, Kenneth W., 1971–
Guodian : the newly discovered seeds of Chinese religious and political
philosophy / Kenneth W. Holloway.
  p. cm.
Includes bibliographical references and index.
ISBN 978-0-19-537145-1
1. Manuscripts, Chinese—China—Jingmen Shi. 2. Philosophy, Chinese.
3. Philosophy and religion—China. I. Title. II. Title: Newly discovered
seeds of Chinese religious and political philosophy.
Z6605.C5H66 2009
091—dc22   2008021581

9 8 7 6 5 4 3 2 1
Printed in the United States of America
on acid-free paper

In loving memory of my mother,
Dr. Caroline Holloway Lynn

Preface

ONE MIGHT EXPECT A SMALL village named Guodian to have around twenty houses, a post office, and a general store—perhaps a Chinese version of a Norman Rockwell painting. Actually, the village is quite different. It is a cluster of roughly five houses at the dead end of a narrow dirt road surrounded by rice paddies. One house has a traditional walled courtyard, while the others are of a design that is more recent, but certainly not modern. Important necessities such as electricity do not appear in short supply, but real luxuries are scarce. This is not where you would expect to find one of the most important archaeological discoveries of the twentieth century.

My journey to the site began in the summer of 1995, when I took time off from my graduate studies at the University of Pennsylvania to spend a year reading classical Chinese with Yang You-wei, a retired professor from Taiwan Normal University. His enthusiasm for teaching is legendary, and I left with a strong desire to write a Ph.D. dissertation on the *Analects* of Confucius. The following year, I studied with an early student of Professor Yang's, Roger Ames of the University of Hawaii, and took part in his seminar that was a prelude to his *Analects* translation. Upon my return to Penn, Paul Goldin became my Ph.D. advisor. I suddenly found it difficult to formulate a dissertation proposal that would make an original contribution to scholarship on the *Analects,* a text that has been analyzed by countless great minds over the past two millennia.

As luck would have it, soon after I completed my comprehensive exams, the Guodian texts were published. In hindsight, none of these events could have been planned more perfectly. However, I could not have accomplished this without the help of numerous people. Professor Zhang Guangda, formerly of Peking University, was immensely helpful during the entire course of the project and lent insight into the structure of the central text of my project, "The Five Aspects of Conduct." I am of course deeply indebted to Paul Goldin and my secondary dissertation readers, Victor Mair and Michael Puett. In addition, the following read and provided valuable comments on portions of my work: Steven Heine, Owen Lock, Robin Yates, Beno Lowe, and Peter Tobia.

Early in my writing stage, I was fortunate to gain important feedback from my presentations at several Warring States Working Group meetings organized by Bruce and Taeko Brooks. In July 2000, Edward Shaughnessy and Donald Harper invited several renowned scholars to conduct a workshop on excavated manuscripts at the University of Chicago for ten North American graduate students. Having the opportunity to learn from Qiu Xigui, Zhou Feng-wu, Lin Sue-ching, and Wang Bo was of great benefit to my understanding of Guodian. Professor Xu Shaohua of Wuhan University generously invited me to the International Conference on New Discoveries of Chu Bamboo Strips in June 2006. It was only then that I had a chance to travel to Guodian and see its priceless treasures, ancient texts written on bamboo. The experience still leaves me at a loss for words.

I am grateful to my editor Cynthia Read, who has been both patient and supportive during this long project. The Levenson family was extremely generous in endowing my chair in Asian studies. Also, in my first two years here, I received two summer research stipends and the Frances Edelman research fellowship.

Finally, my book could not have been written without the constant support of my wife, Shuling Holloway, who has been with me since my first day of graduate school. Although my work would not have been possible without the help of so many, there are inevitable shortcomings in this book, and the responsibility for these is mine alone.

Contents

GUODIAN

Introduction

GUODIAN 郭店[1] IS THE name of a village in the central province of Hubei China. In the early 1990s, grave robbers looted a tomb there that had gone undetected for over two millennia. They left behind what they saw as a worthless pile of bamboo strips.[2] In fact, these strips were a fantastic collection of manuscripts dating from around 300 B.C.E. These Guodian manuscripts[3] are transforming our understanding of the formative era of China's religious and political philosophy. This book will analyze these manuscripts with an eye toward reconstructing their worldview and will provide a window into a pivotal moment in Chinese history.

Long before Guodian, in the Shang 商 (pre-1046) and Western Zhou 西周 (1046–771 B.C.E.), both tombs *and* temples were sacred spaces for ancestor worship. Later, during the Warring States 戰國 (453–221 B.C.E.), the ritual focus shifted to tombs, making them an important site for understanding the religious beliefs of the time.[4] Texts from a tomb such as Guodian that was closed in the late Warring States have an implicit connection to religion. However, understanding the details of these beliefs can be very elusive.

The importance ascribed to the Guodian texts stems from their burial occurring long after Confucius (ca. 551–479 B.C.E.), but still early enough to allow their authors to have been active either before or during the life of Mencius 孟子 (ca. 390–305 B.C.E.). Since the Guodian texts were unseen for more than

two millennia, they provide valuable new insight into the formation of Confucian religious beliefs that became central to the
later tradition. Although the tradition can underscore the importance of these manuscripts, this book will be primarily concerned with analyzing the Guodian texts themselves rather than
emphasizing the ways that they might fit into religious views described in transmitted sources that were edited and transcribed
in the subsequent millennium. Snap assumptions of congruency
and consistency between newly discovered and long-familiar
data sources will be carefully avoided.

The difficulty of this task can be seen in the example of one
Guodian text, "The Five Aspects of Conduct" 五行篇, which is
believed by many scholars to have been written by the grandson
of Confucius. Chapter 2 of this book will discuss the impact
of this hasty labeling in overshadowing the important religious
ideas of "The Five Aspects of Conduct." This text is unique for
locating ethical transformations firmly within our corporal bodies, which can be seen in the first line of the text: "The five
aspects of conduct are: When humanity forms within [your
heart][5] it is called virtuous conduct. If [humanity] is not formed
within it is called a mere act." 五行: 仁形於內謂之德之行, 不形
於內, 謂之行。[6] At first blush, the location of ethics within the body
might seem to be the mark of a system of atomic individualism,
since there is nothing to connect us with others in society. However, the development and practice of virtue is elsewhere in the
text described as inseparable from its social context. Interacting
with others is a necessary part of becoming an ethical person. It
is at precisely this point that "The Five Aspects of Conduct" is
transformed from being a self-help text into a religious treatise.
A leap of faith is involved in believing that humanity exists, is a
physical presence in the body, that the presence is the result of
being converted by another, and that embodying humanity will
alter the moral impact of one's actions.

Religion has long been studied from the perspective of its social manifestations, and this has even been tied in recent years to
the bodies of believers through the analysis of the impact of faith

on physical well-being.[7] The connection between practice and faith in this book will not involve the typologies of earlier work in the field.[8] Instead, we will focus on the critical role of faith in the process of self-cultivation, as it develops from within the bodies of practitioners into a social system that is spread through human contact. The importance of understanding Guodian theories of religious social praxis is further underscored when we consider the high status of the tomb occupant.

It has been theorized that the Guodian tomb master was the tutor to the heir apparent. This would raise the possibility that the religious and political views evident in his tomb texts were those that were held by Chu kings.[9] In addition to Guodian tomb number one, "The Five Aspects of Conduct" 五行篇 was also found in Mawangdui 馬王堆 tomb number three, dating from 168 B.C.E. Although Guodian had been looted, Mawangdui contained elaborate tomb furnishings and weapons that point to the occupant having significant social status.[10] Although we are not sure of the identity of the master of the Guodian tomb, the Mawangdui tomb contained the son of the Lord of Dai 軑侯, a very powerful individual. The combination of these factors indicates that "The Five Aspects of Conduct" was circulated among those in elite circles. Having been selected for inclusion in these two tombs, it raises the strong possibility that the text was more than merely familiar, but a pivotal treatise that described the religious and political views of the time. The importance of "The Five Aspects of Conduct" in the excavated record makes it an appropriate starting point for the analysis of other Guodian texts.

It is particularly difficult to understand the unique characteristics of Guodian texts because the early development of China's religious and political philosophy has been filtered through the school-centric lens of Han 漢 dynasty scholarship. This lens is the product of the Han commentarial tradition and other scholarship from the same era such as Sima Tan's 司馬談 essay on the Six Schools. The grouping of multiple complex texts into schools prevents us from understanding their particular nuances at the passage and paragraph level. In the Han, this trend toward systemization and organization preserved texts that would have otherwise been lost, but the rub has been difficulty in seeing early China without Han glasses. One example of progress toward overcoming this handicap has been recent scholarship demonstrating an important lack of cohesion among works previously considered to belong to particular schools of thought such as Confucianism and Daoism.[11] This scholarship has allowed us to understand the distinct religious and philosophical ideas of Confucius 孔子, Mencius, and Xunzi 荀子.

Dating from before the Han, the Guodian tomb provides an entirely new avenue to questioning the inclusion of schools among the standard tools for analyzing Chinese religious history. Several of these tomb texts were lost for more than two millennia, so they might not have even been known to the Han scholars who created the school divisions. Despite the numerous problems inherent in applying the Han categories of schools to lost manuscripts, some scholars today remain committed to these traditional categories, and they have felt that a good way to begin their analysis of excavated texts is to attempt to fit newly discovered texts into long-established notions of intellectual affiliations. The affiliations they posit are not only highly speculative, but they threaten to mask the philosophical nuances among excavated manuscripts *and* their purported counterparts in the received tradition of transmitted sources.

"The Five Aspects of Conduct," for example, is concerned with the cultivation of humanity 仁, righteousness 義,[12] the rites 禮, wisdom 智, and sagacity 聖 as a group. This is a set of vocabulary shared by several received texts, including those of Confucius, Mencius, and Xunzi, but the same groupings of characters cannot be found. These groupings will be discussed in subsequent chapters of this book.[13] Based on this shared vocabulary, and some common issues such as family-based social harmony, scholars have proposed calling "The Five Aspects of Conduct" Confucian. More specifically, they describe it as a work from "the school of Zisi, Mencius and 'The Five Aspects of Conduct.'"[14] The first problem with this label is the inclusion of Zisi, a figure whose biographical information is ambiguous if we confine our analysis to pre-Han sources. Second, including Mencius in the troika is highly suspect, since "The Five Aspects of Conduct" does not include the character for "human nature" *xing*性, a central philosophical element of Mencius's program for self-cultivation.[15]

In light of these problems, the category of Confucian seems less than useful for analyzing "The Five Aspects of Conduct." The category becomes even less suitable when we consider the archaeological context of the discovery. In both tombs where "The Five Aspects of Conduct" was discovered, the text was buried alongside early editions of the *Laozi*老子. The term "buried alongside" can have a range of meanings, from being discovered in the same tomb to literally being side by side. In the case of "The Five Aspects of Conduct" and the *Laozi*, both meanings actually apply. The reason for this relates to the fact that the Guodian texts were written on bamboo strips, and the Mawangdui scribes used silk. Although the bamboo strips were originally in bundles, their cords rotted long ago. The order of the strips was painstakingly researched based on the size and shape of strips, and the continuation of sentences. However, we do not know the ordering of discrete texts because of their disarray when excavated. In the case of Mawangdui, the tomb had not been disturbed and the silk was in good enough condition to show that in fact "The Five Aspects of Conduct" came directly after the *Laozi* on a single piece of silk. Obviously, the two texts would have been read one after another, which means that we would have to assemble a significant body of evidence prior to concluding that they might have been understood as belonging to separate and possibly competing schools of thought at the time of their burial.[16] Much of the evidence that has been presented by other scholars for separating "The Five Aspects of Conduct" from the *Laozi* has relied heavily on transmitted sources, and that diminishes its persuasive power.[17]

Various problems arise from these hasty attempts at connecting recently excavated texts with received texts. One of the more significant is that it implies that the received texts are more valuable and that other material is simply a new tool for confirming the depth of the tradition in pre-Han times. While there is no question that excavated texts can provide insight into the received tradition, they must first be analyzed in their own right or risk being permanently misconstrued. Therefore, the notion of schools should be put aside at least until a careful analysis of Guodian qua Guodian has been completed. The humble first phase of this project is presented in the subsequent chapters of this book.

Chapter 1 will outline general principles of Guodian religion. The focus of the religious system is unification that involves the bringing together of distinct individuals in society. Individuality is underscored by the physical presence of morality in each of our bodies, requiring us to recognize minority as well as majority concerns within the society. As such, Guodian texts describe a system that is intended for an entire society of individuals. It also requires a belief in the ability of others to act morally. The transition from the individual to the society requires faith, in that it relies on others for its maintenance and propagation. This chapter will provide a detailed analysis of the important transition between individual ethics and a socially conceived system, which it will argue is the foundation of religious sentiment in Guodian texts.

Since our understanding of early China has been filtered for so long by Han era perspectives, chapter 2 of this book will properly situate the Guodian texts as a new set of ideas that relate to but are separate from our former understanding of the tradition. This will also provide a critical overview of other scholarship that is interested in connecting "The Five Aspects of Conduct" to transmitted texts. Chapter 3 of this book will depart from previous oversimplifications of this intellectual milieu by proceeding with a nuanced study of the differences between "The Five Aspects of Conduct" and the *Mencius*. In "The Five Aspects of Conduct," rhetoric is an important part of self-cultivation, but this is not true of the *Mencius*. The *Mencius's* ethical system is primarily concerned with developing the moral framework of the people. A central concept for developing this framework is human nature, an innate source of goodness that enables us to act as moral agents. Human nature is something we all share that allows us to connect with heaven[18] and, by extension,[19] each other. Although Mencius believes human nature is inherent within us, it requires cultivation or it will decay,[20] and the connection will be lost. Human nature is entirely absent from "The Five Aspects of Conduct," which instead employs rhetoric as a means of interlinking people. Rhetoric and human nature initially seem to be entirely different concepts, and there are significant dissimilarities. However, an analysis of the religious function of these two concepts uncovers a similarity from the perspective of the social application: they bridge ruptures that otherwise separate individual processes of self-cultivation.

For example, in "The Five Aspects of Conduct," moral cultivation involves rhetoric. Hearing the way from others helps morality to form within us. Instead of being inborn like human nature, morality has to first develop internally and then become manifest externally through changes in our bodies and our voices. Part of the propagation of morality to others involves their observing and hearing our outwardly manifest ethical signs. Hearing the words and recognizing the appearance of a morally superior individual is part of developing sagacity and wisdom.[21] Of these two manifestations, the auditory is privileged as the higher level of attainment. What we hear is transformative, as the words of a morally superior person are believed to have the power to convert others. As such, these words relate to a religious form of rhetoric, since they create a change in our moral development and bridge the rupture that would otherwise divide the ethical development of individual humans. This is different from human nature, but it is still an innate ability.

In other words, hearing the way is not described in "The Five Aspects of Conduct" as being the exclusive purview of a select subset of individuals. From this perspective there is a small degree of compatibility, since both human nature and rhetoric are conceived of as being universally accessible to all humans.

Chapter 4 will further consider the issue of interpersonal connectedness in the excavated version of the *Laozi* and "The Five Aspects of Conduct." Both of these texts emphasize realizing a unity composed of binary opposites,[22] but there is an important difference from the analysis in chapter 3, in that rhetoric is not important to the *Laozi*. Unity is important to Guodian religion in a general sense, since it involves a faith in the moral system that connects us. This issue of unity will also be shown to be central to the Guodian texts "Tang Yu zhidao" 唐虞之道, and "Taiyi shengshui" 太一生水. Finding four texts that share a consistent concern for unity is insufficient to reconstruct a complete understanding of Guodian religion, but it is hoped that this will provide a starting point for future research. One question that this raises is why the specific texts of Guodian were selected for burial. Warring States tombs tend to contain the valued possessions of the tomb occupant, so it would be natural to expect to find similar concerns addressed in one individual's manuscript collection.

Continuing in the direction of analyzing the function of the tomb texts in Guodian, chapter 5 of this book will discuss specific issues raised by the social implications of the religious concern of unity in Guodian texts. Chapter 5 will discuss the application of unity to the issue of succession. It will be argued that "Tang Yu zhidao" and "The Five Aspects of Conduct" are similar in that they value a unity based on a hybrid composed of humanity and righteousness.

Balancing humanity and righteousness entails unifying two competing centers of moral authority, the central government and the family (lineage group). Because the categories employed by the Guodian texts encompass such a large segment of the population, they can be seen as comprehensive. Thus, it will be argued that they pertain to far more than simply the occasional selection of a sovereign. The balancing of humanity and righteousness will be shown to represent a religiously based political philosophy that is articulated with greatest clarity in Guodian, but is also reflected in the beliefs of certain texts in the received tradition.

ONE

Religious Characteristics
of Guodian Texts

THE GOAL OF RELIGION IN Guodian texts is to propagate a belief in the moral value of harmonious unification. This unification involves faith that morals have a physical existence in our bodies that is transformative both to our actions and to the actions of those we encounter. Subsequent chapters of this book will argue that this belief in unity is central to a significant number of Guodian texts, including "The Five Aspects of Conduct," "Tang Yu zhidao," "Taiyi shengshui," and the *Laozi* fragments. Unity is created out of the tension between moral elements within our bodies that also connect externally to the social segments of individual, family, and group in "The Five Aspects of Conduct" and "Tang Yu zhidao." These two texts see unity in a similar way as the concept of communitarian connectedness in that there is a concern for all individuals in society, including a commitment to the moral development of members of the minority as well as the majority.[1] "Taiyi shengshui" and the *Laozi* fragments, however, discuss unity as an organic characteristic of our universe that people should strive to understand and embrace.

In "The Five Aspects of Conduct," five distinct ethical principles are individually valuable, yet necessary to cultivate as a united group. These ethical principles relate to a variety of emotional responses that range from joy to tearful sadness, yet the entire spectrum of sentiments is important to self-cultivation. Since these ethical principles also shape our various actions, they represent a comprehensive sketch of the text's worldview.

By valuing this broad range of emotional responses, actions, and ethical tenets, "The Five Aspects of Conduct" embraces the human condition in a holistic manner. Spreading this holistic perspective, inseparable from self-cultivation and manifest in unity, is the broad religious goal of the text. It is seen as imperative to implement this cultivation, so proper understanding involves practicing each principle as part of a system of nondiscrimination and equality. Embracing pleasant and unpleasant emotional states is a reflection of the text's inclusive tendencies. This equality is not hypothetical but must be applied to our interactions with individuals we encounter in society. Individuality should be embraced in the same way that various emotional states are all seen as simply part of the human condition. This again reflects communitarian connectedness, in that each individual would have to be equally valued. It should be noted that social interconnectedness is not seen as an artificial construction in the text. Instead, it is an organic state that develops in our bodies and is then passed to others spreading harmony.

"Tang Yu zhidao" exhibits similar tendencies but is concerned with only one pair of moral concepts that are interestingly also part of the five discussed in "The Five Aspects of Conduct." These two concepts are humanity and righteousness, which the text relates to minority versus majority concerns. Humanity is described as rooted in the family, and when expanded to a government perspective emphasizes the aristocratic inheritance of bureaucratic positions. In contrast, righteousness is the promoting of the most skilled individual and can be seen as government by meritocracy. Balancing these two terms is performed in a process similar to that in "The Five Aspects of Conduct," since it is a product of the human body. In "Tang Yu zhidao," the bodies that created this harmony are specific sages in antiquity,

Yao and Shun. The fascinating contribution of the text is that it does not really see a difference between aristocracy and meritocracy, since both similarly contain strengths and weaknesses that must be balanced to create unity. In that the text is specific, it focuses on the application and not the cultivation of harmony. This is different from "The Five Aspects of Conduct," where the discussion of cultivation is central, and specific individuals are mentioned only in passing.

The presence of a common method for attaining harmony in "The Five Aspects of Conduct" and "Tang Yu zhidao," along with a shared focus on unity in "Taiyi shengshui" and the *Laozi* fragments, is significant as it indicates purpose and order in the selection process of texts to be interred in the tomb. While the term "purpose" is accurate, it is also a minimalist accounting of this assemblage of texts. These texts are describing a moral space, and a consistent trend in such an arena should be properly termed a religion or at least a religious perspective.

The title "The Five Aspects of Conduct" refers to the harmonious unification of five ethical principles that are distinct and different in the specific qualities of their development and practice. Unity can be achieved only by celebrating the unique characteristics of the elements that constitute a composite whole. The beginning paragraphs of the text focus on the equal value of these five terms, but later paragraphs highlight the different elements that constitute unity.

By observing the intersection of equivalency, differentiation, and unification of specific terms in "The Five Aspects of Conduct," we can understand that the text is advocating a unity that is not fully homogeneous. Instead, it requires the presence of distinct members to function properly. The five distinct principles of the text are in fact five types of knowledge, thinking, and acting. They are intended to encompass the diverse range of ethical activities that a person could encounter. The breadth implied by the five terms is evident in paragraph 2: "There are five aspects of virtuous conduct, that, when united, are called virtue itself. When only four of these actions are united it is called being adept [at virtue]. Adeptness is the way of humans ❹ while virtue is the way of heaven." 德之行五和, 謂之德, 四行和, 謂之善。善, 人❹道也。德, 天道也。[2] Uniting the distinct ways of acting virtuously provides access to a wide breadth of understanding, extending to either the various ways people can be moral or even the greater universality of heaven.

Since these five terms are considered a comprehensive representation of moral principles and behavior, their equal treatment in the parallel sentences of the first paragraph of the text reinforces the message that no one is privileged above another. It must be remembered that even in the later development of a unity from wisdom and sagacity, it remains important to include the individual elements of humanity, righteousness, and the rites. Although we can create a distinction by pointing to one who has attained the higher level of self-cultivation that is on par with heaven, or a lower level of humans, each stage remains composed of and inseparable from a holistic understanding of ethical conduct.

Part of cultivating the array of moral tenets in "The Five Aspects of Conduct" involves appreciating a similarly broad group of what we today would characterize as emotions. These emotional responses range from happiness and joy to anxiety and extreme sadness. One example of this occurs in paragraph 4 of the text, which describes the absence of proper moral understanding. The results of this absence are explained through a modified quotation from the odes. The received version states, "When I do not see my lord, my sorrowful heart is agitated. Now that I have seen him, now that I observe him, my heart can be happy." 未見君子憂心惙惙亦既見止亦既覯止我心則說。[3] However, in "The Five Aspects of Conduct," the scenario is reversed, since it is describing the opposite reaction, one that a person without morals would experience. It states, "'When I do not see my lord, my sorrowful heart ❾ cannot be agitated.' Now that I have seen him, my heart cannot be happy." 未見君子, 憂心❾不能惙惙; 既見君子, 心不能悅。[4] The important difference between these two versions is that in "The Five Aspects of Conduct," the heart is not able to be agitated. This means that the reaction of the agitated heart is the proper and desired reaction to the situation, so its absence is cause for alarm. This example illustrates the importance of what appears to be a simple emotion that would today be categorized as a negative or unhappy emotional response. Despite its appearing unpleasant, it remains an important part of the process of self-cultivation.

Another text from Guodian, "Xing zi ming chu," expresses an even clearer example of the importance of a range of emotions to self-cultivation:

> The *qi* of joy, anger, sorrow and sadness are given by nature. When it comes to their being manifested on the outside, it is because things have called them forth. Nature comes from the decree, and the decree is handed down from heaven.

> 惪（喜）蒸（怒）悑（哀）悲之　（氣），眚（性）也。及其見於外，則勿（物）取之也。眚（性）自命出，命自天降。[5]

This passage is different from "The Five Aspects of Conduct" in that it discusses nature 性(*xing*).[6] Despite this important difference, there is an interesting similarity in the role that joy and sorrow play in self-cultivation. It is inappropriate to translate *qing* (情) as emotion in pre-Han texts, but this passage lists a range of precursors to reactions that would today be classified as emotional responses to situations. As long as we are clear that what is meant by emotions in Guodian is not something that should be suppressed, but a core part of self-cultivation, we can continue to use "emotions" as an analytical category. In "Xing zi ming chu," these emotional responses are part of what every human experiences, and they have the ability to connect us to a higher power, heaven. These responses are also important examples of moral cultivation being produced in the corporal bodies of individuals.

Many positive emotional responses are also included in discussions of self-cultivation in "The Five Aspects of Conduct." In the final paragraph of the text, we see that "those that hear the way and are happy are those that like humanity. . . . Those who hear the way and are musical are those who like virtue." 聞道而悅者, 好仁者也。。。。聞道而樂者, 好德者也。[7] The types of emotions that are part of self-cultivation are again inclusive of a broad range, which can be seen as an appreciation of the totality of the human condition, including joy and tears. However, this broad range does not mean that the text lacks standards. Rather, standards for judgment are based on context. The various moral principles and related emotional responses are always described and understood relationally. Individual distinct elements are deemed equally valuable but also unable to be fully understood in atomic isolation; they exist in society. The importance of societal context becomes clear when "The Five Aspects of Conduct" describes the proper way to act as a judge.

Late in "The Five Aspects of Conduct," we find an example of how one should judge a legal case. There are two types of cases provided, and they are similar in also illustrating a range of responses. The first type of case is a major crime that is said to be deserving of capital punishment. The second type involves the commission of a minor crime, where the criminal should be set free without punishment. At the end of chapter 4, I will discuss the first type as an application of righteousness, and the second as humanity. In applying the ethical principles of the text broadly to the context of society, a problem arises. It is important to harmonize humanity and righteousness in a way that still recognizes the individual characteristics of each of the moral principles. However, there is a case to be decided, and a choice must be made. One cannot execute a felon and then set him free, at least not in a way that is meaningful to the accused individual in question. Still, a sage is supposed to be able to harmonize humanity and righteousness. There is no clear indication how this seemingly impossible task might be accomplished in "The Five Aspects of Conduct" itself.

The solution to this conundrum can be found by referencing a similar problem posed by "Tang Yu zhidao." Here, when faced with the question of who should succeed a ruler in government, two methods of succession are presented, abdication and inheritance. When a king abdicates, he selects a successor based on merit and does not allow his position to be inherited by his son. The situation with inheritance is of course exactly opposite. The abdication option is related to righteousness, and inheritance is the way of humanity. These two ethical principles are the same as we found in the example of the legal case in "The Five Aspects of Conduct." Fortunately, in "Tang Yu zhidao," the problem is discussed in detail and a solution is presented.

Before discussing the solution to this conflict, we must be clear about the goal of "Tang Yu zhidao." Abdication and inheritance can be misleadingly secular terms. Although there is a strong social component to the application of ethics in the text, this should not overshadow its religious message, which is the cultivation and dissemination of upright ethical behavior. It is believed that a populace can be encouraged to cleave toward ethics with support of the government in these two texts by achieving unity that creates a moral community equal to that of Yao and Shun, sages of antiquity. There is an implication that this unity would not have ended with the shift from meritocracy to aristocracy, since both systems are really just tools for bringing balanced morality to the people. This morality is to be fostered through what might seem to be morally neutral channels, inheritance, and abdication. However, these choices are far from neutral, since they are major decisions that create resonances across the empire. That the choice of a sovereign can even be understood as touching the people is an example of the pervasive holism in "Tang Yu zhidao."

"Tang Yu zhidao" begins with a statement that contains two possible succession choices. Abdicating is related to righteousness, and the statement follows the same binary style, with humanity as an alternate method of succession. "Being filial is the crown of humanity. ❼ Abdicating is the utmost of righteousness." 孝, 仁之冕也。 ❼禪, 義之至也。[8] Both humanity and righteousness are ethical principles with positive connotations, which indicate the presence of an enigma similar to that of "The Five Aspects of Conduct."

The beginnings of a solution can be found when "Tang Yu zhidao" provides a more detailed description of the problem. "Loving the family one forgets the outstanding; you are humane but not righteousness. Elevating the outstanding distances one from the family; you are righteousness but not humane." 愛親忘賢，仁而未義也。尊賢遺親，義而未仁也。[9] First, we see the extent of the dilemma; acting based on the ethics of the family promotes humanity at the expense of outstanding individuals. Promoting the outstanding would be in the best interest of the government by making use of the talents of useful individuals born outside of important lineages. The problem is that this would marginalize the importance of the lineage group in government. In either instance, there is a give-and-take between what benefits the minority interests of the family and the majority interests of the government. One path to a solution can be found in the fact that this passage does not contrast inheritance with abdication, as is found in the first line of the text. Instead, the passage substitutes "loving the family" 愛親.

A historical precedent is brought in to support this solution as one viable means of overcoming the dilemma of how to promote both righteousness and humanity. "Yao and Shun acted to love their families and elevate the outstanding. Loving ❻ your family therefore is filial, elevating the outstanding therefore is abdicating." 堯舜之行，愛親尊賢。愛❻親故孝，尊賢故禪。[10] It is important to remain cognizant of the message that the text begins with, which is that individuals have the power to balance abdication and inheritance. The historical example of the early sage kings is but one solution, leaving room for the opposite situation of later kings passing their position down through inheritance and finding some other means of empowering the outstanding. What is important is to find a way of balancing the two priorities of humanity and righteousness.[11]

The crux of the solution that "Tang Yu zhidao" proposes is that in one instance, you may act based on humanity, but in other situations, righteousness can be applied. While righteousness marginalizes the family, this is balanced out by subsequent opportunities in which you are not righteous and the family increases in importance. The sum of these situations creates a balance, with harmony occurring between conflicting priorities. If we apply this same solution to "The Five Aspects of Conduct," the manner in which the legal case is described becomes instructive. Two separate scenarios are described in the text. The first is a minor crime; the second is a major crime. By applying humanity in the first situation and righteousness in the second, the result is again a balance. The cultivation and application of ethical principles does not exist in abstraction; it is a part of life, differing from day to day. The application of ethics from one situation to the next is different, yet each situation is equally important. Furthermore, the combination of these distinct situations creates a unified harmony both within the individual and among those encountered.

"Tang Yu zhidao" and "The Five Aspects of Conduct" connect the ethical principles of humanity and righteousness to people both as individuals and as a group. This connection will be related in greater depth to individual examples of unity in chapter 5 of this book. The structure of binary contrasts remains consistently understandable as relevant to either a larger social grouping of the majority or a smaller grouping of the minority, but this relevance is relational and thus fluid. For example, in "Tang Yu zhidao," the king's abdication is righteous, which could be seen as resulting in a marginalization of the rest of the royal family by elevating an individual strictly based on his virtue. The royal family is a member of the majority in that it controls the state, but subsequent to abdication, the ruling house becomes part of the minority, since it is reduced to a single lineage among the many others in the state. The same type of transformation, this time from minority to majority, occurs when considering the selection of a single outstanding person to rule instead of passing through inheritance.

These transformations illustrate the two basic choices a religious community must make. Should power lie in the hands of individuals without consideration of their lineage ties, or should families be the primary authority in directing state affairs? The question of power in either families or individuals is not one simply of political influence but also of moral authority. Righteousness is an ethical principle that does not derive meaning from family values. It drills down to individuals and considers them as corporal bodies directly related to the state, which then sees the world as a conglomerate of atomic, disconnected entities. Humanity is also an ethical principle, but it sees the state as a collection of families where individuals have meaning only when contextualized by their lineage. With humanity, it is natural that a position would be inherited, since the single person selected to rule is of lesser importance than family background. It is assumed that family-based ethics are the basic building blocks of the state, and it is meaningless to view the actions of a single even highly talented individual outside of a familial context.

A government that favors righteousness sees the state as composed of disconnected individuals, which can be beneficial to the government in that it recognizes talent on a smaller scale than humanity. The problem with focusing on disconnected individuals is that it is difficult to develop cohesion in society. Disregard for family ties in selecting individuals for government service decreases the importance of family to society. The obligation and connection of an individual to his parents can also be attenuated if these connections do not relate to activities in the broader society. Such a situation would make it more difficult for the individuals to feel connected to the society, since humanity, an organic element of interpersonal relations, has been marginalized.

There are equally pressing problems raised by following only humanity, in that a focus on the family raises the possibility that individuals of talent would be overlooked if they were born into families of lesser moral or political standing. In the Guodian ideal, a righteousness-based concern for individuals must be balanced by a humanity-based government of families. Without this balance, either the concerns of the family or the talents of individual contributors would be overlooked.[12]

Connecting self-cultivation to the way we understand the value of majority and minority views is particularly important to the way that "Tang Yu zhidao" helps clarify "The Five Aspects of Conduct." The reason this clarification is needed is that much of "The Five Aspects of Conduct" is difficult to connect specifically to the way that self-cultivation would affect our interactions with others. In other words, simply because ethical principles must be understood individually and as a group does not necessarily mean we should have the same concerns for actual people.[13] However, taking into account the similarities between the application of humanity and righteousness in succession issues in "Tang Yu zhidao" and the judgment of a legal case in "The Five Aspects of Conduct," the importance of ethical principles shaping our interpersonal relations is manifest.

Cultivating humanity, righteousness, the rites, wisdom, and sagacity is termed "virtuous action" in the first paragraph of "The Five Aspects of Conduct." However, we do now know what virtuous action is in any sort of precise manner. When using "Tang Yu zhidao" as context, it seems the virtuous actions we are expected to carry out in "The Five Aspects of Conduct" should be those that contribute to the construction of a unified society. This society is one where individual egalitarianism is balanced with communitarian connectedness to create a harmony between the priorities of the majority and minority groups in our society.

While it might be tempting to conclude that Guodian texts advocate democracy, there are problems with what this word conjures, such as the image of an entirely modern government. In particular, a church-state split is not present in Guodian texts. Despite this, there are elements of Guodian religion that seem very modern in being concerned with the priorities of the majority and minority. The obvious difference is that in early China, religion, ethics, and elements of ancestor worship were part of a government's responsibility. The fact remains that marginalizing the family by selecting a single outstanding individual has greater importance to the religious concerns of the state than the term "democracy" would imply. These texts were of course excavated from a tomb, where their immediate purpose was inseparable from a concern for providing for the deceased in his afterlife, so religious questions are important. If we fail to consider this context, we might mistakenly read these texts as only shaping the society of the living and thus being disconnected from their relation to ideas of a life after death.

Being buried in a tomb requires us to see them as being just as relevant to the dead as to the living, even raising the possibility that such a split would be foreign and inconsistent to the worldview of those that interred these texts. In other words, the burial of texts advocating moral action might not have been seen as less important than ensuring the employment of talented individuals in government. For example, the Mawangdui tomb number three contains a famous letter to the underworld that indicates a government bureaucracy is present after death that is largely similar to the world of the living.[14] This would then indicate a plausible reading of Guodian tomb texts that explored their viability as guides to serving the bureaucracy of the afterlife. Following this line of reasoning, it is possible that the authors did not see a rupture between the ethical workings of life and afterlife. Despite "The Five Aspects of Conduct" describing the importance of the physical embodiment of ethical principles, it could be that the death of the tomb master would not be understood as inhibiting his ability to practice moral behavior in the afterlife.

There are indications that ethics can transcend physical boundaries in "The Five Aspects of Conduct." One example of this is morality being transmitted through rhetoric as will be discussed in chapter 3 of this book. This is different from morality extending to the afterlife, since rhetoric appears to have meaning only when it influences another living being. A more compelling example can be found in the relationship between people and heaven. In paragraphs 2 and 11 of "The Five Aspects of Conduct," we see that "Being Virtuous is the way of heaven." 德, 天道也. This is inseparable from the actions of humans, since the first paragraph of the text states that forming ethical principles within ourselves is virtuous conduct. The relationship between individuals and a higher power is also evident in paragraph 17: "sages know the way of heaven" 聖人知天❷❻道 也. These sages are people who have succeeded in internalizing and practicing all of the five ethical principles discussed in the first paragraph of the text, which connects them to the higher power of heaven.

The relationship between ethical conduct and heaven means that the estimable affects of our actions can be traced to both the tangible, as in the impact on individuals, and the intangible through transcendent connection with heaven. Details describing the impact that this relationship might have on either the practitioner of ethical conduct or heaven are scant in "The Five Aspects of Conduct." However, the power of a connection between a sage and heaven is certainly important in the text's main objective, the ability to harmonize diverse ethical principles.

Losing My Religion

In "The Five Aspects of Conduct," moral principles must be formed in our bodies before we can act with morality. By forming the five moral principles of the text within the body and practicing them, it was believed that we could bring morality to others. It is important to be clear that this is not described in the text as a transformation. "The Five Aspects of Conduct" itself does not call the cultivation of morality a transformation. Instead it uses the character for formation (形 xing) that produces manifestations both internally and externally. The results of this process are described in the beginning portions of paragraphs 5 through 7, such as having "essential thoughts," "extended thoughts," and "light thoughts." The external manifestations are looking and sounding like jade. Changes resulting from self-cultivation are described as transforming the body, but the morality itself is simply a formation. These personal changes also have the ability to affect others. Some of this impact is described in very concrete terms, as in the judgment of a legal case. This example is concerned with bodies of the accused, as they are to be either set free or executed. Additional changes that occur in relation to the bodies of others are more subtle. These involve the ability to hear and see a moral person, which is also an important part of spreading self-cultivation.[15]

Interestingly, the formation of ethical principles results in a transformation of the physical form of the body. This metamorphosis into an embodiment of virtue can also be reversed, and we then lose our virtue. Understanding how cultivation may be undone requires a careful review of instances in "The Five Aspects of Conduct" where we find examples of moral principles presented in the negative. The first example we find of a lack of ethics is in paragraph 1 of the text, where the formation of ethics within the body is contrasted with a lack of its formation. Degrees of attainment are not described; either you possess ethics, or you do not. Lacking gray areas, it would seem that this might not be a case of losing morals, but rather a contrast of either having developed them or having never had them. Ethical cultivation is described as a complex process in the rest of the text, which could indicate that the process of either attainment or loss would be lengthy. Surprisingly, there is little evidence that the text sees a decline of morality as protracted. Instead, the text points to single moments in time when the change toward decline appears, or the moment when the decline reached a critical juncture. This explanation is supported by descriptions of declines in morality in paragraphs 2 and 3 that both contain single instances of when the decline begins.

Paragraph 2 contains the first detailed example of the unraveling of morality. This is presented in a sorites or chain argument, which begins with a lack of concern in the inner heart of a noble man that progresses to a lack of wisdom and concludes with a lack of virtue. "If a noble man's inner heart lacks concern, then he will lose his inner heart's wisdom. If his inner heart lacks wisdom, his inner heart will lack ❺ happiness. If his inner heart lacks happiness, he will not be at ease. Not being at ease he will lack music and without music he will lack virtue.■" 君子無中心之憂則無中心之智。無中心之智則無中心❺（之悅.無中心之悅，則不）安。不安，則不樂.不樂，則無德。■¹⁶ The same sorites is also present in the Mawangdui edition, but there it is repeated verbatim with one character substituted. In the second repeated sorites, sagacity is substituted for wisdom. Paragraph 2 is significant for providing a seemingly single instant that produces ethical decline. The subject in the paragraph is a noble man, and "The Five Aspects of Conduct" consistently uses the term "noble man" in the moral sense, representing one who has achieved a high level of ethical attainment. This is seen in paragraph 3: "If someone forms the five aspects of conduct within his inner heart and at the appropriate time practices them ❻ he is said to be a noble man." 五行皆形於内，時行❻之，謂之君（子）。¹⁷

It is interesting that the moment that causes the decline in paragraph 2 is an internal factor, or a failure on an internal level. The starting point is when the noble man's inner heart lacks concern. From the first paragraph of the text, we know that it is important to form humanity, righteousness, the rites, wisdom, and sagacity internally, but there is no mention of concern or happiness. Internal factors are important for self-cultivation, but it seems that attaining wisdom requires other factors, particularly concern. The character for concern (憂 *you*) occurs only once more in the text, in paragraph 4, where it appears in a *Book of Odes* quotation, again in the form of "concern in the heart" (憂心 *youxin*); the same passage also mentions happiness in the heart. Paragraph 4 relates this to a lack of wisdom, indicating that there is a relationship between losing concern, happiness, and wisdom. The exact nature of this relationship is somewhat unclear, but we can be sure that the process of self-cultivation is something that can be reversed, and seems similar in either building or decline. In other words, the process of building begins internally and is later manifest externally, while the decline also begins from within.

In paragraph 3, we have another example of a loss of self-cultivation that is similar to that in paragraph 2.

3. If someone forms the five aspects of conduct within his inner heart and at the appropriate time practices them ❻ he is said to be a noble man. When a gentleman has his goals set on the way of a noble man he is said to have the goals [appropriate to] a gentleman. Being adept [at virtue] but not practicing it, you will not make progress. Being virtuous but lacking ❼ a goal your [virtue] will not be completed. Being wise but not thinking you will not comprehend. Thinking without essence, you will not have keen insight. Thinking without extension, you will not comprehend. Thinking without lightness, [the five aspects of conduct] will not be formed. Not being formed you will not be at ease. Not being at ease you will not be musical, not musical ❽ you will lack virtue.■

3. 五行皆形於內, 時行❻ 之, 謂之君（子）。士有志於君子道，　謂之之志士。善弗為無近, 德弗❼志不成, 智弗思不得。　思不精不察, 思不長　[不得, 思不輕][18]　不形。不形不安, 不安不樂, 不樂❽無德。■[19]

Both of these paragraphs begin with the five aspects of conduct being formed within. The topic of the paragraphs is related to how one could decline from a full attainment of moral understanding. While paragraph 2 lists a single starting point for the decline, a lack of concern, paragraph 3 lists three areas: The first is a failure to practice, the second is lacking the proper goal, and the third is not thinking. In the instance of the first failure, the result is a lack of progress, but it is not stated what you are supposed to be getting closer to as far as an objective. The second failure is one where lacking a goal, you will not attain completion.

These two failures are similar in that they leave some question as to what you will be failing to make progress toward, or what you will fail to complete. In each case, the character that begins the sentence appears significant. In the case of progress, the sentence begins with being adept, and in completion, the sentence begins with virtue. It would seem that in each instance, the character at the beginning of the sentence is telling us what we would be unable to attain by the end of the sentence. There is also a sense of progression from the first to the second failure in that in paragraph 2, being adept is having four aspects of conduct and being virtuous is having all five. There is a hierarchy between the two terms, and failing at the lesser of the two terms results in a failure to progress, so virtue cannot be attained. The third failure, of being wise but not thinking, results in a lack of attaining or comprehending. Following this are three phrases about not thinking properly, which involve thinking without essence, extension, and lightness.

The discussions of a lack of ethics in "The Five Aspects of Conduct" can be found in paragraphs 2 and 4, 12 through 14, and 17 through 19 of the Guodian edition. Interestingly, these paragraphs also contain an important similarity. All of these paragraphs stand out when compared with the Mawangdui edition. The first section of the Mawangdui edition does not contain what scholars have termed the Explanation (說 Shuo) and paragraphs 2 and 4 are part of that section. The Mawangdui edition contains two portions, a Classic and an Explanation portion. The Classic at Mawangdui is largely the same as the text found in Guodian. The Explanation repeats phrases from the Classic and adds brief suggestions as to what the phrase might mean. This commentary is not present at all in the Guodian edition. In addition, paragraphs 12 through 14 and 17 through 19 are reversed in the Mawangdui edition. The sections where negative examples are found stand out from the rest of the text for different reasons, and there are no clear patterns to explain how these paragraphs relate to the loss of morality.

However, there is a pattern regarding the general way that the loss of morality is discussed in "The Five Aspects of Conduct" that becomes clearer when contrasted with the *Mencius*. The *Mencius* contains several important passages that discuss moral decline. Among the more famous examples of this is the

Ox Mountain analogy of 6A.8, which describes the struggle to maintain morality as a constant battle. Ox Mountain is described as a place originally covered in lush vegetation, but after a continuous assault, the vegetation succumbs to humans cutting down the trees, and animals finish off the destruction by biting off the shoots that attempt to regrow during the recuperative periods of the night. The vegetation represents the moral standing of an individual; once laid barren by daily degradation, it is unrecognizable from the original state as morally upright and ethically fertile.

> Mencius said, "There was a time when trees were luxuriant on the Ox Mountain, but as it is on the outskirts of a great metropolis, the trees are constantly lopped by axes. Is it any wonder that they are no longer fine? With the respite they get in the day and in the night, and the moistening by rain and dew, there is certainly no lack of new shoots coming out, but then the cattle and sheep come to graze upon the mountain. That is why it is as bald as it is. People seeing only its baldness tend to think that it never had any trees. But can that possibly be the nature of the mountain?"[20]

> 孟子曰.牛山之木嘗美矣。以其郊於大國也。斧斤伐之。可以為美乎。是其日夜之所息。雨露之所潤。非無萌蘗之生焉。牛羊又從而牧之。是以若彼濯濯也。人見其濯濯也。以為未嘗有材焉。此豈山之性也哉。[21]

This story is fascinating in that it sees the process of developing morality as a lifelong struggle. The assault on our morality is a daily event. In addition, in describing the locus of morality in natural terms such as vegetation, the text has selected structures that are not directly recognizable in terms of organic elements of the body. Natural descriptions such as this are different in important ways from "The Five Aspects of Conduct." The attempt to regrow the sprouts represents Mencius's understanding of human nature as a receptacle for morality. This receptacle, while understood as residing within us, is also in some ways a foreign construct. Human nature is a tool by which we may connect with heaven in 7A.1, and the source of goodness in 6A.1–3.

"The Five Aspects of Conduct" does not describe maintaining morality as a constant struggle as is the tendency of the *Mencius*. Instead, the excavated manuscript describes the process in progressive terms. Morality forms within the body, is put into practice, and spreads to others. The reverse is also possible, as in the unraveling of a piece of cloth; once put into motion, decline can be as complete as the ascent. However, there is no sense that building morality is a struggle as in the Ox Mountain sprouts trying to overcome the continuous threats to their existence. In addition, natural metaphors are not used in a negative fashion, and animals in particular are not used to illustrate a decline of morality in "The Five Aspects of Conduct." The process of acquiring morality is confined to the body, which is able to be completely and successfully controlled by the mind and by the physical presence of morality. This is unlike *Mencius* 6A.1–3. The contrast with a system that sees the body as complete unto itself without the foreign construct of human nature is significant. In "The Five Aspects of Conduct," paragraph 25 sees the mind in absolute control of the senses and the body in its totality.

> Ears, eyes, nose, mouth, hands and feet are the six that the mind employs. If the mind says yes[22] none dare not say yes. If it [says to] agree, none dare disagree. If it [says to] ❹❺ advance none dare not advance. If it [says to] withdraw none dare not withdraw. If it [says to] go deep none dare not go deep. If it [says to] go shallow, none dare not go shallow. When there is harmony there is equality; when there is equality there is adeptness [at virtue]

25. 耳目鼻口手足六者，心之役也。心曰唯莫敢不唯；若莫敢不諾；❹❺進莫敢不進；後莫敢不後；深莫敢不深；淺莫敢不淺。和則同同則善。■❹❻

Examples of concepts that could be seen as having any similarity to a metaphor from nature such as is found in Ox Mountain are limited in "The Five Aspects of Conduct" to things that have been fully transformed into ritual objects. These are the bronze and jade, which are used to describe the voice and body of a moral individual. The only other mention of nature is in a quotation from *The Odes*: "'Only when you are able to display your wings unevenly' do you understand the utmost sadness." Here, the image of a bird with uneven wings is an aid in attaining an appreciation of sadness. By thinking about the uneven wings, we are brought to a deeper understanding than we could attain on our own. In this case, the animal is not gnawing at the vulnerable sprouts of our morality as in the *Mencius*, but instead is raising our awareness to new heights. This awareness seems to come from an appreciation of sadness common between man and beast, and when we understand this, we are touched. When we see this shared emotion, our understanding of our own circumstances is heightened and the animal has provided assistance to our process of self-cultivation. It should be mentioned, of course, that the bird analogy is also filtered through the ritualized text of *The Odes*. The quotation is fully separated from the context of the bird in nature. All we see are uneven wings. Even the full body of the bird is absent from the description. This appreciation of nature when processed through ritual reflects a consistent focus on morality as resident in the body and then shared from one body to another through society.[23] These differences between Mencius and Guodian texts challenge the consensus of most Chinese scholars, as will be discussed in chapter 2 of this book.

"Tang Yu zhidao" is a text that is less concerned with the internal development of ethical behavior, and more concerned with its application in government. This application is seen as inherently difficult, and the text illustrates this difficulty by referencing the experiences of the ancient king Shun. There is far less detail in the excavated manuscript "Tang Yu zhidao" than in the *Book of Documents* version of the story.[24] "Tang Yu zhidao" mentions Shun as being filial toward his blind father and compassionate to his brother, but that is the extent of what the text tells us about these two individuals. By continuing to refer to Shun's father as blind, there is an implication that he is seen as the same morally benighted person of the *Book of Documents*. It is possible that this indicates "Tang Yu zhidao" sees the process of transforming others as very difficult. If the great Shun was unable to change his father's ways, what chance do others have?

If we are correct in seeing the transformation of society as difficult in "Tang Yu zhidao," then "The Five Aspects of Conduct" could seem like an outlier. However, in "The Five Aspects of Conduct," there are indications that internal formation and external practice are in fact different. First, the sorites must be understood as occurring in two groups. The internal sorites of paragraphs 5 through 7 do not contain terms that imply conflict. They simply describe the process beginning with purely internal phenomena and continuing to external manifestations.

This is different from the sorites involving the practice of morality externally, in society, in paragraphs 12 through 14 and 19 through 21.[25] The external sorites contain the word "admonishment"[26] as part of the process of obtaining righteousness. We learn later in the text that admonishment is capital punishment and that righteousness is hard while humanity is forgiving, and softness. The inclusion of "admonishment" in both of these sections means that the term is related to executing criminals, a very harsh way of dealing with someone that is beyond rehabilitation. Humanity is different. There are no terms associated with humanity that indicate a loss of hope; in fact, it is related to forgiving criminals.

This split between the internal and externals sorites means that while practicing righteousness, we will be asked to deal harshly with criminals, but internal cultivation is not similarly conflicted. There is no indication that the internal side is problematic as Mencius describes in 6A.15. In contrast, we see internal harmony that then runs into conflict only when applied in the society. The result of this internal harmony is seen near the end of "The Five Aspects of Conduct," where it states, "If the mind says yes, none dare not say yes."[27] The mind works in perfect concert with the various other parts of the body, and this is a clear example of the consistent religious belief in Guodian texts that harmonious unification is a powerful force.

TWO

Guodian and Traditional Views of China

THE FIRST FOUR STRIPS OF "The Five Aspects of Conduct" describe the process of internally cultivating humanity, righteousness, the rites, wisdom, and sagacity—the five terms referred to in the title of the text.[1] We can only uncover the way each of these five terms is interrelated by analyzing the web of their co-relationships. This web is constructed of the pervasively used rhetorical device of the sorites. For example, humanity, wisdom, and sagacity appear in three parallel sorites from strips 12 through 16.[2] Each sorites begins with changes in one's thoughts (思 si) and ends with reference to having a jade-like countenance (玉色 yuse) or being like jade sounds (玉音 yuyin). Although the use of sorites makes it difficult to penetrate too deeply into the exact details of what each process entails, what is being described are three parallel processes of internally developed moral traits that ultimately result in external manifestations, here described as jade-like. Jade refers to a person attaining the ritual importance of jade in a religious or ceremonial context. The significance of this is that the internal process of self-cultivation at the end of the sorites becomes visible and apparent to an outside observer. This shift from internal moral development to a broader social and governmental context begins here and marks the second major attribute of the text.

Strips 37 through 41 provide an example of how you can judge a legal case by applying humanity and righteousness. The text describes two choices: being lenient toward a person who has committed a relatively minor crime, or meting out capital punishment for a serious crime. The former is said to be the soft and is the method of humanity, while the latter is the hard or the method of righteousness. Based on the context provided in strips 32 through 33, we can see that humanity's association with the family[3] might explain why minor crimes can be forgiven. The *Analects* 論語 13.18 story of Upright Gong sets a precedent where certain crimes should be dealt with among family members to the exclusion of state involvement. The difference is that 13.18 does not mention humanity. Furthermore, the pairing of humanity and righteousness as contrasting sides of moral cultivation is specific to Guodian texts but conspicuously absent in 13.18 or elsewhere in the *Analects*.[4]

Another text found in Guodian, "Liu De" 六德 section 7:2, also pairs humanity and righteousness in a manner similar to "The Five Aspects of Conduct." In "Liu De" we see that "humanity is family; righteousness is state.[5] The rites and music are shared. The inner establishes the father, son, and ❷❻ husband. The outer establishes the ruler, minister and married women." ■仁，內 也。義，外也。禮樂，共也。內立父、子、❷❻夫也，外立 君、臣、婦也。[6] A description of mourning rituals follows this quotation that is similar to those we find in the *Book of Rites* 禮 記 and *Yili* 儀禮. This "Liu De" quotation is similar to "The Five Aspects of Conduct" in that the inner cultivation of humanity in the family is followed by the outer cultivation of righteousness in the state. The "Liu De" contrast is clearest in comparing the inner of father and son with the outer of ruler and minister. In "The Five Aspects of Conduct," we see consecutive paragraphs ending with the following: "Loving your father and extending this to love others you are Humane." 愛父，其繼愛人，仁也。[7] "Venerating the noble, those with rank, and elevating the outstanding, is righteousness." 貴貴，其等尊賢，義也。[8] This pairing of human-ity and righteousness in Guodian texts provides a clear contrast with the *Analects* and *Mencius*. The issue will be revisited in relation to a wider range of texts in chapter 5.

Analects

In the *Analects*, we first encounter the idea that humanity is related to one's family in passage 1:2: "Acting filial and frater-nal are the roots of humanity" 孝弟也者，其為仁之本與![9] This passage understands humanity as a concept that one begins to learn as a child in the home through being filial.[10] The appro-priate treatment of parents and siblings establishes a precedent that is continued when interacting in the community at large. In this passage, humanity is fundamental to the process of self-cultivation, but the implications of what this process entails can be interpreted several ways. First, it is possible that humanity is the link that provides continuity from the smaller scale of learn-ing appropriate behavior in the family to the larger scale of prac-ticing it in the community. Second, it is possible that humanity relates to either or both of the smaller and/or larger spheres of interaction. The third and most likely explanation is that the en-tirety of humanity is confined to neither of these possibilities.

The implication of this third explanation is that *Analects* 1:2 reflects one part of the system of morality seen in "The Five As-pects of Conduct." Following one's early education in morality at home, humanity should then be applied in the larger context of the society.[11] This understanding of humanity is also compat-ible with the "Liu De" passage where humanity is listed prior to righteousness, implying an application in ever-widening circles, beginning with the family and continuing with the state and/or empire. It is important to recognize, however, that a pair-ing of humanity with righteousness is completely absent in the *Analects* and represents an important difference in the under-standing of self-cultivation. This pairing was shown in chapter 1 of this book to represent the core religious ideal of "The Five Aspects of Conduct," where cultivation begins internally with humanity and then extends to the empire with righteousness.

Mencius

Mencius contains three passages that discuss humanity and righteousness in a manner with some similarities to "The Five Aspects of Conduct" and "Liu De." The first is 7A.15, which states: "Loving parents is benevolence; respecting one's elders is rightness."[12] 「親親，仁也。敬長，義也。」[13] The relationship between humanity and a person's parents in this passage could be seen as congruent with the previously mentioned *Analects* passage 1:2. In both instances, humanity is related to a person's innermost circle of interaction, the family. This is followed in 7A.15, where righteousness is described as being related to respecting elders. By itself, the prospect of respecting elders is ambiguous as to the intended object of respect. There is no indication that respect in this passage might be intended as a concept that is confined to either one's family or a larger social sphere. The best way to understand what Mencius might mean by respecting elders in 7A.15 is to refer to similar passages for guidance.

In Mencius's debate with Gaozi in 6A.4, we see the idea of respecting elders as referring to the respect of those outside of one's family and even one's state:

"Why do you say," said Mencius, "that benevolence is internal and rightness is external?" [Gaozi[14] said,] "That man there is old and I treat him as elder. He owes nothing of his elderliness to me, just as treating him as white because he is white I only do so because of his whiteness which is external to me. That is why I call it external."[15]

孟子曰：「何以謂仁內義外也？」曰：「彼長而我長之，非有長於我也。猶彼白而我白之，從其白於外也，故謂之外也。」[16]

This is a problematic passage to use because Mencius is arguing against Gaozi. However, Mencius's point of contention is not that Gaozi is incorrect but rather that his statements represent a lesser understanding. In other words, Mencius's view encompasses and expands upon Gaozi's position.[17] Despite problems unraveling the specifics of Mencius' objections, we find righteousness relating to the respect of elders in 7A.15, without consideration of familial bonds.

Mencius 3A.4 also discusses righteousness in terms related to a larger social sphere:

> This gave the Sage King further cause for concern, and so he appointed Hsieh as the minister of Education whose duty was to teach the people human relationships: love[18] between father and son, duty[19] between ruler and subject . . .[20]

> 「聖人有憂之，使契為司徒，教以人倫：父子有親，君臣有義 . . . 」[21]

In this passage, we can see that rulers and ministers have different standards of conduct than fathers and sons. Righteousness is being distinguished as a term that corresponds to a broader societal level than the family. Humanity is of course not mentioned. Although 7A.15 and 3A.4 are the closest parallels to the Guodian pairing of humanity and righteousness in the *Mencius*, they also contain important differences.

The final examples in Mencius further highlight this difference as the distinctions between humanity and righteousness as contrasting social segments are unlike Guodian. *Mencius* 4A.27, states:

> The content of benevolence is the serving of one's parents; the content of dutifulness[22] is obedience to one's elder brothers; the content of wisdom is to understand these two and to hold fast to them; the content of the rites is the regulation and adornment of them . . .[23]

> 孟子曰：「仁之實，事親是也。義之實，從兄是也。智之實，知斯二者弗去是也。禮之實，節文斯二者是也。[24]」

While humanity relates to a familial context in this passage, there is also a blurring of the previously observed distinctions between humanity and righteousness, since both terms are here related to the family. One explanation for this is that the terms "humanity" and "righteousness" are complex concepts that comprise many variant attributes. Distinguishing righteousness and humanity as relating to larger and smaller social spheres is but one aspect of the meaning of these terms. This meaning can be found when trying to establishing a parallel with "The Five Aspects of Conduct," but a large number of passages in the *Mencius* use the terms "humanity" and "righteousness" as near equivalents.[25]

The usage of "humanity" and "righteousness" as rough synonyms can also be seen in 4A.20: "When the prince is benevolent, everyone else is benevolent; when the prince is dutiful,[26] everyone else is dutiful; when the prince is correct, everyone else is correct."[27] 「君仁莫不仁，君義莫不義，君正莫不正 . . . 」[28] Here, "humanity" and "righteousness" do not imply any of the specific meanings discussed in previous passages. The terms are approximately equivalent because there is nothing to indicate how an individual would act differently when following humanity and righteousness. Therefore, "humanity" and "righteousness" must represent general terms for proper behavior in 4A.20, and this is unlike the usage of these terms in Guodian.

In conclusion, "The Five Aspects of Conduct" and "Liu De" use "humanity" in a similar manner with the *Analects*, but there is no crossover in the pairing of humanity with righteousness. *Mencius* contains a few passages that hint at a Guodian usage of "humanity" and "righteousness," but there is no consistent pairing. Neither the *Analects* nor *Mencius* contains enough similarities in the usage of "humanity" and "righteousness" to demonstrate a close affinity with "The Five Aspects of Conduct." It should be noted that while early scholarship[29] on the *Analects* often used the *Mencius* to explain difficult passages, recent scholarship has tried to treat texts more distinctly.[30] Therefore, it is not surprising to conclude that the *Analects* and

Mencius use "humanity" and "righteousness" in a manner distinct from Guodian texts. Furthermore, as chapter 5 will demonstrate, there are important distinctions in the perspectives of abdication and inheritance within the *Mencius*. This makes it impossible to nail down a specific Mencian position on these concepts. This is important because it challenges the category of "Mencian" as an analytical device. Specific passages might contain certain similarities to "The Five Aspects of Conduct," but the *Mencius* as a whole cannot, since it does not consistently employ key terminology.

The Discovery of "The Five Aspects of Conduct"

Scholars have sought to connect "The Five Aspects of Conduct" to the *Mencius* since its discovery in 1973. In that year, a cache of silk manuscripts was found in Mawangdui tomb number three in Hunan Province 湖南省. This was the first extensive collection of silk manuscripts unearthed from such an early period: 168 B.C.E., during the Han 漢 dynasty (206 B.C.E.–220 C.E.).[31] Guodian village in the province of Hubei was the site of another exciting discovery in October 1993.[32] Here archaeologists uncovered a tomb they labeled M1 from 300 B.C.E. in the pre-Qin 秦 state of Chu 楚 that contained texts written on 804 bamboo strips. These two tombs are separated by one of the most significant period-defining events in ancient history, Qin Shihuang's 秦始皇 unification of China. Excavated manuscripts now bridge this historic divide. Some are early editions of major works known from the received tradition. Others were previously unknown, having been lost for over two millennia.

The discovery of multiple copies of texts indicates wide circulation. This is not surprising for the Daodejing, which was never lost. Based on recent excavations, it seems "The Five Aspects of Conduct" was of comparable import from the late Warring

States through early Han. Furthermore, the interment of these two texts in both tombs must be more than coincidental. In Mawangdui, the two texts were written on a single piece of silk, which would facilitate reading them in tandem. This resulted in "The Five Aspects of Conduct" originally being entitled "The Ancient Lost Text That Comes after Copy A of the Laozi" 老子甲本卷後古佚書.[33] Finding these texts connected in this manner is noteworthy, since "The Five Aspects of Conduct" is primarily concerned with the cultivation of humanity and righteousness, moral values that appear prominently in the *Analects* and the *Mencius*.

By avoiding the pitfalls that schools pose for a careful analysis of excavated manuscripts, we can begin to see through the clouds of the Han institutionalization of Confucianism that has filtered our understanding of the formative period of Chinese political philosophy. According to Pang Pu 龐樸, the archaeological record shows the transmitted version of the *Laozi* exaggerates the rancorousness of the debate with followers of Confucian ideas. In fact, the side-by-side discovery of a Confucian text with versions of the *Laozi* in both Mawangdui and Guodian indicates that in early China their ideas must have been understood as related. Since recently excavated manuscripts have shown that the *Laozi* developed alongside Confucian ideas,[34] old notions of schools of thought are in need of being reconsidered.[35]

Guo Qiyong's 郭齊勇 work shows that Guodian has also changed our dating of the formation of the classics, a group of texts revered by traditional scholars for their ability to convey ancient morals to later generations. Prior to these discoveries, it was believed that the classics were first grouped together in the Han dynasty. The earliest citation for this had been the *Zhuangzi*'s 莊子 "Heavenly Revolutions" 天運 chapter that lists the *Book of Odes* 詩經, the *Book of Documents* 尚書, the *Book of Rites* 禮記, the *Book of Music* 樂經, the *Book of Changes* 易經, and the *Springs and Autumns* 春秋, which it labels the Six Classics 六經. The "All Under Heaven" 天下 chapter also lists these titles as a group but does not refer to them as "the Six Classics."

Since the discovery of the "Liu De" 六德[36] text at Guodian, we have learned that the classics were grouped together at least as early as the late Warring States period. This is much earlier than previously supposed, and means that Guodian has moved the date for the first grouping of the classics back to long before the Han dynasty.[37]

Another example of Guodian contributing to our understanding of pre-Han religious and intellectual history is "Xing zi ming chu" 性自命出, which provides new insight into the term "nature" 性. The later importance of this term to Neo-Confucianism resulted in considerable interest by current scholars in understanding the landscape that might have contributed to the development of the term in the *Mencius*. In the "Xing zi ming chu," we see that "Nature comes from mandate, mandate descends from heaven. The way begins with essence (*qing*),[38] essence is born of nature." 性自命出, 命自天降。道始於情, 情生於性。[39] The important difference between this quotation and the later text of the *Mencius* is the incorporation of "essence" into a discussion of the relationship between "nature" and "heaven."[40] It is significant that "essence" forms a link with "nature" and the "way," since "essence" and "nature" are both discussed in *Mencius* 6A.6 and 6A.8. However, in the *Mencius* there is no mention of a relationship between the terms.[41] Finally, "nature," "essence," and "heaven" are discussed in sorites, or linked arguments in "Xing zi ming chu," which is also the dominant rhetorical style in "The Five Aspects of Conduct."

The two editions of "The Five Aspects of Conduct" are highly similar, but their differences have prompted a debate as to the original form of the text. The first difference we notice between the Mawangdui and Guodian editions is actually the medium of choice employed in each tomb. The version of the text found in the Guodian tomb was written on fifty bamboo strips that measure 32 to 32.4 cm in length and are .45 to .65 cm in width, being slightly sharpened on each end. The Mawangdui edition was written on silk. The substantial difference in the content of the texts is that the Mawangdui edition contains a Classic (經 *Jing*) and an Explanation (說 *Shuo*), whereas the Guodian edition contains only the Classic.[42]

Li Xueqin 李學勤 believes that because the Mawangdui tomb was closed roughly a hundred years after the Guodian tomb, the Explanation is the work of later commentators.[43] Ikeda Tomohisa 池田知久 disagrees and argues that the Explanation must have been extant at the time of the Guodian tomb but was omitted by the person who copied the text. His reasoning is that the Explanation was necessary for the Classic to be intelligible.[44] Both scholars could be correct to some extent if the Explanation was the work of a group in existence at the time of Guodian that did not write down their teachings until a short time before Mawangdui was closed. The difference is that this book will argue for the intelligibility of the Classic or Guodian version without use of the Explanation.

Much of the disagreement over which edition came first is concerned with the question of the correct placement of two sections of the text that are ordered differently in the Mawangdui and Guodian editions. Therefore, the question of which edition came first is also an attempt to answer the question of which edition has the correct placement of these sections. If we number the strips based on their appearance in the Guodian edition, we find that the second half of strip 20 through the first half of strip 21 is placed before strip 23 in Mawangdui.[45] Another important discrepancy between the two editions of the texts can be found in the Mawangdui version moving paragraphs 19 through 21 of the Guodian version[46] forward in the text to appear after paragraph 13.

Pang Pu attributes these differences to changes in understanding among the people who were responsible for copying the text. He believes that the placement of paragraphs in the Mawangdui edition indicates the text follows the order of humanity, righteousness, the rites, wisdom, sagacity; he sees the order of paragraphs in the Guodian text as first emphasizing sagacity and wisdom. From the logic and thematic development of the text, he feels the Mawangdui version is more reasonable and may represent the original order of the text.[47]

The problem with Pang Pu's explanation is that depending on how one interprets lacunae, the Mawangdui version could appear to emphasize sagacity and wisdom more than the Guodian version. The second paragraph of the Mawangdui version contains a pair of mirroring sentences that discuss sagacity and wisdom.[48] In the Guodian version, the half of the mirrored sentences relating to wisdom is present, but the sentence relating to sagacity is entirely missing.[49] The absence of this sentence may simply be an oversight or copyist error in the Guodian edition, or it may be seen as an indication that the pairing was deemed more important to the Mawangdui editors.

Liao Mingchun 廖名春 believes that the Mawangdui edition represents a change in the proper order of the text. He feels that the Guodian edition is more internally consistent than the Mawangdui edition and therefore represents the earlier form of the text.[50] Liao argues that the differences in the placement of sections are the work of later Mawangdui editors who changed the order of paragraphs 19 through 21 of the Guodian text because they repeat and expand upon paragraphs 12 through 14.

Paragraph 27 of the Guodian edition contains an important epigraphic issue that can clarify our understanding of its relationship to the Mawangdui text. The characters for "heaven" (天 *tian*) and the coordinating conjunction written as 而 (*er*) in modern Chinese are often indistinguishable in the Guodian script; both are written 天. Strip 20 of the text, for example, has a character that can be transcribed either way. The Mawangdui edition, being written after the standardization of characters by the First Emperor, differentiates the two characters. Therefore, it is interesting that in section 18 of the silk manuscript version of the Classic[51] from Mawangdui, there is a copy error where the character *er* 而 is written instead of *tian* 天. The Guodian text states: "Sages know and lead." 聖人知而道. The Mawangdui text states: "Sages know the way of heaven." 聖人知天道也. It is clear that this is an error, since it is corrected in the corresponding explanation 18,[52] where the passage is repeated. There is no question that the Mawangdui text was copied and buried later than the Guodian edition. However, finding a copy error in the Mawangdui edition that would have easily been a product of the script used in the Guodian edition establishes a paleographic connection in the transmission of the texts.[53]

Schools and Authors

Much of the recent scholarship on "The Five Aspects of Conduct" has been concerned with ascertaining who might have written the text, and the current consensus is that Zisi 子思 was the author.[54] If we could be certain about what Zisi stood for philosophically, this would be a major contribution to scholarship. Instead, we have simply matched a text without an author to an author we know little about from sources that are pre-Han.[55]

There are three ways that scholars relate "The Five Aspects of Conduct" to Zisi.[56] The first way relies on evidence found in Xunzi's 荀子 chapter "Contra Twelve Masters" 非十二子, where he criticizes Mencius 孟子 and Zisi's 子思 *Wuxing* 五行; these happen to be the same two characters used in the opening line of "The Five Aspects of Conduct." The second relates to the appearance of two sentences in the Mawangdui Explanation that are attributed to Shizi 世子. The third reason cites the presence of other texts attributed to Zisi that were also found in the Guodian tomb, increasing the likelihood that "The Five Aspects of Conduct" was by the same author.

We will begin with reasons that relate to "Contra Twelve Masters." The Tang 唐 dynasty (618–907) scholar Yang Liang 楊倞[57] interpreted the characters "Wuxing" 五行 in this chapter of the Xunzi as representing "humanity," "righteousness," "the rites," "wisdom," and "living up to your words" 信.[58] Since the discovery of a text also entitled *Wuxing* in the Mawangdui tomb, Pang Pu has wondered if Yang Liang might have been wrong.

Instead, Pang Pu proposes that these characters could refer to the title of the recently discovered text "The Five Aspects of Conduct" (*Wuxing*).[59] If this is the case, then we are now able to read a text that was singled out as a target for criticism in the *Xunzi*:

> Some men follow the model of the Ancient Kings in a fragmentary way, but they do not understand its guiding principles. Still their abilities are manifold, their memory great, and their experience and knowledge both varied and broad. They have initiated a theory for which they claim great antiquity, calling it the Five Processes theory [五行].[60] Peculiar and unreasonable in the extreme, it lacks proper logical categories. Mysterious and enigmatic, it lacks a satisfactory theoretical basis. Esoteric and laconic in its statements, it lacks adequate explanations. To give their propositions a cloak of respectability and to win respect and veneration from them they claim: "These doctrines represent the genuine words of the gentleman of former times. Zisi provided the tune for them, and Mencius harmonized it." The stupid, indecisive, deluded Ru of today enthusiastically welcome these notions, unaware that they are false. They pass on what they have received, believing that, on account of these theories, Confucius and Zi-gong[61] would be highly esteemed by later generations. It is in just this that they offend against Zisi and Mencius.[62]

> 略法先王而不知其統。猶然而材劇志大。聞見雜博。案往舊造説。謂之五行。甚僻違而無類。幽隱而無說。閉約而無解。案飾其辭而祗敬之。曰。此真先君子之言也。子思唱之。孟軻和之。世俗之溝猶瞀儒嚾嚾然不知其所非也。遂受而傳之。以為仲尼子游為茲厚於後世。是則子思孟軻之罪也。[63]

Although these characters in the preceding quotation are translated "Five Processes theory," they are the same as the title of "The Five Aspects of Conduct." However, we have no way of knowing if these characters refer to the excavated manuscript we found in Guodian and Mawangdui. Xunzi could just as easily be referring to the Five Processes theory of metal 金, wood 木,

water 水, fire 火, and earth 土. This creates a significant problem for Pang Pu's theory that cannot be resolved with certainty
based on existing evidence.

The opening sentence of the Xunzi quotation states, "Some
men follow the model of the Ancient Kings in a fragmentary
way." Jiang Guanghui 姜廣輝 argues that here Xunzi is criticizing Zisi for not knowing about the broader principle of succession that grew after Yao 堯 to Shun 舜 and Yu 禹. Jiang feels that
Zisi is a proponent of the principle of abdicating the throne. His
evidence for this claim is the Guodian text "Tang Yu zhidao,"
which he sees as supporting a king abdicating and then selecting a worthy person as a successor rather than passing his position down hereditarily.[64]

Pang Pu concludes that the following sentence indicates that
Xunzi is critical of "The Five Aspects of Conduct": "They have
initiated a theory for which they claim great antiquity" 案往舊
造說. He states that this shows Xunzi was primarily displeased
with Zisi, who culled his ideas from disparate ancient sources to
establish a new paradigm for discussing virtues. Pang Pu then
sees "mysterious and enigmatic" 幽隱 and "esoteric and laconic"
閉約 as being concerns relevant to Xunzi's primary objection.
This analysis seems rhetorically unproblematic as Pang Pu is
simply assuming that the arguments are being presented in
order of importance.[65]

Regardless of the differing analyses that we find of "Contra
Twelve Masters," we can be certain that Xunzi is somehow displeased with what he terms Zisi, Mencius, and *Wuxing*. Unfortunately, the text is not explicit in stating if Xunzi is referring to
individuals, groups, texts, or even schools of thought, so we are
left to wonder about the true target of his criticism. In my opinion, the question remains unresolved, as this is the only passage
in which Xunzi addresses the subject.

Therefore, despite the best efforts of the scholarship dis-
cussed here, I feel we lack sufficient evidence to conclude that
Xunzi believed that Zisi wrote "The Five Aspects of Conduct."
I agree with Yameng Liu, who has also found only a loose overall

connection between any of the twelve masters in Xunzi's work. When discussing "Contra Twelve Masters," Liu states, "The accusations are, rather, eclectically based and rhetorically charged labels pointing to only one thing in common among the critiqued: their doctrines all deviate, in one way or another, from Xunzi's version of Confucianism."[66]

Returning to the second of three ways that scholars relate "The Five Aspects of Conduct" to Zisi, Li Xueqin believes that Shizi 世子 is important to our assessment of this issue. The characters "Shizi" appear in the Explanation of the Mawangdui edition of the text, and Li believes that Shizi was the author of the Explanation portion. Although there is only a very brief section of the text that is attributed to Shizi, there are no sections from other individuals. Li then argues that Shizi must have been Shishuo 世碩, a disciple of one of Confucius's seventy students. The implication of one of Confucius's seventy students having written the Explanation to "The Five Aspects of Conduct" means to Li that the author of the Classic must have been a person of even greater stature, such as Zisi.[67]

One problem with this theory is that if Shizi wrote the Explanation, there is a potential problem with the sequence of events. Naturally, the Classic portion of "The Five Aspects of Conduct" would have to have been written before Shizi could write his Explanation. However, Shizi is supposed to have died long before the 300 B.C. date of the Guodian tomb. If Shizi actually wrote the Mawangdui Explanation, then it would have been a likely candidate for inclusion in Guodian. Li resolves this problem by assuming that Shizi's writings could have been recorded and compiled after his death by his students in a similar manner as the *Great Learning* 大學, which is supposed to have been recorded by Zengzi's 曾子 disciples.[68] Unfortunately, Li cites no evidence for this assumption, so it must be treated as purely speculative.

A comparison with other texts from Guodian forms the third method of arguing that "The Five Aspects of Conduct" should be associated with Zisi. "Black Robes" and "Duke Mu of Lu Asked Zisi" are clearly connected with Zisi, and these two texts share some similarities with "The Five Aspects of Conduct." Our first evidence that Zisi wrote "Black Robes" comes from the "The Annals of Music" in the *Sui Dynastic History* 隋書, where three chapters of the *Book of Rites*: "'Zhongyong,' 'Biaoji,' 'Fangji,' and 'Ziyi' are all parts of the 'Zisizi.'" 《禮記: 中庸》,《表記》,《坊記》,《緇衣》 皆取 《子思子》. Liang Tao 梁涛 cites the preceding passage and notes that the writing style is similar in the "Biaoji," "Fangji," and "Black Robes." They all use the format of "The Master Said . . ." 子曰 and quote frequently from the *Book of Odes, Book of Documents, Book of Changes*, and *Springs and Autumns*. Among these texts, the *Book of Odes* is quoted more frequently than the rest.[69]

"The Five Aspects of Conduct" is similar in that it favors quotations from the *Book of Odes*, but it also contains important differences. First, it never uses the phrase "The Master said." Second, it is more of a unified philosophical work than the "Black Robes." Liang believes that one possible explanation for these discrepancies is that they might represent two phases in the development of the Zisi School. The earlier phase relied more on quoting and interpreting the words of Confucius, while the later school developed its own philosophical treatises.[70]

Liao Mingchun provides a physical analysis of the bamboo strips to support the association of "The Five Aspects of Conduct" with "Black Robes." He finds that the shapes of the strips of "The Five Aspects of Conduct" and "Black Robes" are essentially the same. His conclusion is that this increases the likelihood that the texts were written by either the same individual or individuals with a common background.[71]

The final evidence of the ideas of Zisi being present in the Guodian tomb can be found in the title of the document "Duke Mu of Lu Asked Zisi." It is interesting that the connection between Duke Mu of Lu and Zisi is also attested to in *Mencius* 6B6, where Chunyu Kun 淳于髡 states, "In the time of Duke Mu of Lu, Gong Yizi was in charge of affairs of state, and Ziliu and Zisi were in office, yet Lu dwindled in size even more rapidly than before."[72] 魯繆公之時。公儀子為政。子柳子思為臣。魯之削也滋甚。[73]

There are two problems with citing the presence of texts attributed to Zisi as evidence that "The Five Aspects of Conduct" should be related to the school of Zisi. First, there are texts attributed to many different authors in the tomb, and Zisi does not even constitute a majority. Second, the only text that "The Five Aspects of Conduct" has been consistently found next to is the *Laozi*, and the two texts were clearly not written by the same author.

The idea that there is even a separate school of Zisi thinking originates in the Xianxue 顯學 chapter of the *Hanfeizi* 韓非子, where it states that in the generation after Confucius, the Confucian school split into eight parts.[74] Pang Pu, for one, questions whether the number of eight should be taken literally.[75] We also must be cautious about drawing conclusions about a Confucian school based on the Hanfeizi because one of the dominant themes in the text is the criticism of the Confucians for being unable to provide a unified voice. Instead, Hanfeizi says that all the Confucians and Mohists can provide is endless debates that distract the emperor.[76]

If we do accept that there was a separate entity known as the Zisi School, the question of what distinguishes it from other Confucian schools remains at present unanswered. One way of ordering the schools is to group Mencius and Zisi together. As discussed earlier, this grouping is the result of Mencius and *Wuxing* being criticized jointly in the *Xunzi*. The problem with this assumption is that we cannot be sure that the *Wuxing* mentioned in *Xunzi* is the same as the *Wuxing* found in Guodian and Mawangdui.[77] Prior to the rediscovery of "The Five Aspects of Conduct," there was considerable disagreement as to how to interpret the *Wuxing* mentioned in *Xunzi*. Liang Qichao 梁啓超 (1873–1929) questioned Yang Liang's standard interpretation, since Yang's fifth item, "living up to your words," 信 is not often used by Mencius. However, Liang was confident that Yang Liang's explanation of the other four items of humanity, righteousness, the rites, and wisdom were plausible, since Mencius himself groups them together in passages 6A.6 and 7A.21.[78]

The earliest mention of the term *Wuxing* is in the *Book of Documents*, "The Speech at Kan" 尚書甘誓: "The prince of Hu wildly wastes and despises the five elements . . ." 有扈氏威侮五行 . . .[79] After the Guodian discovery, it seems that the *Wuxing* alluded to here might not be the five elements or Five Phases *Wuxing* of metal, wood, water, fire, and earth. Instead, there is a possibility that the term *Wuxing* represents five virtues.

In conclusion, it should be noted that there is not unanimous acceptance of the theory that the *Wuxing* of *Xunzi* refers to "The Five Aspects of Conduct." One scholar who disagrees is Ikeda Tomohisa, who believes that "The Five Aspects of Conduct" is a mixture of ideas present in the *Mencius, Xunzi*, and elsewhere. Mencius's work represents the "way of heaven," which Ikeda argues is the result of emphasizing inborn characteristics that we have received from heaven.[80] Xunzi's work represents the "way of humans," according to Ikeda, since it emphasizes the impact of social forces on the development of good behavior. Ikeda further argues that in *Mencius* 6A.15, the relationship between the mind and body is unclear. Commentators claim that this passage implies that the mind is in control of the body, but the text itself is open to interpretation. The difference that Ikeda sees in Xunzi is that the mind is clearly separate from the rest of the bodily organs and controls them.[81] In "The Five Aspects of Conduct," Ikeda also sees the mind as being in control of the body, which he feels may have influenced Xunzi.[82]

The above analysis has shown that the more nuanced approaches of Ikeda Tomohisa and Pang Pu provide valuable insight into the development of the ideas of Mencius, Xunzi, and "The Five Aspects of Conduct." Ikeda points out ways that these three texts have important similarities in their basic assumptions about self-cultivation, while Pang questions some of the ways that "The Five Aspects of Conduct" has come to be linked with Zisi.[83] Further exploration of these connections will continue to enhance our understanding of the intellectual history of early China. Conversely, attempts to determine the author of "The Five Aspects of Conduct" prior to sorting through its philosophical implications seem problematic, as it is likely to limit the range of theories scholars are willing to consider as to how this text relates to others from Guodian. As has been stated, "The Five Aspects of Conduct" was found alongside the *Laozi* on two occasions. A search for further affinities between these two texts should provide fruitful and interesting results.

Analytical Methodology

The analytical challenge presented by "The Five Aspects of Conduct" is that it is highly repetitive and convoluted, making it difficult to identify a clear philosophical position for many single passages. Despite this, there is no indication that the text is simply a random collection of statements; there are consistent patterns in which certain characters tend to be repeated together while others are never used in conjunction with each other. Analyzing the text thus involves understanding what is signified in the usage patterns that occur in the work as a whole. Uncovering these patterns is aided by the presence of black squares on the bamboo strips of the Guodian tomb that indicate section breaks roughly akin to modern paragraphs. The fifth through seventh of these paragraphs, for example, are stylistically very similar in that the character beginning each paragraph is also repeated at the end. These repeated characters are 仁 humanity, 知 wisdom, and 聖 sagacity. There are several other similarities, such as the second through fourth characters being the same in all three paragraphs. Consistent patterns among these three paragraphs indicate they are related, but the most important distinguishing factors are the initial and final characters, which indicate their topics—an exploration or examination of humanity, wisdom, and sagacity.

Since these three paragraphs contain chains of terms with characters repeated at their beginning and end, they are epanaleptical sorites. Sorites are a frequently occurring rhetorical device in "The Five Aspects of Conduct," but they are not all epanaleptical. This presents a difficulty, as sorites are inherently problematic to analyze. They are linked arguments wherein the predicate of each link in the chain of reasoning is used as the subject of each subsequent link. Paradoxical sorites are the most famous of these and have been discussed since Greek times.[84] Recent approaches have considered degrees of truth as a way of ascertaining value in sorites. Michael Tye and Terence Horgan have proposed measuring the degree of vagueness among parts of a sorites to attempt to find value in linked arguments that would otherwise be problematic to analyze.[85]

The problem with applying this methodology to "The Five Aspects of Conduct" is that the moral principles in the text are difficult to measure in objective terms so as to understand the degree of vagueness in the connection between one link and another. This necessitates a search for a yardstick by which to gauge the level of affinity present among terminology that in "The Five Aspects of Conduct" is otherwise highly difficult to quantify. The difficulty in quantifying the terminology will be overcome in this book by carefully building an understanding of value from within "The Five Aspects of Conduct" that will then be tested against and supported by comparison to other excavated Guodian texts. Very little of this type of analysis has been attempted by other scholars, since the bulk of scholarship has looked at the text's relation to the received tradition.

It seems necessary to defend calling the terms used in "The Five Aspects of Conduct" difficult to quantify when the majority of terms employed could be understood by their similar usage in a host of received texts including the *Analects, Mencius, Xunzi*, and so forth. Among these three texts, *Mencius* and *Xunzi* were composed after "The Five Aspects of Conduct," so their hermeneutic value is greatly diminished. While the exact content of the *Analects* circa 300 B.C.E. is a topic of significant debate, the 定州 Dingzhou *Analects* dated to 55 B.C.E. could give a rough approximation of what was available a century and a half earlier.[86] Although this early edition of the *Analects* can provide some degree of clarity to "The Five Aspects of Conduct," these two texts are philosophically unique and thus cannot serve as exact guides to terminological understanding. In addition, due to the penchant for supporting arguments with quotations from *The Odes*,[87] if the author of "The Five Aspects of Conduct" had wanted the reader to understand his text in light of the *Analects*, or any other text, he or she would have provided quotations.

THREE

Rhetoric as Self-Cultivation: A Question of Language

WHEN INDIVIDUALS DEVELOP MORALITY IN "The Five Aspects of Conduct," they break through the confines of what is internal cultivation and convert others in the society. This societal involvement occurs only after their internal cultivation reaches a certain degree of maturity. Although the process can be called self-cultivation, it must be understood as necessarily encompassing a social element and not being limitable to an atomic self.

The mechanism by which morality surpasses internal confines is difficult to understand. It involves morality, an intangible concept, connecting what would otherwise be separate and distinct individuals. There is a degree of difficulty involved in appreciating this particular type of self-cultivation, since it is also described in the text as being manifest in changes in voice and appearance. Believing that morals have such power is a leap of faith. Whether or not this transformation actually occurs, however, is not the concern of the following analysis. Instead, the task is to employ the analytical methodology outlined at the end of chapter 2 to understand the mechanics by which these transformations bridge the rupture that separates individual processes of self-cultivation.

The faith involved in bridging individuals takes on two forms: First, faith is necessary when introducing the inevitable variables involved in including another person in the process of individual moral cultivation. The second type of faith will be discussed in subsequent chapters of this book, but briefly, it relates to the unification or harmonization of conflicting moral principles. This process is understood as occurring diachronically. A single event is insufficient to manifest fully the harmonization of different types of morality, so there is a leap of faith necessary when believing that subsequent events and opportunities will be available to create the desired balance and harmony. This is particularly important, since the bridging of individuals is the key to understanding the societal and religious implications of "The Five Aspects of Conduct."[1]

The basic mechanics of cultivating morality in "The Five Aspects of Conduct" entails two sides, an internal building up and an external manifestation that also includes a transmission to others. Language will be shown to play a role in both moral cultivation and transmission. This role is apparent in paragraph 16, where the text describes external manifestations as part of the process of developing wisdom and sagacity. Very broad terms are used in this description so the actual statements in isolation merely tell us that seeing is part of the cultivation of wisdom, and hearing is part of the cultivation of sagacity. "Seeing something and knowing it is wisdom; hearing something and knowing it is sagacity." 見而知之，智也。聞而知之，聖也。[2] Sensory acuity is the common element here as the visual and aural faculties are both linked to ethical cultivation.

Exactly what we should be hearing or seeing remains somewhat ambiguous in paragraph 16, but clarity can be had by referencing similar statements in paragraphs 6 and 7. These earlier paragraphs describe the seeing and hearing of the moral achievements of those around us. "Having keen vision you will be able to perceive an outstanding person" 明則見賢人[3] appears in paragraph 6, which concerns wisdom. "Having keen hearing you will hear the way of the noble man" 聰，則聞君子道[4] is in paragraph 7, which discusses sagacity. These two paragraphs continue by describing similar phenomena that are resultant from sensory input. Specifically, we are able to produce verbal articulations and manifest physical changes that are both described as resembling jade. By relating ethical cultivation to the beauty of jade, paragraphs 5 and 6 are persuading the reader of the benefits of morality via the medium of language. Here we can see the first clear connection between language and morality; "The Five Aspects of Conduct" itself is creating this connection by using language that could persuade a reader to act morally. The frequent use of quotations from *The Book of Odes* in the support of other statements also indicates language is seen to have persuasive power. This connection will be discussed in detail later in the section entitled The Rhetoric of Self-Cultivation.

Before we can begin to address a possible connection to rhetoric in paragraphs 5, 6, and 16, it is important to be sure that it is not music that we are intended to be hearing. The musical side is initially compelling, since jade is seen elsewhere in early China as musical. Scott Cook discusses a potential connection with the jade pendants described in the *Li Ji* 禮記 "Yu zao 玉藻" chapter, but he ultimately concludes, based on the Mawangdui version, that "The Five Aspects of Conduct" is likely referring to jade-like words rather than jade music.[5] That having been said, since the terms should be put into practice, their linguistic manifestations are merely one component of what they fully represent. The choice of jade is not random. Jade is used in the performance of rituals, and the text uses the term in relation to a person's actions. Since the choice of jade-like as a description is consistently used in the text,[6] we should understand the words we produce and hear as being part of moral cultivation that is upright in a way akin to proper ritual music and jade chimes.

"The Five Aspects of Conduct" sees sagacity as related to language when we are told that we hear the way of the nobleman in paragraph 7. Therefore, sagacity serves as a medium by which we can affect others in society. Words that transform others can be considered a type of rhetoric, since they transmit our internal understanding of sagacity and wisdom in order to persuade others. The process is also cyclical: After completing the cultivation of sagacity by hearing the way from another, I should then seek to convert others to this same understanding through my own words. After others reach this understanding, they perpetuate the cycle by also relying on language to continue the propagation of moral understanding.

There has been significant interest in the relationship between language and ethics in early China.[7] This is no surprise, since Confucius, Mencius, Laozi, Xunzi, Zhuangzi 莊子, and many others address this issue. However, a detailed survey of these transmitted sources would be far too lengthy a detour for a book on Guodian. Instead, the relationship between rhetoric and self-cultivation will be analyzed within "The Five Aspects of Conduct." Then the significant differences with self-cultivation in the *Mencius* will be explored. The reason for selecting the *Mencius* is to continue to refute the claims of scholars discussed in chapter 2 of this book. Prior to embarking on this comparison, it is important to understand the structure in which the crucial elements of sagacity and wisdom relate to the language of moral cultivation in "The Five Aspects of Conduct."

The Hierarchy of Sagacity and Wisdom

Sagacity and wisdom appear together as concepts that bridge the rupture between individual processes of self-cultivation and thus have the power to unite the society as a whole. This provides an important requirement for a religious system, since there is a single standard of morality that brings people together. By analyzing paragraphs 17 and 18 of "The Five Aspects of Conduct," it will be argued that an important hierarchy exists between sagacity and wisdom. Both paragraphs begin with sagacity and wisdom, respectively, but the structures of the paragraphs provide evidence that they are seen as existing in a hierarchy.[8] Specifically, paragraph 17 states that sagacity is the harmonization of five aspects of conduct, while paragraph 18 states that wisdom is the harmonization of only four. This means that sagacity is greater in scope than wisdom.[9] The scope in question here relates to the ultimate question of the text, how self cultivation allows us to join conflicting parts of our ethical world.

The first clue to this unification is in paragraph 17, where we see that sagacity and wisdom are transferred through linguistic and visual signs:

> Hearing the way of the noble man is having keen hearing; hearing something and knowing it is sagacity. Sages know the way of heaven ❷❻. Knowing something and putting it into practice is righteousness. Practicing something with the appropriate timing is virtue. Recognizing an outstanding person is having keen vision. Recognizing something and ❷❼ knowing it is wisdom. Knowing and being at peace is humanity. Being at peace and reverential is [following the] rites. Where sageness, wisdom, ritual and music are born is the harmonious combination of the five ❷❽ aspects of conduct.

> 聞君子道, 聰也。聞而知之, 聖。聖人知天❷❻道也。知而行之, 義也。行之而時, 德也。見賢人, 明也。見而知之, ❷❼ 智也。知而安之, 仁也。安而敬之, 禮也。聖, 知禮樂之所由生也, 五❷❽ [行之所和]也。[10]

The practice of self-cultivation is composed of five important moral concepts that connect to each other in a variety of ways. There are consistencies in these relationships such as wisdom relating to keen hearing and sagacity's association with keen vision, but their important function in paragraph 17 is to act as catalysts that allow us to connect humanity, righteousness, and the rites. The paragraph begins with sagacity, which might indicate it is deemed of greater importance in relation to the connections with terms subsequently mentioned. The problem with this is that paragraph 18 begins with wisdom but then contains a similar discussion of the intertwining of humanity, righteousness, and the rites. A clarification of this relationship can be had by referencing the way the interconnection of five moral characteristics is seen in paragraph 2: "There are five aspects of virtuous conduct, that when united is called virtue itself. When only four of these actions are united it is called being adept (at virtue). Adeptness is the way of humans ❹ while virtue is the way of heaven." 德之行五和謂之德，四行和謂之善。善，人❹道也。德，天道也。[11] This brings us full circle to "virtue" and "heaven," which were both related to sagacity in paragraph 17: "Sages know the way of heaven ❷❻. Knowing something and putting it into practice is righteousness. Practicing something with the appropriate timing is virtue." 聖人知天❷❻道也。知而行之，義也。行之而時，德也。[12] Here, sagacity is part of a more advanced stage of self-cultivation, which also entails a unification of other moral traits. The consistency between paragraph 2 and paragraph 17 means that we can conclude that sagacity represents the highest form of cultivation in the text, a unification of all other virtues, and a connection with heaven.

In that the basic style of argument in "The Five Aspects of Conduct" is sorites, one might argue for a connection between sagacity in the second sentence of paragraph 17 and the phrase that follows: "knowing something and putting it into practice is righteousness." Such an assumption would see righteousness as more closely related to sagacity than humanity, since it follows in closer proximity in the passage. This would be incorrect based on evidence from paragraphs 5 through 7, each of which discusses a single moral concept: humanity, wisdom, and sagacity, respectively. These three paragraphs are stylistically very similar and constitute an important exploration of the path of cultivation, starting from within our bodies and proceeding to external manifestations. This also relates to a central theme of the text that sees the path of cultivation requiring an external side and religious element. However, in these paragraphs, righteousness is not mentioned, which means it is not consistently connected to sagacity.[13]

The issue of consistent and inconsistent usage in the text is an interesting one. There is a consistency within binary pairs, but other terms appear and disappear in an irregular manner. Sagacity and wisdom are used consistently in that sagacity is always the mark of higher cultivation and wisdom is slightly lower. However, when we expand our analysis to include their relationships with humanity and righteousness, there is a lack of consistency. The trend that appears out of this is that juxtapositions between binary pairs tend to maintain consistency, but larger groupings, such as four concepts, do not exhibit such clear inclinations.

For example, following the mention of righteousness in paragraph 17, we find humanity related to wisdom, but it is not directly linked to the term "sagacity," which begins the paragraph. Subsequent to the statement containing "humanity," there is an additional connection with the rites. The text states that "being at peace and reverential is [following the] rites." One reading of this statement is that it could mean that wisdom plus peace and reverence is the rites. An alternate reading would be that humanity with the addition of reverence is the rites. Since there was not an explicit connection between righteousness and sagacity in the later part of the paragraph, there is no reason to think that there is a special relationship between the rites and wisdom either. Regardless of how we understand how "the rites" fits into this statement, we can see that sagacity and wisdom are used more consistently than subsequent broader connections. However, we must remember the importance of these two terms is that they are able to unify different sides of our moral conduct.

A more precise, understanding of how the lower stage of self-cultivation still involves unity can be seen in paragraph 18:

> 18. Recognizing something and knowing it is wisdom. Knowing and being at peace is humanity. Being at peace ❸⓪ and practicing it, you are righteous. Practicing it and being reverential [is to follow] the rites. Humanity, righteousness and the rites are what emerge when you unify the four aspects of conduct.

Having harmonized ❸❶ them you can bring them together; when together you are adept [at virtue].

見而知之，智也。知而安之，仁也。安❸❶而行之，義也。行而敬之，禮。仁義，禮所由生也。四行之所和也，和❸❶則同。同則善。■¹⁴

The preceding quotation relates to wisdom and not sagacity. The first reason for this is obvious; sagacity is not mentioned. While this might seem overly simplistic, it can lead us to a better understanding of what distinguishes wisdom from sagacity. In the next to the last sentence, there is mention of the unification of four aspects of conduct. Unifying only four aspects is related to being adept, a term that appears in the last sentence of the passage. Without a harmonization of all five ways of acting morally, a person cannot attain either sagacity or virtue, two terms again absent from the passage. This means that terms here encompass the various attributes of a lower level of attainment, unlike those found in paragraph 17.

By comparing the attributes of self-cultivation in paragraphs 17 and 18, we can understand what is meant by lower versus higher levels of attainment. The first feature that should be mentioned is that both levels include the three aspects of conduct: righteousness, humanity, and the rites. We could assume that these aspects of conduct are understood as either not having distinctions of higher or lower attainment or else pertaining to a person of both levels of attainment. Since there is no instance in the text where "humanity," "righteousness," or "the rites" is clearly limited to either higher or lower levels of self-cultivation, it is logical to assume that these terms relate to both levels.

Important similarities between paragraphs 17 and 18 further supports the theory that the advanced stage of self-cultivation is developed from the lower stage. This can be seen by observing the consistent usage of the terms "humanity" "righteousness," "the rites," and "wisdom." First, the relationship between humanity and wisdom is identical. In both instances, it is stated that wisdom with the addition of peace is humanity. This reinforces the sense that sagacity is slightly above but encompassing of wisdom, since it comes after a statement related to sagacity in paragraph 17. Second, righteousness in both instances follows the word 行 *xing*, which has been translated "acting." Finally, the word 敬 *jing*, or "being reverential," is what precedes the rites. Each of these associations—peace with humanity, practicing with righteousness, and reverence with the rites—can be seen repeated several times in the text.

The differences between paragraphs 17 and 18 are, then, subtle. One example of the subtlety can be seen by comparing paragraph 17, where righteousness is "knowing and acting," with paragraph 18, righteousness is "being at peace and acting." One possible explanation for this slight difference is that the paragraphs are describing different levels of attainment. When fully harmonizing all five aspects of conduct, righteousness is knowing and acting, but a person who can harmonize only four aspects of conduct understands righteousness as being at peace and acting. If we accept this explanation, it must be that a superior understanding of the rites is one that involves peace and reverence while an inferior understanding is one that involves practicing and reverence. The problem with both the explanation of righteousness and how such an explanation informs our understanding of the rites is that, as previously stated, humanity is described in the same manner in both paragraphs. It seems unlikely that humanity is the one aspect of conduct that is the same regardless of one's level of attainment. The most plausible explanation of this is that the text is not attempting to make a distinction in terms of the specifics of how one cultivates morality in beginning and advanced stages.

Furthermore, we cannot conclude from these paragraphs that peace is an attribute of wisdom while knowing is an attribute of sagacity. The first reason this is not true is that knowing itself is an attribute of wisdom in the sense of seeing and knowing. The second reason is that in paragraph 17, the rites are described as being at peace and being reverent, whereas in paragraph 18 the rites are described as acting and being reverent. In both paragraphs, the term "rites" comes after "wisdom" and is the last Aspect of Conduct to be discussed, so we cannot conclude that peace is an attribute of wisdom.

So far, the only substantial differentiation between the attainment of four aspects of conduct in paragraph 18 and the attainment of five aspects of conduct in paragraph 17 is that the former relates to sagacity. However, an interesting difference can be seen in the following sentence in paragraph 17 that contains the character "music" 樂. "Where sageness, wisdom, ritual and music are born is the harmonious combination of the five ❷❽ aspects of conduct." 聖，知禮樂之所由生也，五❷❽ (行之所和) 也。The other three terms that are to be harmonized are aspects of conduct: sagacity, wisdom, and the rites. It is not surprising that sagacity, wisdom, and the rites would be part of the harmonization because there are abundant other examples of this in "The Five Aspects of Conduct." Music, however, is not described as one of the main aspects of conduct and is thus a surprising inclusion. It is important to look at other instances of the word in the text to understand the importance of this difference.

"Music" 樂 is used ten times in the text. The exact same statement regarding music appears three times. This statement is, "Without peace you are not musical; without music you lack virtue." It occurs in paragraphs 2, 3, and 11 and accounts for six of the occurrences of the character in the text, since the character appears twice in each instance. In paragraphs 2 and 3, it follows similar situations in which a person does not possess or properly apply wisdom. In paragraph 11, it follows a statement describing a lack of sagacity, wisdom, and humanity. The next three instances of music occur in paragraph 17. The first is in the anomalous instance we are seeking to clarify that is quoted earlier. The next two instances from paragraph 17 are in the sentence that follows: "Being unified you are musical. If there is music there is virtue and a state and its families can arise." Once again, we can see that the word "music" is being used in the same context as wisdom and sagacity. The final instance of "music" is in the last sentence of the text: "Those who hear the way and are musical are those who like virtue." Since the most consistent context for the occurrence of the word "music" in the text is virtue, the two terms should be related. Virtue represents the highest level of attainment in the text, and music occurs within two characters of every instance of virtue. Despite paragraph 17 being slightly different, it still relates to a high attainment of self-cultivation. This confirms that paragraph 17 is subtly distinguishing itself as a higher level of self-cultivation than paragraph 18. Such confirmation is important when trying to measure the vagueness of a sorites and understand the way that moral behavior is interrelated.

It is important to remember that this high level of attainment that relates to music and unification can only be achieved with the help of our sense of hearing in "The Five Aspects of Conduct." This highlights the first important difference between "The Five Aspects of Conduct" and the *Mencius*. The role of hearing the way from another in the process of self-cultivation represents an outside influence that Mencius would downplay. In 2A.6, Mencius states that we all have four sprouts just as we have four limbs. These sprouts are humanity, righteousness, the rites, and wisdom, but Mencius sees them as innate abilities similar to our four appendages. These four sprouts are what orient us toward good behavior such as saving a baby about to fall into a well. Lacking these sprouts is described as not being human.[15] This decline is described in 6A.15 as resulting from the lesser parts of our bodies seducing our greater parts. In this, we see a recurrence of internal factors being described as a source of goodness and problems only arising from external factors. Interestingly, in 6A.15, the means by which these external factors can destroy our innate goodness is through the organs of hearing and sight, precisely the means by which we absorb goodness in "The Five Aspects of Conduct."[16]

Mencius deals more specifically with the relationship between language and self-cultivation in 2A.2, where he opposes Gaozi's statement "If you do not get it from words, do not seek it in the heart; if you do not get it from the heart, do not seek

it in *qi*."[17] 不得於言。勿求於心。不得於心。勿求於氣。[18] Men-
cius sees things quite differently from "The Five Aspects of Conduct," since he sees the heart taking precedence over words. It
is interesting that the statement by Gaozi cited by Mencius is
a sorites. Since we are concerned with the inner structure of
sorites argument in "The Five Aspects of Conduct," it is instructive to reference Alan K. L. Chan's observations of the passage in
that he reduces Gaozi's statement to a simple hierarchy between
"words" 言, "the heart" 心, and *qi* 氣.[19]

Chan's hierarchy is demonstrated in the following statement where Mencius sees the power of words as secondary to
inner sources of moral cultivation: "From biased words I can see
wherein the speaker is blind; from immoderate words, wherein
he is ensnared; from heretical words, wherein he has strayed
from the right path; from evasive words, wherein he is at his wits'
end."[20] 詖辭知其所蔽。淫辭知其所陷。邪辭知其所離。遁辭
知其所窮。[21] In his analysis of this quotation, Chan states, "This
confirms the general relationship between *yan, xin* and *qi* discussed earlier. It also highlights Mencius' disagreement with
Gaozi, who places 'words' in a privileged position in the shaping
of the heart."[22] Instead of searching outward while cultivating
morality, Mencius advises us to turn to internal sources such as
our human nature.

"The Five Aspects of Conduct" is a text that is concerned
primarily with unity, so there is no inherent tension between
internal and external, self and other.[23] Our cultivation is internal in that we must form sagacity and wisdom internally. It
is also external, since we must listen to the words of another.
Ultimately, these divisions must disappear as even the divisions
between sagacity and wisdom are replaced by a purely harmonious combination of all aspects of moral conduct. The term
"self-cultivation" is even somewhat of a misnomer, as the process cannot function within the confines of only one individual.
Rhetoric bridges the divide between individuals and allows the
development of sagacity to become infinite, since it is continued
in those we touch.[24]

The Rhetoric of Self-Cultivation

The previous section demonstrated that in "The Five Aspects of Conduct," moral articulations are an important part of self-cultivation. One crucial area is the question of what might be important to be heard by a person seeking to cultivate sagacity. Two rhetorical devices that are predominantly used by this text can clarify what we are to listen for, quotations from *The Book of Odes*, and sorites.[25] *Odes* quotations play a supporting role in that they consistently appear at the conclusions of statements about moral cultivation, as axiomatic evidence to bolster claims that are logically distinct from the meanings of the quotations themselves. These quotations are seen as important and are treated as maxims in the text. The function of *Odes* quotations is to demonstrate the correctness of other statements and thus serve as clarification and amplification. One example of an *Odes* quotation appears after a sorites on sagacity:

7. Sagacious thoughts: [they] are light; being light they form, forming they will not be neglected, not neglecting you will have keen hearing;[26] having keen hearing you will hear the way of the noble man; hearing the way of the noble man you will be like jade sounds; being like jade sounds you will be formed; being formed you will be ❶❺ Sagacious. ■

7. 聖之思也輕，輕則形，形則不忘，不忘則聰。聰，則聞君子道，聞君子道則玉音，玉音則形，形❶❺ 則聖。■

8. "A good person, a noble man, his manner is unified."[27] Only after you are able to unify [your manner] can you be a noble man. Then you are always concerned about your uniqueness.[28] ■ ❶❻

8.「淑人君子，其儀宜一也。」 能為一，然後能為君子。[君子] 慎其獨也。■ ❶❻

9. "I looked until I could no longer see her and cried like rain."[29] "Only when you are able to display your wings unevenly"[30] do you understand the utmost sadness. A noble man is concerned about his ❶❼ uniqueness.∎

9.「(瞻望弗及)，泣涕如雨。」能「差池其羽，」然後能至袁。君子慎其❶❼（獨也。∎）

A direct approach to explaining how these Odes quotations relate to sagacity is difficult. The aesthetic congruence between these lines of poetry and the development of morality is intentionally vague. Our only viable wedge for understanding these lines is the conspicuous repetition of the term "noble man" 君子. Two sides of the term "noble man" are important to understand in the text. The first is what constitutes a noble man. This relates to what is involved in such a person's process of self-cultivation and what may be construed as to the outlines of a definition of the term. The second aspect of the term is how a noble man affects those he encounters. Although the text provides clues as to how the actions of a noble man are carried out, there are no clear or exact definitions of what is meant by the term. The text also does not contain entirely specific details as to how a person should carry out the tasks of a noble man in a particular circumstance. However, a general understanding can be pieced together from fragmentary evidence in "The Five Aspects of Conduct."

First, as far as the status of the term in the text is concerned, the noble man represents a person who has achieved a high level of attainment in self-cultivation. This can be seen in the fact that the noble man is described in the text as at a higher level than the gentleman 士 *shi*. We can derive this hierarchy from paragraph 3, which states that the gentleman should focus his goals on way of the noble man. The term "gentleman" does not appear frequently in the text; it is used on only one other occasion. However, "the way of the noble man" is repeated several times. The instance that begins the third paragraph is particularly important. It states that the noble man embodies all five aspects of conduct that are central to the text and then practices them at the appropriate time.

It might seem that in order to be called a noble man, a person must have completed the process of self-cultivation and be a paragon of morality. The problem with this assumption is that paragraph 10 states: "Regarding a noble man's being adept [at virtue], there is something that he takes as the beginning and something that he takes as the end. Regarding a noble man being virtuous, ❶❸ there is something that he takes as the beginning but nothing that he takes as the end." This passage implies that the term "noble man" can be associated either with being adept, the second-highest level of self-cultivation, or with virtue, the highest level of self-cultivation. A plausible explanation for this is that when the noble man encounters different situations, he acts differently.

However, in the beginning of paragraph 3, a distinction is drawn between being adept, as a combination of four Aspects of Conduct, and being virtuous, a combination of all five: "If someone forms the five aspects of conduct within his inner heart and at the appropriate time practices them ❺ he is said to be a noble man." This idea was reinforced in paragraph 7, which relates the noble man to sagacity—the higher level of cultivation. One conclusion that can be inferred is that a person who has mastered the higher level of cultivation can perform actions that were prerequisite to attaining that higher level if necessary. This is predicated on a notion of cultivation as a process that begins low and progresses to higher levels. In this, there would be continuity between the higher and lower levels. It would then be natural for a noble man with the higher level of cultivation to continue performing actions perfected earlier while working to attain more advanced levels.

One description of a noble man's actions that was mentioned earlier is the timely application of morality. In addition to this attribute, in paragraph 2, we see that lacking concern leads a noble man to lack wisdom. From this, we can see that the opposite should also be true: concern is an attribute important to the noble man. This is evident in paragraph 4, where lacking wisdom and humanity led an individual to lack concern in the face of a noble man's absence. This introduces the idea that a noble man is a person who not only exhibits concern but also engenders concern in others.

Further traits of the noble man appear in paragraph 24: "A noble man puts the great parts together." The sentences following this quotation contain terms related to humanity and righteousness.[31] Because of this connection, it is possible that the two parts that a noble man puts together are humanity and righteousness. An alternative is that it could also refer generally to the unification of moral conduct. While it is likely that the noble man is one who brings humanity and righteousness together, the ability to unify conflicting moral principles is also highly valued in the text as a whole.[32] Thus bringing greater parts together is generally a highly prized attribute. The idea that a noble man brings things together is further reinforced in paragraph 8, where the quotation from the *Book of Odes* (毛 詩 152) states, "A good person, a noble man, his manner is unified."

What we can conclude about the *Ode* quotations in paragraphs 8 and 2 is that they are specifically restating attributes of the noble man that are also apparent in other sections of the text. These two attributes are, respectively, the ability to unify, and the development of concern. The rhetorical function of the *Odes* is thus axiomatic; it is cited as an authority on proper cultivation that reinforces the words of the author. These quotations are not defended or justified; they are simply provided as unassailable truths. The *Odes* quotations are also the only ones used in the text, so they are the best candidate for considering what one might be intended to hear that would enable one to attain an understanding of sagacity. Finally, *Odes* quotations might represent an example of what one might say to others after mastering self-cultivation.

Understanding Sorites

Paragraph 11 of "The Five Aspects of Conduct" provides one example of rhetoric's importance to the process of self-cultivation:

11. A bronze [bell] voice is adept [at virtue] while jade vibrancy is sagacious. Being adept [at virtue] is the way of humans ❶❾ while being virtuous is the way of heaven. Only those who have virtue, can have a bronze [bell] voice and jade vibrancy. Not having keen hearing you will lack keen vision; not having keen vision you will lack sagacity; no sagacity no ❷⓿ wisdom; no wisdom no human-ity; without humanity you will not be at peace; without peace you will not be musical; without music you will lack virtue.

金聲，善也。玉音，聖也。善，人❶❾道也。德，天（道也）。唯有德者，然後能金聲而玉振之。不聰不明，［不明不聖］，不聖不❷⓿智，不智不仁，不仁不安，不安不樂，不樂無德。[33]

The structure of the beginning of the quotation is A:B; A:B with "bronze tone," "being adept," and "the way of humans" being "A," and "jade voice," "sagacity," "being virtuous," and the "way of heaven" being "B." As has been discussed, this structure shows the relationship between wisdom and sagacity as hierar-chical, with the way of heaven "B" being greater than the way of humans "A." The grouping of the "A" side as a unit is unprob-lematic as "being adept" is repeated and serves as a common ele-ment tying "bronze tone" together with "the way of humans."

However, the grouping of the "B" side is less obvious, since neither "virtue" nor "sagacity" is repeated. That we have the be-ginnings of parallelism in "A" does not mean that we can be confident that the same pattern will be followed in "B." The best evidence for "B" belonging as a group can be found later in the text, where paragraph 17 states that "sages know the way of heaven ❷❻" 聖人知天 ❷❻ 道也。[34] This is still not as concrete a grouping as the "A" side, since a connection between "sage" and "heaven" does not necessitate a relationship with "jade voice" and "being virtuous," but there is a strong probability that this is the case.

Relating bronze and jade sounds with sagacity and wisdom can also be found in *Mencius* 5B.1, which D. C. Lau translates as follows:

> Confucius was the one who gathered together all that was good. To do this is to open with bells and conclude with jade tubes. To open with bells is to begin in an orderly fashion; to conclude with jade tubes is to end in an orderly fashion. To begin in an orderly fashion pertains to wisdom while to end in an orderly fashion pertains to sageness . . .[35]

> 孔子之謂集大成。集大成也者。金聲而玉振之也。金聲也者。始條理
> 也。玉振之也者。終條理也。始條理者。智之事也。終條理者聖之事
> 也。[36]

In the *Mencius*, bronze and jade sounds are ritual signifiers[37] of the beginning and *end* of the process of cultivating wisdom and sagacity. It would seem that this passage from the *Mencius* would be instrumental in explicating the cultivation process in "The Five Aspects of Conduct," since terminological similarities are abundant.

However, "The Five Aspects of Conduct" is very different. In paragraph 10, we see that "regarding a noble man being adept [at virtue], there is something that he takes as the beginning and something that he takes as the end. Regarding a noble man being virtuous, ❶❽ there is something that he takes as the beginning but nothing that he takes as the end. One who has a bronze tone and jade tremolo is a virtuous one." 君子之為善也, 有與始, 有與終。君子之為德也, ❶❽[有與始, 無與][38] 終。金聲而玉振之, 有德者也。[39] In this quotation, we find the same pairing of "being adept" with "bronze" and "being virtuous" with "jade" that appears in paragraph 11 and the *Mencius* in conjunction with wisdom and sagacity. The difference is that paragraph 10 tells us that while being adept and wise is a finite process, being virtuous and sagacious is infinite, so there is no "end" as in the *Mencius*.[40]

One way of explaining the finite and infinite in the context of wisdom and sagacity is to see that the former pertains to the initial stage of self-cultivation, whereas the latter pertains to the more advanced stages. Since a truncated version of the wisdom and sagacity hierarchy also appears in *Mencius* 5B.1, such an explanation should raise no objections. However, the specific implications of finite and infinite self-cultivation are quite complex.

First, although *Mencius* 5B.1 does discuss the development of morals in the general context of the infinite, it is explicit in another passage, 7A.1. "Mencius said, 'For man to give full realization to his heart is for him to understand his own nature, and a man who knows his own nature will know heaven.'"[41] 孟子曰。盡其心者。知其性也。知其性則知天矣。[42] In 7A.1, fully realizing ourselves leads to a higher level of understanding, which includes making a connection with what is beyond our capacity to understand through direct contact.[43] What we come to understand is of such immense proportions that it is in fact infinite. Continuing from this perspective, when we compare 7A.1 and 5B.1, we see that the key difference is human nature when deciding if self-cultivation will lead to the infinite or the finite. I believe that what is meant by finite in the progression from sagacity to wisdom in 5B.1 is that the end point of this action is our human nature, which in turn serves as our only means of comprehending heaven. In other words, progressing from wisdom to sagacity is finite, since it is part of realizing our human nature and nothing more.

"The Five Aspects of Conduct" and the *Mencius* have important terminological similarities in their description of this progression from wisdom to sagacity; they both believe this is analogous to bronze and jade sounds. However, the author of "The Five Aspects of Conduct" was not concerned with human nature, and the term does not appear in the text. This is not a minor difference. Without a consideration of human nature, there was no impediment to cultivation beginning with wisdom, progressing to sagacity, and then concluding with a direct comprehension of heaven and the infinite.

Exactly how one obtains an understanding of heaven is not immediately clear in "The Five Aspects of Conduct." I do not believe that sagacity itself is the link between the individual and infinite or heaven. Instead, the process of self-cultivation can be divided into two parts: The initial stage of cultivation features having keen vision, wisdom, being adept, and the way of humans and is finite. The latter stage includes having keen hearing, sagacity, virtue, and the way of heaven and is infinite. Components within the initial stage of cultivation are interconnected and appear in contrast to members of the second stage and vice versa. This is similar to the way that the noble man relates to initial and advanced stages of cultivation.

One term found in the second stage of self-cultivation that is conspicuously absent from the *Mencius* is keen hearing. The importance of hearing is that it bridges the divide between people. By taking the place of human nature, it forms a link between the individual and the infinite. This linking of individuals is of course vital to the religious structure of "The Five Aspects of Conduct." As was pointed out earlier, in paragraphs 10 and 11, sagacity and wisdom involve both the production of ritual articulations as signified by jade and bronze sounds and the ability to identify correctly these manifestations of self-cultivation. This means that self-cultivation is in fact inseparable from interacting with other individuals and the formation of a religious community. If we are unable to hear from others or observe the manifestations of their cultivation, we are missing an important aspect of sagacity and wisdom. In addition, if we do not express to others what we have realized through our cultivation, in both visible and audible signs, we are not fully possessed of sagacity and wisdom.

This means that rhetoric is inseparable from moral cultivation. Sagacity and wisdom are expressed to others through the practice of rhetoric. Such a claim is not mere self-expression; this is an act of religious transformation both for the audience and for the person producing the rhetoric. By producing morally persuasive rhetoric, we transmit sagacity and wisdom to others and simultaneously realize it for ourselves. Support for this assertion is evident in paragraph 15, where it states:

> One who has never ❷❷ heard the way of the noble man, is said not to have keen hearing. One who has never seen an outstanding person, is said not to have keen vision. If you hear the way of the noble man but do not know ❷❸ it is the way of the noble man this is called not being sagacious. If you see an outstanding person but you do not know he has virtue, this is called not being wise.❷❹

> 未嘗❷❷聞君子道，謂之不聰。未嘗見賢人，謂之不明。聞君子道而不知❷❸其君子道也，謂之不聖。見賢人而不知其有德也，謂之不智。❷❹[44]

This passage follows the same A:B; A:B pattern observed in earlier passages related to sagacity and wisdom. Part "A" associates hearing with sagacity, and "B" connects seeing with wisdom. Hypothetical believers might see it as possible to remain unaffected after contacting a noble man or an outstanding person, but it would be the result of a failure to understand sagacity and wisdom. When we are moved by the words of a noble man, we are fulfilling an important step in the cultivation of sagacity. This is more advanced than wisdom, which involves only visual recognition. Rhetoric is thus responsible for transferring sagacity from one individual to another.

The connections among sensory acuity, sagacity, and wisdom are pervasive in the text. Every paragraph that mentions sagacity and wisdom also mentions keen hearing and vision. A person must possess both of these abilities in order to complete the search for understanding.

This results in the interconnectedness of individuals, not unlike the way that the sorites represent a chain of connections.

Specifically, individual items in chains relating to humanity, righteousness, the rites, wisdom, and sagacity are then repeated in another section of the text, building connections between sections. The sectioned nature of the text is evident in the square blocks on the original bamboo strips, indicating logical breaks in ideas quite similar to modern paragraphs. For example, the mention of sensory acuity in relation to both sagacity and wisdom is a way these two terms interconnect. The highest goal of the text is a harmonization and appreciation of five different aspects of conduct, and it seems that the sorites provide insight into how this can be accomplished.

This harmonization is not immediately apparent in the text, since wisdom corresponds to a harmonization of four of the aspects of conduct; sagacity corresponds to a harmonization of all five. In addition, sagacity is the way of heaven, whereas wisdom is the way of man. From this, it is clear that sagacity represents a higher level of attainment than wisdom, since sages are able to be equal to heaven, but the wise do not have this power. It is important to remember that the ultimate purpose of the text is not to distinguish and separate the aspects of moral conduct, but rather teach us how to bring them together. This harmonization is not fully homogenized without distinctions but is, rather, a celebration of diverse and distinct elements that work together to construct a coherent unity. The importance of individual moral elements that maintain distinct unique characteristics in the text is of course consistent with the aim of a religious system that is built on individual cultivation.

The importance of distinct moral elements is akin to the importance of distinct individuals in the society. The social structure is composed of disparate elements, each of which is unique and separate. Social hierarchy is important, but there is recognition that it is the contributions of all elements that represent the highest level of achievement. If even one-fifth of the group is excluded, then it is a failure to achieve the fully integrated harmonization that the text advocates.

The previously discussed theory is that the difference between the infinite and the finite in "The Five Aspects of Conduct" and the *Mencius* stems from human nature's presence or absence. While human nature does not represent the entirety of the differences between the texts, we do see that humans can be equal to heaven in "The Five Aspects of Conduct," but this is not the case in the *Mencius*. There is a clear hierarchy in the *Mencius*, and heaven is much more powerful. In particular, this becomes an issue in relation to the role of humans in deciding who should rule, as will be discussed in chapter 5.

FOUR

Attaining Unity in Guodian Texts

THE STATE AND FAMILY, INNER and outer, even self and cosmos, are unifiable in the Guodian texts. This is accomplished by harmonizing and integrating what the benighted would consider distinct, or even in diametric opposition. Unity provides a coherent religious message that self-cultivation is more than an individual project, but part of a larger system for the society. The prevalence of this theme will be shown in four texts: the *Laozi* fragments, "Taiyi Shengshui,"[1] "The Five Aspects of Conduct," and "Tang Yu zhidao" 唐虞之道. The *Laozi* fragments and "The Five Aspects of Conduct" will receive greater attention, since they provide insight into the process of attaining unity.

In the Guodian *Laozi* fragments, we are asked to overcome our usual fixation with opposites such as beauty and ugliness, being and nonbeing, and so forth. Average people become burdened by these opposites, while enlightened individuals see them as interrelated and sharing a common origin. Similarly, "The Five Aspects of Conduct" advocates an internal unification of five different aspects of moral conduct, while "Tang Yu zhidao" sees government as ideally being a hybrid that employs methods that relate to both humanity and righteousness. Each of these texts explores unity from a slightly different perspective, but a harmonization of binary opposites remains the key to achieving the highest levels of understanding.

A concern for the proper understanding of pairs of opposites has long been recognized as an important part of the *Laozi*,[2] fragments of which were of course included in the Guodian tomb. What is unique is that texts that are seen by many as offspring of Confucius's writings such as "The Five Aspects of Conduct" share this perspective.

The use of terms like "harmonization" and "integration" in the following discussion is meant to illustrate the Guodian penchant for the merging of dissimilar entities to form a new whole. This integration can be divided into two types: The first is a harmonization of the positive with the negative, which is prominent in the *Laozi* fragments. In this text, by seeing beyond the normal categories that others accept, an enlightened person can understand the true nature of the world. The second type of integration that is observed in the Guodian is comprised of positive attributes. These include humanity and righteousness, morals that form the core of Confucian ethics. Although they share a positive connotation, these morals remain distinct and are developed, practiced, and understood differently. Their integration represents the highest achievement of self-cultivation in "The Five Aspects of Conduct" and forms the basis of good government in "Tang Yu zhidao."

Interestingly, a harmonious unity of state and family concerns is precisely the type of government advocated by the long-contested Grand Unity 大同 passage of the *Book of Rites*:

> When the Grand course was pursued, a public and common spirit ruled all under the sky; they chose men of talents, virtue, and ability; their words were sincere, and what they cultivated was harmony. Thus men did not love their parents only, nor treat as children only their own sons. A competent provision was secured for the aged till their death, employment for the able-bodied, and the means of growing up to the young.

They showed kindness and compassion to widows, orphans, childless men, and those who were disabled by disease, so that they were all sufficiently maintained. Males had their proper work, and females had their homes. (They accumulated) articles (of value), disliking that they should be thrown away upon the ground, but not wishing to keep them for their own gratification. (They labored) with their strength, disliking that it should not be exerted, but not exerting it (only) with a view to their own advantage. In this way (selfish) schemings were repressed and found no development. Robbers, filchers, and rebellious traitors did not show themselves and hence the outer doors remained open, and were not shut. This was (the period of) what we call the Grand Union.[3]

大道之行也天下為公選賢與能講信修睦故人不獨親其親不獨子其子
使老有所終壯有所用幼有所長矜寡孤獨廢疾者皆有所養男有分女有
歸貨惡其弃於地也不必藏於己力惡其不出於身也不必為己是故謀閉
而不興盜竊亂賊而不作故外戶而不閉是謂大同。[4]

It is possible that this quotation is indebted to the Guodian focus on harmony, since Graham believes the Grand Unity passage dates from the Han.[5] Hsiao Kung-chuan provides a lengthy treatment of the subject and concludes that Qian Mu and others who date the "Li Yun" as Han are overzealous followers of the 1920s and 1930s movement to doubt antiquity. He feels the ideas of the Grand Unity can be justified as Confucian and need not be seen as Mohist, Huang-Lao, or anything else.[6] It might seem that recently excavated texts are confirming Hsiao's theory that the Grand Unity is compatible with Confucian philosophy; however, a lack of school distinctions in Guodian challenges this from a methodological perspective. One significant difference between the Grand Unity and Guodian is a lack of binary opposites being joined to construct unity. The only obvious binary opposites are male and female, but these are not seen as existing in tension. Instead, male and female equally partake in unity. Chapter 5 of this book will explore the Guodian notion of balancing the selection of talented individuals with passing on through inheritance. There is a hint of this line of thinking at the start of the Grand Unity in that the selection of talented people results in not loving only one's parents and children. In Guodian, however, this would be balanced by recognizing the importance of emphasizing the family alone, and to the exclusion of the talented. This type of conflicting binary opposites is missing in the Grand Unity.

We will begin with the *Laozi* fragments, since unity here can be demonstrated with greater ease than with other Guodian texts where we must also show that the harmonized morals are also distinct entities. In the following discussion, every attempt will be made to limit the analysis to texts found in the Guodian tomb. In Guodian, it has become customary to divide texts as related to Laozi versus Confucius.[7] While much has already been said on this subject in previous chapters, I feel the connections between opposing groups are closer in the Guodian than we might assume from reading many other sources. One example is the changing of the received *Laozi* chapter 19's criticism of humanity and righteousness into a condemnation of craftiness and profit in the Guodian.[8] A second example is abdication (禪讓 *shan rang*), which has been traditionally associated with the writings of Mozi 墨子.[9] However, it is related to the harmonious unification of humanity and righteousness in "Tang Yu zhidao," a text that is consistently classified as Confucian.

Laozi

The *Laozi* fragments advocate a harmonious unification of positive and negative attributes. The first example we will examine is in *Laozi* A9 (2):[10]

> When everyone in the world knows the beautiful as beautiful, ugliness comes into being.

When everyone knows the good, then the not-good comes into being. [In this way we must understand] the mutual production of being nonbeing,

The mutual completion of difficult and the easy,
The mutual formation of long and short,
The mutual filling of high and low, but
The mutual harmony of tone and sound,
And the mutual following of front and behind.[11]

天下皆智（知）散（美）之為散（美）也，亞（惡）已；皆智（知）善，其不善已。又（有）亡之相生也，戁（難）惕（易）之相成也，長耑（短）之相型（形）也，高下之相涅（盈）也，音聖（聲）之相和也，先後之相墮（隨）也。[12]

This quotation contains a collection of binary opposites that we are asked to understand as interrelated. Although common logic would indicate that beauty and ugliness are distinct entities, the text describes beauty as begetting ugliness, long and short as coming from each other, and so forth. Assuming this is meant to represent a range of items and not an exhaustive list, we see that all our perceptions and any conclusions about our world we might derive from them are flawed. These flaws come from a failure to observe the true connection among things in the universe, things that normally appear to us as distinct and separate entities. Understanding these connections involves embracing a unity that most are not able to understand.

The unity of things could have several meanings: First, it might be that the world is simply a homogeneous mush with no true discernible lines between one thing and another. This interpretation is supported by passage A1 (19), where the elimination of knowledge is seen as beneficial to the people.[13] However, a complete absence of knowledge does not seem to be what the text is after, since the overall goal is to attain knowledge of the way. True knowledge of the way is not what the author was hoping to eliminate. This is reinforced by other passages that discuss attaining knowledge and understanding in a favorable manner.

Benjamin Schwartz describes this type of knowledge as the state of being where things are undifferentiated, "the harmonious hazy state in which they naturally abide."[14] However, I believe he is incorrect. Although beauty and ugliness are connected, there remains something discernible that the text terms beauty and something else called ugliness. Although a person can eventually see through common distinctions, this process begins with separate entities.[15]

This leads to the second possible reading: What we normally take to be either beautiful or ugly is in fact flawed. This seems more plausible but leads to the question of wherein the mistake lies. All we know from A9 is that common perceptions are mistaken and that we are challenged to find a new way to understand the interconnection between what most would call distinct entities.

Mark Csikszentmihalyi offers a detailed and insightful discussion of different commentarial perspectives on self-contradictions in *Laozi*. He demonstrates that there are two phases in the commentaries. Prior to the introduction of Buddhism, contradictions were explained by finding solutions that remained logical but counterintuitive. Later commentaries embrace *Laozi*'s contradictions as indicating that there is no real distinction among phenomenon. The earlier nontranscendent explanation has some similarities to the Guodian context of being based in a functional society.[16] Similar to earlier commentaries, there seem to be logical solutions for many of the contradictions in "The Five Aspects of Conduct" and "Tang Yu zhidao," as will be explored in chapter 5. The difference is that these Guodian texts seek to harmonize the differences between two opposing ways of acting: humanity and righteousness. This does not make the texts transcendent, but it does point to the presence of a type of higher understanding where the distinctions of common people disappear, similar to the post-Buddhist interpretations.

A second theory as to what *Laozi* thinks might be the cause of our mistaken understanding can be found in Jane Geaney's *On the Epistemology of the Senses in Early Chinese Thought*. She argues that *Laozi* is advocating moderation: "I will argue that in the *Laozi* this is achieved by prohibiting sensory excess, in order to boundlessly expand satisfaction in moderation."[17] Although Geaney is not using the Guodian version of the *Laozi*, several passages also present in the Guodian version do admonish us to avoid desire; two that she discusses are A3 (46) and A6/C4 (64). Geaney's interpretation is supported by A3 where it states, "Of disasters—none is greater than not knowing when one has enough. The contentment one has when he knows that he has enough—This is abiding contentment indeed."[18] 化（禍）莫厚虖（乎）不智（知）足。智（知）足之為足，此互（恆）足矣。[19] Benjamin Schwartz similarly feels that "it is thus quite correct to call the Tao-te-ching a 'primitivist' tract, an attack on the entire project of civilization."[20] He argues that through society's influence, the human mind becomes separated from the Dao.

However, A6/C4 (64) begins to hint at something other than simply the avoidance of sensory excess: "The sage desires not to desire and places no value on goods that are hard to obtain. He teaches without teaching, and backs away from matters in which the masses go to excess."[21] 聖人谷（欲）不谷（欲），不貴難得之貨，孝（教）不孝（教），復眾之所𤸷（過）。[22] The desire to not desire is clearly deemed admirable in this passage. This is the difference between what the sage and the masses value, since the latter leads to the wrong type of desire. This is reinforced by several passages that describe the correct sort of sensory stimulation. The most colorful of these is A17 (55), a passage that compares an infant to one who has embraced *de* 德 (virtue): "He does not yet know the mating of female and male, [yet] his penis stiffens."[23] 未智（知）牝戊（牡）之合然蕊（怒）。[24] Sensory pleasure is evident in the excited state of the infant's penis, yet we are to understand that he is not deriving his stimulation from common sources of sexuality. This is similar to A6/C4 (64) in that it is drawing a distinction between the desires and sensory stimulation of an average person and one who has higher understanding. Schwartz touches on a similar point in his analysis of the transmitted *Laozi* chapter 38 (which admittedly is absent in Guodian); he states, "The possessor of the highest virtue is unconscious of it and, one might say, without any self-consciousness."[25] However, the infant in A17 (55) has attained the highest virtue by embracing *de*, and his excited state would indicate that he is extremely conscious of what has occurred.

The reward for cultivation is hardly couched in terms of moderation in B8 (54):

> If you cultivate your self, your virtue will be pure; If you cultivate your family, your virtue will be overflowing; If you cultivate your village, your virtue will be long lasting; If you cultivate your state, your virtue will be abundant; If you cultivate your empire, your virtue will be universal . . . .[26]

攸（修）之身，其悳（德）乃貞（真）攸（修）之豪（家），其悳（德）德又（有）舍（餘）。攸（修）之向（鄉），其　（德）乃長。攸（修）之邦，其　（德）乃奉（豐）。攸（修）之天[下]　[其德乃愽（溥）普]。[27]

In this passage, abundance and greatness are the result of cultivation. This is quite different from being admonished to seek contentment and avoid excess in A3 (46) and A6/C4 (64). It seems that the difference can be explained by seeing that once we free ourselves from our old conceptions, we will be able to revel in our new understanding. This new understanding can then be applied to our interactions within the village and the state, which is further evidence that the text is not simply proposing primitivism as a solution.[28]

B8 (54) also provides insight into the process of cultivation in that it develops from the individual, the village, and then the state. This growing or spreading of one's cultivation from smaller to greater spheres of the society is particularly interesting, since it can explain the difference between the avoidance of excess and the embracing of abundance. Subsequent to the previously quoted section of B8 (54) where cultivation spreads from the body to the empire, we are told that each layer we encounter should be understood separately. "Use the family to observe the family; use the village to observe the village; use the state to observe the state; use the empire to observe the empire."[29] [以家 觀]豪（家）以向（鄉）觀向（鄉）以邦觀邦，以天下觀天下。[30] From this passage, we can see that differences are to be expected between the various social spheres. While this same type of progression from self to empire is also evident in the *Great Learning*, each level is more distinct in the *Laozi*.

This distinction between smaller and greater levels in the *Laozi* has the potential to answer the apparent contradiction between passages that are either engaged or disengaged from the society. B6 (52 lines 5–10) contain the phrase "Close the gates; Block the holes And to the end of your days you will not toil. Open the hole; Excel in affairs; And you will never reach the end of your days."[31] 閟（閉）其門，賽（塞）其逸（兌）終身不㞷。啟其逸（兌）賽其事，終身不逨來。[32] This seems like an admonition to reject engagement with society. A premature death awaits those who enter society and succeed. However, the two halves of B6 are not identical. One consistent aspect is the hole, presumably referring to our sensory organs. In the first half, they are closed and things go well; then, when they are open, disaster strikes. Clearly, we are better off without our senses leading us astray. We have a difference between the two halves in that the gate is to remain closed in the first half but is not mentioned in the second. This means that the problem is not opening the gate and being engaged in the world but doing so with improperly conditioned sensory organs. If B6 and B8 relate to each other, then it is possible that cultivating the body is the initial stage when one closes the gate and blocks the holes. Then, after completing this stage, one can enter society having reached a level of understanding that will remain intact when assaulted by the improper sensory experiences that exist in that social sphere. This relationship between spheres is also addressed in "Taiyi shengshui."

One exception to the Guodian emphasis on the attainment of unity in our daily lives and society is of course "Taiyi shengshui," which is more concerned with unity on a cosmic level. In this text, the Great One 太一 produces water 水 and heaven 天, which together return to assist in the creation of all things.[33] "The Great One gave birth to water. Water returned and assisted Taiyi, in this way developing heaven. Heaven returned and assisted Taiyi, in this way developing earth."[34] 大（太）一生水，水反輔（輔）大（太）一，是以陸成天。天反輔太一，是以成竈（地）。[35] It is interesting that D. C. Lau's article "The Treatment of Opposites in 'Lao Tzu'" addresses a similar issue in a section devoted to disproving the interpretations of Feng Youlan and Yang Guan. They state that the Dao works through reversion so the hard and soft or high and low develop into each other. Lau argues that their interpretations are incorrect, since this would mean that the terms would lose any sort of fixed meaning.[36] In "Taiyi shengshui," we see the fixed meanings of terms like "heaven" and "water" remain important, but we must also consider their actions, which are reversion and transformation.

As stated earlier, the unity of all things in "Taiyi shengshui" does not arise from self-cultivation but instead appears naturally in the cosmos. This broader focus on what is found outside direct human interactions is different from the *Laozi* fragments described earlier in this chapter that emphasize unity on a human scale. Therefore, the rhetorical function of "Taiyi shengshui" is to reaffirm the importance of individuals cultivating unity by providing a cosmic corollary to our actions. By accepting Xing Wen's theory that "Taiyi shengshui" is philosophically related to the *Laozi*,[37] we can assume that when A9 (2) asks us to see the beautiful and the ugly as interrelated, we are supposed to internally embrace the external cosmic order. The process of cultivation in the *Laozi* fragments is therefore one in which internal perception is brought in line with external truths.

With a cosmic corollary of our actions, the role of reversion and mutuality becomes important to our self-cultivation. Taiyi describes a cosmos where opposites return and assist Taiyi, or repeatedly assist each other to produce the various manifestations of the universe. "Yin and Yang repeatedly assisted each other, in this way developing the four seasons."[38] 陰（易）陽復相輔也，是以成四時。[39] This same process plays out in the *Laozi* when we encounter the different levels of self-cultivation in B8. Each level is distinct and different just as Yin and Yang are not the same as the four seasons. However, in practicing self-cultivation in an interconnected world, what we learn from our selves, our families, state, and so on, is all interrelated and mutually beneficial to our attainment of unity. At the conclusion of our cultivation, we understand that the seemingly opposite concepts of beauty and ugliness are in fact interrelated, and in seeing this unity, we are able to grasp the connectedness of our other experiences. This basic element of unifying the inner and outer can also be found in "The Five Aspects of Conduct."

"The Five Aspects of Conduct"

The following discussion of the harmonization of distinct entities in "The Five Aspects of Conduct" involves two stages: First, we need to demonstrate that harmonization is central to the text. Second, since this is a harmonization of two types of morality, it is necessary to demonstrate the distinct nature of these concepts. This second step is difficult in that "The Five Aspects of Conduct" defines terms in webs of relationships. Many of these webs take the form of sorites, or linked arguments. The result is that while the basic outline of the text may be easily comprehended, a clear philosophical understanding remains elusive unless pursued methodically.

An emphasis on harmonization begins with the first lines of the text. "The Five Aspects of Conduct" begins by repeating the same line five times. Each line states that carrying out virtue (德 *de*) is a process wherein each of the following is formed within: *ren* 仁, *yi* 義, *li* 禮, *zhi* 智, and *sheng* 聖. These terms have commonly been translated as "humanity," "righteousness," "the rites," "wisdom," and "sagacity." One example of the identically repeated sentences is "When humanity forms within [your heart] it is called virtuous conduct. If [humanity] is not formed within it is called a mere act." 仁形於内謂之德之行，不形於内謂之行。This use of repetition establishes the main theme for the text, which is the simultaneous cultivation of these five distinct moral traits. Although distinct and different, these traits must each be harmoniously combined.[40]

This theme of harmonization is reinforced by what follows the quintet of repeated sentences. "■2 There are five aspects of virtuous conduct, that, when united, are called virtue itself. When only four of these actions are united it is called being adept [at virtue]. Adeptness is the way of humans ❹ while virtue is the way of heaven." 德之行五和，謂之德，四行和，謂之善。善，人❹道也。德，天道也。In this passage, we see that the more types of morality one can bring together, the better. When you bring together four types, you have attained the highest a mere person can accomplish, but five makes you on par with a higher power, here translated as heaven.

Later in the text, unifying different types of morality is again emphasized: "Where sageness, wisdom, ritual and music are born is the harmonious combination of the five ❷❽ aspects of conduct." 知禮樂之所由生也，五❷❽〔行之所和〕也。In addition, "Humanity, righteousness and the rites are what emerge when you unify the four aspects of conduct. Having harmonized ❸❶ them you can bring them together; when together you are adept [at virtue]." 仁，義禮所由生也，四行之所和也。和❸❶則同，同則善。Now that we have demonstrated a deep concern for the harmonization of different types of morality in "The Five Aspects of Conduct," the second step in our analysis remains. Exactly how different are these five types of morality? We begin by returning to the two sides of moral cultivation described in the text.

These two sides are the building up of morals internally and then their application, or putting them into practice in society. This split was observed in the first lines of the text, where it states that once these types of morality are built up inside, we must put them into practice. "■3 If someone forms the five aspects of conduct within his inner heart and at the appropriate time practices them ❺ he is said to be a noble man." 五行皆形於內，時行❻ 之，謂之君（子）。Furthermore, in subsequent discussions of moral cultivation, there are certain terms that cleave more closely to the internal cultivation side and others that relate more closely to application in society. The main method the text uses to distinguish these two types of morals is the sorites, or linked argument.[41] The first group of sorites in the text emphasizes humanity, sagacity, and wisdom while the second group discusses humanity, righteousness, and the rites. This grouping is evident in the structure of the text: The first comprises paragraphs 4 through 6, while the second comprises paragraphs 10 through 12 and 17 through 19. The groups are stylistically distinct; epanaleptical sorites make up the first group, while double sorites make up the second.[42] The main difference between the first and second occurrences of these double sorites is that the words used in the first instance are further explicated by being accompanied by additional terms when they appear in the second instance.

The three internal single sorites are as follows:

5. Humane thoughts: [they] are essential; being essential ❶❷ you will have keen insight; having keen insight you will be at ease; being at ease you will be gentle; being gentle you will be happy; being happy your demeanor is pleasant; having a pleasant demeanor you can be intimate; being intimate you will be loving; loving your countenance will be jade-like;[43] having a jade-like countenance you will be formed; being formed you will be humane. ■ ❶❸

5. 仁之思也精。精❶❷ 則察，察則安，安則溫，溫則悅，悅則戚，戚則親，親則愛，愛則玉色，玉色則形。形則仁。■ ❶❸

6. Wise thoughts: [they] are extended; having extended [your thoughts] you will comprehend; once you comprehend you will not forget; not forgetting you will have keen vision; having keen

vision you will be able to perceive an outstanding person; being able to perceive an outstanding person you will have a jade-like countenance; having a jade-like countenance you will be formed; being formed you will be ❶❹ wise. ∎

6. 智之思也長，長則得，得則不忘，不忘則明。明則見賢人，見賢人則玉色，玉色則形，形❶❹則智。∎

7. Sagacious thoughts: [they] are light; being light they form, forming they will not be neglected, not neglecting you will have keen hearing;[44] having keen hearing you will hear the way of the noble man; hearing the way of the noble man you will be like jade sounds; being like jade sounds you will be formed; being formed you will be ❶❺ sagacious. ∎

7. 聖之思也輕，輕則形，形則不忘，不忘則聰。聰，則聞君子道，聞君子道則玉音，玉音則形，形❶❺ 則聖。∎

In analyzing these paragraphs, we must begin by establishing their commonalities. Following this, we discuss why this group should be understood as internal. The parallel nature of these three paragraphs can be seen as follows: First, as we have stated, all three paragraphs are epanaleptical sorites, where the first and last character in each paragraph is one of the five aspects of conduct.[45] The second through fourth characters are *zhi* 之 a possessive particle; *si* 思 thoughts; *ye* 也 intensifying particle. Following this is a list of attributes of identical length related to the aspect of conduct that began the paragraph. This structure can be seen in literal translation in table 4.1.

The basic structure of the paragraph on humanity illustrated in this table is identical to the other two epanaleptical sorites that discuss wisdom and sagacity. The only differences are the initial and final terms, and what is labeled as "attribute" and "repeated attribute." Further evidence of the similarity between these epanaleptical sorites can be seen in the

TABLE 4.1: Humanity Sorites

Humane thoughts: [they] are essential

Repeated Attribute	則 Thus	Attribute	Repeated Attribute	則 Thus	Attribute
being essential	thus	keen insight 察;	having keen insight	thus	at ease 安;
being at ease	thus	Gentle 温;	being gentle	thus	happy 悅;
being happy	thus	pleasant demeanor 戚;	pleasant demeanor	thus	intimate 親;
being intimate	thus	loving 愛;	loving	thus	countenance will be jade-like 玉色;
having a jade-like countenance	thus	formed 形,	being formed	thus	
will be Humane 仁.					

way each paragraph ends. Before repeating the same character the sorites began with, each paragraph contains the word "formed" 形. What being "formed" specifically means can be seen in the first lines of "The Five Aspects of Conduct." "When humanity forms within [your heart] it is called virtuous conduct. If [humanity] is not formed within it is called a mere act."[46] By considering the meaning of "formed" from paragraph 1, we can see that discussing how people go about forming humanity, sagacity, and wisdom in their hearts must be important to paragraphs 5 through 7. The details of this process of cultivation are somewhat unclear, but there is a common theme to the terms used. None involves a direct interaction with an outside individual, since they are all related to internal phenomena.

This brings us to the second commonality among these paragraphs, which is that every term is confined to what goes on internally. The first indication that these aspects of conduct relate to what is internal occurs in the initial characters of paragraphs 5 through 7. Humanity produces essential thoughts, while wisdom extends one's thoughts, and sagacity produces light thoughts. It is significant that each of these passages begins by focusing on one's thoughts, because this is the last time the character "thought" (*si* 思) appears in the text. In addition, these paragraphs represent the longest sections devoted exclusively to sagacity and wisdom. Prior to these paragraphs, *si* occurs seven times, and the usage is consistently associated with "humanity," "sagacity," and "wisdom." *Si* never appears in conjunction with "righteousness" and "the rites."

The closest paragraphs 4 through 6 come to discussing ideas that could relate to another person is the mention of events that could be manifest externally. When cultivation reaches advanced stages, it is described as being visible to an outside observer. This phenomenon is especially apparent if that observer is also one who has attained an advanced stage of cultivation. This manifestation is described as taking the form of a person's jade-like countenance, or having a jade-like voice.[47]

Social Aspect

In contrast with the previous aspects of conduct that relate to internal phenomena, those discussed in this section emphasize interactions with an outside observer. Since the cultivation of these aspects of conduct requires contact with other people, it can be categorized as the social aspect. One reason for grouping paragraphs 12 through 14 and 19 through 21 can be seen because they are all double sorites. The pattern of these double sorites can be seen in tables 4.2 and 4.3.

In these tables we see that attributes found in the first half of the double sorites are repeated in the same order in the second half. The second half thus serves as an explanation of the first half. The trend we see evident is that terms are consistently related to one's interaction with society.

TABLE 4.2: First Half of Double Sorites

Negation 不	Attribute	Negation 不	Attribute	Repeat
If you are not	open to change 變	you will not	be happy 悅	if you are not happy
		you will not have	a pleasant demeanor 戚	if you do not have a pleasant demeanor
		you cannot	be intimate 親	if you are not intimate
		you will not	love 愛	if you do not love
you will not be	humane 仁			

TABLE 4.3: Second Half of Double Sorites

Repeat	Explanation	Attribute From First Half
Introduction:	Your appearance and countenance are mild and changeable. When using your inner heart to interact with others	
		you will be happy 悅
When your inner heart is happy	and you influence your brother's behavior	you have a pleasant demeanor 戚
Having a pleasant demeanor	and living up to your words	you are intimate 親
Being intimate	and affectionate	you will be loving 愛
Loving your father	and extending this love to others	
Conclusion:	You are humane	

Humanity

The first term that appears in a double sorites is "humanity." These doubled paragraphs are separated by five other paragraphs in the Guodian edition, but in the Mawangdui edition, they appear next to each other as we have here:

12. If you are not open to change you will not be happy; if you are not happy you will not have a pleasant demeanor; if you do not have a pleasant demeanor you can not be intimate; if you are not intimate, you will not love; if you do not love you will not be humane.

12. 不變不悅，不悅不戚，不戚不親，不親不愛，不愛不仁。∎

19. Your appearance and countenance are mild and changeable. When using your inner heart to interact with others, you will be happy. When your inner heart is happy, and you influence ❸❷ your brothers' behavior you have a pleasant demeanor. Having a pleasant demeanor and living up to your words you are intimate. Being intimate and affectionate you will be loving. Loving your father and extending this to love others you are humane.

19. 顏色容貌溫變也。以其中心與人交，悅也。中心悅旃，遷❸ ❷ 於兄弟，戚也。戚而信之，親　　［也］。親而篤之，愛也。愛父，其繼愛人，仁也。∎

Many of the terms that appear in paragraph 12 are not initially recognizable as requiring the participation of another individual to be carried out. It is necessary, therefore, to look at paragraph 12 in the context provided by paragraph 19 to understand the implication of these terms. A clear example of this is the term *yue* 悅, which has been translated as "happy." Generally speaking, happiness is a feeling that does not necessitate the participation of another person. Based on this, we might see it as a mental attribute and not a social one. However, the nineteenth paragraph explains that the term "happiness" refers to a specific type of happiness. This is the happiness you experience "when using your inner heart to interact with others." The same observation may be made of "having a pleasant demeanor" (戚 *qi*). Normally, this would not require outside participation. However, in the second half of the double sorites, we see that this occurs in the context of interacting with one's brother. This pattern can best be seen in tables 4.2 and 4.3.

The endings of the paragraphs continue to relate humanity to familial relations. The first example is the presence of the term "intimate" (親 *qin*), which means acting in a familial manner. The second term that is related to the way one interacts with one's family is "loving" (愛 *ai*). The relationship between "loving" and one's family is explained in the second half of the sorites, where the term "love" is explained as "loving your father and extending this to love others." From this, we can see that the love being discussed here is not broadly defined but instead is to be understood as the specific sort of love that one applies to one's father. Since none of the terms that appear in the double sorites related to humanity may be carried out without other people, these paragraphs should be categorized as part of the social aspect.

Righteousness

Righteousness is the second term that appears in double sorites:

13. If you are not upright you will not be steadfast; not being steadfast, you will not be courageous; not being courageous ❷❶ you will not admonish; not admonishing you will not act [appropriately]; not acting [appropriately], you will not be righteous. ■

13. 不直不肆,[48] 不肆不果, 不果❷❶不簡, 不簡不行, 不行不義。■

20. When your inner heart ❸❸ distinguishes and is appropriately put into practice you are upright. If you are upright and attain you are steadfast. If you are steadfast and are not intimidated by those who are strong and powerful you are courageous. You should not ❸❹ allow lesser concerns to jeopardize greater concerns, thus you admonish. If there is a serious crime with a

capital punishment, this is called acting [correctly]. Venerating the noble, those with rank, and elevating the outstanding, you are righteous. ■❸❺

20. 中心❸❸辯然，而正行之，直也。直而遂之，肆也。肆而不畏強禦，果也。不❸❹以小道害大道，簡也。有大罪而大誅之，行也。貴貴，其等尊賢，義也。■❸❺

Even in isolation, paragraph 13 contains terms that exceed the boundaries of merely internal phenomena. This can be seen in the concluding two terms: admonishing and acting. Admonishment relates to the judgment of a legal case.[49] As such, it is clear that admonishment involves an obvious social context. The term "acting" (行 *xing*), when taken outside of the context of paragraph 20, is not obviously related to the social aspect. However, the usage of acting in this paragraph is clearly something that refers to acting morally, which could involve other people.

When paragraphs 13 and 20 are analyzed in conjunction, we see the social characteristics of righteousness more clearly. The term "acting" (行 *xing*) appears in the context of admonishment and thus involves the meting out of severe punishments for serious crimes as in paragraph 22 of the Guodian edition. The term "courageous" (果 *guo*) does have an implied social context, and this is seen in paragraph 20 where it states that acting courageous is not being "intimidated by those who are strong and powerful." Therefore, every term appearing in the righteousness sorites relates to a social context.

Rites

The third and final double sorites focuses on the term "the rites":

14. If you do not keep the appropriate distance you will not be reverent; if you are not reverent, you will not be stern; if you are not

stern you will not show honor; if you do not show honor you will not
be polite; if you are not polite you will not [follow the] rites. ■

14.　不遠不敬，不敬不嚴，不嚴不尊，不尊不恭，不恭不禮。■

21. When using your external heart to interact with others you
[maintain the appropriate] distance. [Maintaining the appropri-
ate] distance and being stern, is reverence. Being reverent, but
not [overly] frugal or regulated this is stern. Being stern and
having awe ❸❻ you venerate. Venerating, but not being arrogant,
you can revere. Revering and widely interacting with others is [to
act in accordance with] the rites. ■

21.　以其外心與人交，遠也。遠而莊之敬也。敬而不儞，嚴也。嚴而畏
❸❻之，尊也。尊而不驕，恭也。恭而博交，禮也。■

The social characteristics of the rites are clear from every term
that appears in paragraph 14. The first term, "keep the appropriate distance" (遠 *yuan*), implies there is another person present,
since even an isolated person must be distant from someone or
at least something. Paragraph 21 agrees with this assumption
and states that keeping distance relates to how we interact with
others. The next four terms—"being reverent" (敬 *jing*), "being
stern" (嚴 *yan*), "showing honor" (尊 *zun*), and "being polite"
(恭 *gong*)—will be dealt with as a group: Each of these words
refers to the proper way that a person behaves when interacting with another. In addition, without the presence of another
person, these terms largely are without meaning. The only possible exception is being stern, which a person could carry out in
solitude. From this, we can see that everything that relates to the
rites requires a social context.

The discussion on the previous pages provides one way of cat-
egorizing the key terms in "The Five Aspects of Conduct." Belonging to a category merely implies a degree of similarity. For example,
the text also distinguishes the rites from humanity and righteousness. This is apparent, since humanity and righteousness are said

to relate to what is within one's heart, while the rites is said to the external heart. For the rites, the text says, "When using your external heart to interact with others you [maintain the appropriate] distance."[50] Humanity is said to be "When using your inner heart to interact with others, you will be happy."[51] Finally, righteousness is said to be "When your inner heart distinguishes and is appropriately put into practice you are upright."[52] From this, we can see that the three internal terms have important differences. Despite this, these three terms possess greater dissimilarities when compared with two social terms,[53] which is why they deserve to be grouped together.[54]

"Humanity" is a term that is more difficult to categorize in this text as it appears in both the social and the internal sorites. Interestingly, when it appears in the social sorites, it relates to the family. The family would seem to constitute the most intimate social sphere in which a person would interact. We see this in humanity being related to "loving one's father" and interacting with one's brother in paragraph 19. Humanity's relationship to a smaller social sphere continues when we compare it with righteousness. In paragraphs 22 and 23, righteousness is related to executing a criminal for an unusual or rare crime. The same paragraphs relate humanity with forgiving a criminal for a lesser crime. The familial context of paragraph 19 tells us that the more intimate sphere social sphere of forgiveness is different from the occasional need to execute criminals who commit heinous crimes that impact the society at large. In this way, the text is distinguishing humanity and righteousness as being related to greater and lesser social spheres.

Now that we have established the distinctions between different types of moral cultivation, we turn our attention to an example of how exactly the text advocates their harmonization. This can be found in paragraph 20:

You should not ❸❹ allow lesser concerns to jeopardize greater concerns, thus you admonish. If there is a serious crime with a capital punishment, this is called acting [correctly]. Venerating the noble, those with rank, and elevating the outstanding, you are righteous. ■❸❺

不❸❹以小道害大道，簡也。有大罪而大誅之，行也。貴貴，其等尊賢，義也。■❸❺

This quotation provides an explanation of the result of admonishment, which is the execution of those who commit serious crimes. It also tells us what is entailed in the process of admonishing: "You should not allow lesser concerns to jeopardize greater concerns." It is not immediately clear what is meant by greater or lesser concerns in this passage. In several instances the character *dao* 道 has been translated "concerns," since it does not imply a broad entity that exists through a continuum as "way" implies.

When *dao* refers to "way" in the text, it exists as a continuum that is not contradicted when changing from lesser to greater. The two instances of this are the "way of man" and "the way of heaven": "11: Being adept [at virtue] is the way of humans ❶❾ while being virtuous is the way of heaven" 善，人❶❾ 道也。德，天（道也）。A hierarchy is evident in these two categories; the way of man is lesser than the way of heaven. Furthermore, the lesser way of man is actually a subset of what is encompassed in the universal way of heaven. This can be seen in the following: "■2 There are five aspects of virtuous conduct, that when united are called virtue itself. When only four of these actions are united it is called being adept [at virtue]善. Adeptness is the way of humans ❹ while virtue is the way of heaven" 2. 德之行五和，謂之德，四行和，謂之善。善，人❹道也。德，天道也。There is a clear distinction between "the way of humans" and "the way of heaven." The difference is that the way of heaven involves mastering the harmonization of all five aspects whereas the way of man involves only four. Since the lesser way of man would not be seen as jeopardizing the greater way of heaven, the lesser *dao* and greater *dao* in paragraph 20 do not refer to the way of humans and heaven, respectively.

The lesser concerns that one must weigh in admonishment in paragraph 20 should refer to the decision-making process one goes through when deciding a legal case. This is how one's decision affects a smaller versus larger subset of society. "Greater concerns" refers to a decision based on broader social concerns such as the state as a whole, while "lesser concerns" refers to deciding based on smaller social concerns such as one would develop in the family. These lesser and greater concerns in turn reflect a connection to humanity and righteousness, respectively. Greater and lesser concerns therefore indicate the social scale that one is using when making decisions.[55]

When understanding admonishment and leniency, it is important to see that each type of action is related to a different type of situation:

22. Without admonishment you cannot act [appropriately]. Not being lenient you cannot have insight into the way ❸ ❼. Meting out a capital punishment for a serious crime is admonishment. Issuing a pardon for an insignificant crime is being lenient. Not ❸ ❽ meting out a capital punishment for a serious crime is not acting [properly]. Not issuing a pardon for an insignificant crime you cannot have keen insight into the way.

22. 不簡，不行。不匽，不辯❸ ❼於道。有大罪而大誅之，簡也。有小罪而赦之，匽也。有大罪而弗❸ ❽大誅也，不行也。有小罪而弗赦也，不辯於道也。■

This passage describes two situations, one in which there is a serious crime and another in which the crime is insignificant. It is the severity of the crime that dictates what sort of action one should take. Serious crimes call for executions while minor crimes should be forgiven. Each of these decisions then affects the subject in a different manner: In the first, one has the opportunity to act correctly, while in the second, one has the opportunity to gain insight into the way. However, the text simply described different results arising from different actions that correspond to different situations.

Here we must ask ourselves whether these two situations can be seen as completely separate. The simple answer is that no, the situations are not entirely different as they both involve deciding what to do in the event of a crime. As obvious as this may seem, it leads us in an important direction. It is important to see that the situations encountered are distinguished only by severity, and there is an implied connection between the two actions undertaken. The difference between forgiving and punishing is the same as the difference between admonishment and leniency or righteousness and humanity. The connection is that the former is the hard approach and the latter is the soft approach.[56] Ultimately, what the text is asking us to do is to find out how to unify these five different ways of acting morally. When one encounters a criminal and decides he should be forgiven, it is because his crime is somehow deemed petty. In contrast, when a criminal is punished, some element of his crime is deemed heinous and forgiveness would be inappropriate. Decisions based on the terms "humanity" and "righteousness" do not exist in isolation; it is only by harmonizing them that the highest ideals of the text may be obtained.

Conclusion

"Tang Yu zhidao" discusses two methods of succession: inheritance and abdication: "Tang Yao and Yu Shun's way was to abdicate and not pass [through inheritance]." 唐虞之道, 禪而不傳。[57] Here the text is opposing hereditary transmission and supporting abdication in favor of one deemed more capable of ruling. Later, these two methods of succession, heredity and abdication, are again described as having an inherent tension: "Loving the family you forget the outstanding; you are humane but not righteous. Elevating the outstanding ❽ distances you from the family; you are righteous but not humane." 愛親 忘賢, 仁而未義也。尊賢 ❽ 遺親, 義而未仁也。[58] This quotation links humanity with governing that emphasizes hereditary transmission, while righteousness is related to elevating the most capable person. In deciding who will succeed a king, one must choose to love one's family and maintain the power of the family through humanity or follow righteousness and search for the most capable person for the job.

Only the great sages Yao and Shun are able to overcome this conflict and both love their families and elevate the outstanding. "The practice of Yao and Shun was to love family and elevate the outstanding." 堯舜之行，愛親尊賢。[59] Here we see that the potential exists to overcome the inherent tension between state and family. Harmoniously unifying these two social structures allows us to follow the lofty examples of Yao and Shun.

Guodian texts emphasize different aspects of attaining unity, but the prevalence of this trend is unmistakable. The grouping of humanity and righteousness with the smaller and larger social structures of family and state in "Tang Yu zhidao" is similar to that in "The Five Aspects of Conduct," where humanity is related to the internal or familial while righteousness is related to broader category of the state or society as a whole. Both of these texts have similar projects of self-cultivation that emphasize the unification of the state and family. The *Laozi* fragments ask us to embrace the unity of our cosmos seen in "Taiyi shengshui." By internalizing this external unity, we come to enjoy the connections between concepts like the beautiful and the ugly, high and low, long and short that unenlightened people fail to understand. "The Five Aspects of Conduct" also advocates cultivating a harmonious unification of inner and outer. The inner involves the individual and the family, while the outer pertains to the state, or collection of families. This inner-outer relationship is described as inherently problematic in "Tang Yu zhidao," since issues of succession naturally create tension between the priorities of the state and the family. This was overcome in antiquity when sage rulers such as Yao and Shun abdicated the throne but embraced the family by acting filial. Yao and Shun are praised as models who overcame the tension between inner and outer, creating a harmoniously unified state.

FIVE

Harmonizing Aristocracy and Meritocracy

PREVIOUS CHAPTERS OF THIS BOOK have discussed problems with the theory that "The Five Aspects of Conduct" 五行篇 is philosophically related to the *Mencius*. This chapter will recenter the discussion of this relationship by comparing two recently excavated texts, "The Five Aspects of Conduct" and "Tang Yu zhidao" 唐虞之道, to several received texts, namely, the *Mencius, Xunzi*, and *Mozi*. The goal will be to measure the degree of congruency between these texts by analyzing specific tenets of their philosophical systems. Despite including transmitted sources, our focus will remain on Guodian.

"Tang Yu zhidao" explores a philosophy of balance through a discussion of the sages Yao 堯 and Shun 舜, who are said to have harmonized aristocratic and meritocratic priorities when they chose their successors based on aptitude but remained faithful to their lineages by cultivating filial and humane qualities. Aristocracy here means an emphasis on family as the basis for a strong state.[1] As such, aristocracy is different from meritocracy, where finding capable individuals from around the state is the primary concern, and familial relations are not considered. It is somewhat counterintuitive, but a focus on meritocracy is a more macro perspective as the particular context of the individual's background is not considered. Aristocracy is the micro-focused methodology, since it cares more about one's unique background. These two systems can actually be harmonized, since they are not working at cross-purposes. Differences in the scope of their primary foci dictate different priorities, which when harmonized can be seen as a two-pronged approach to developing a religious community. In "The Five Aspects of Conduct," these categories of macro and micro or state and family are also applied to a framework for considering a legal case.[2]

Understanding the harmonization of aristocratic and meritocratic priorities in recently excavated texts will help clarify what otherwise appears to be contradictory views in the received texts *Mencius, Xunzi*, and *Mozi*, each of which contains passages that support *and* passages that oppose the elevation (尊 *zun*) of those who are judged to be outstanding (賢 *xian*). "Tang Yu zhidao" begins with a discussion of the elevation of the outstanding as a tenet of a meritocracy that should be harmonized with aristocratic principles. This meritocracy privileges talent over hereditary concerns in government staffing decisions and benefits the state, since the best-qualified person will be found for the job. It is logical to conclude that staffing decisions based on merit alone would have negative implications for the families of those in government, since in a meritocracy birth into the family of an officeholder will not ensure continued power. Because of this, "Tang Yu zhidao" states that elevating the outstanding is but one way to rule, and must be balanced with other methods that build upon familial virtues. The text argues that the highest ideal of succession is the harmonization of the priorities of the state and the family into a meritocracy/aristocracy hybrid.

This hybrid is not merely a political or social ideal. It is consistently described as a practical application of the ethical terms humanity and righteousness. The goal of the system is to allow both ethical practices to flourish and prevent one from eclipsing the other through disharmony. In Guodian texts, humanity and righteousness are crucial to the creation of this political hybrid. Hints at this pairing can also be found at times in the *Mencius, Xunzi,* and *Mozi.* Righteousness is one of the merits sought after in a meritocracy, and humanity is the means by which families encourage the development of talented individuals in an aristocracy. The trend of treating humanity and righteousness in parallel is so regular that their cultivation and practice must also have been understood as occurring in concert. Since these two terms are also signifiers of moral conduct, this is not an exploration of a purely political apparatus. Instead, the government is fostering a harmony that is also deeply religious in its composition.

These terms meritocracy and aristocracy imply a comprehensive system of government, yet "Tang Yu zhidao" is concerned with succession, which is but a small part of a political system. This raises a fundamental question. If we are to construct an understanding of the political aspects of religious philosophy in Chu around the time of the closing of Guodian, we must decide if these excavated manuscripts present a religious system robust enough to accomplish this objective. A discussion of this problem is provided in the following section.

Guodian Texts

Many times, the most important decision a ruler had to make in his lifetime was the selection of his successor. He could follow the dictates of aristocracy and select a family member or follow the methods of a meritocracy and select the most talented individual. Being limited to a single individual, royal succession could not simultaneously utilize both meritocratic and aristocratic methods. However, government as a whole had to maintain a balance in order to be successful. "Tang Yu zhidao" begins by describing the abdication of Yao to Shun, an action encapsulating the earliest succession method in China. Since rulers were selected based on ability, this system of government should be called a meritocracy. The text then states that this method is one that follows righteousness and the elevation of outstanding people. The problem with a meritocracy is that it can be plagued by power struggles when individual families compete to maintain dominance over a collection of families—the state. If a family fails to exhibit talent, power slips to another. This is inherent with a system of abdication, where a ruler is expected to select the most capable person in the empire as his successor.

Recognizing this inherent problem with meritocracies, the text turns to a second term, "humanity." This is an important shift as "humanity" and "righteousness" are consistently used in pairs throughout the Guodian texts. In "Tang Yu zhidao," "humanity" has the same connotation as in other Guodian texts in that it is associated with the family and is a counterbalance to righteousness. Humane governments emphasize the family, but in "Tang Yu zhidao," concerns for the strength of family through aristocracy and the concerns of a meritocracy from righteousness are given equal weight:

唐虞之道, 禪而不傳。³ 堯舜之王, 利天下而弗利也。禪而不傳, 聖之❶盛也。利天下而弗利也, 仁之至也。故昔賢仁聖者如此。身窮不貪,⁴ 沒❷而弗利, 窮⁵ 仁矣。必⁶ 正其身, 然後正世, 聖道備矣。故唐虞之(道, 禪)也。❸

夫聖人上事天, 教民有尊也; 下事地, 教民有親也; 時事山川, 教民❹有敬也; 親事祖廟, 教民孝也; 大學⁷ 之中, 天子親齒, 教民弟也; 先聖❺與後聖, 考後而甄⁸ 先, 教民大順之道也。

堯舜之行, 愛親尊賢。愛❻親故孝, 尊賢故禪。孝之施,⁹ 愛天下之民。禪之傳, 世亡隱德。孝, 仁之冕也。❼ 禪, 義之至也。六帝興於古, 皆¹⁰由此也。愛親忘賢, 仁而未義也。尊賢❽遺親, 義而未仁也。古者虞舜篤事瞽盲,¹¹ 乃戴¹² 其孝; 忠事帝堯, 乃戴其臣。❾愛親尊賢, 虞舜其人也 . . . 古者堯之與舜也: 聞舜孝, 知其能養天下之老也; 聞舜弟, 知其能事天下❷❷之長也; 聞舜慈乎弟[象_ _ , ❷❸知其能] 為民主也。故其為瞽盲子也, 甚孝; 及其為堯臣也, 甚忠; 堯禪天下❷❹而授之, 南面而王天下, 而甚君。故堯之禪乎舜也, 如此也. . . .¹³

Tang Yao and Yu Shun's way was to abdicate and not pass [through inheritance]. Yao and Shun's rule benefited all under heaven but did not [focus on] benefit. Abdicating and not passing is the flourishing of sagacity ❶. Benefiting all under heaven but not [focusing on] benefit is the utmost of humanity. Therefore, in ancient times, outstanding, humane and sagacious ones were like this. In body, destitute but not greedy, being without ❷ but not seeking advantage, this is the utmost of humanity. You must make the body upright and then make our time upright, this is the completion of the way of the sage. Therefore Tang Yao and Yu Shun's (way was abdication). ❸

The sage serves heaven above and instructs the people ❹ to have respect. He serves earth below and instructs the people to be intimate. At the appropriate time, he serves mountains and streams and instructs the people to be respectful. His family serves the temple and teaches the people to be filial. In the grand learning, the son of heaven is intimate with the aged, and teaches the people fraternal respect. Regarding the former sages ❺ and the latter sages, he examines the latter and discerns the former, teaching the people the way of great accordance.

Yao and Shun acted to love their families and elevate the outstanding. Loving ❻ your family therefore is filial, elevating the outstanding therefore is abdicating. Filial's method is to love the people of the state. Abdicating's transmission eliminates concealed virtue in our time. Being filial is the crown of humanity. ❼ Abdicating is the utmost of righteousness. The six emperors that arose in antiquity all came from this. Loving your family you forget the outstanding; you are humane but not righteous. Elevating the outstanding ❽ distances you from the family; you are righteous but not humane. In ancient times, Shun of Yu politely served his blind father. Then he upheld filial piety and devoted himself to serving emperor Yao. Thus, he honored his loyalty. ❾ Loving family and elevating the outstanding, Tang Yao and Yu Shun were such people. . . .

In ancient times Yao bestowed upon Shun. Hearing Shun was filial he knew he could nurture the state's[14] ❷❷ elderly. Hearing Shun was fraternal, he knew he would be able to serve those older than him in the state. Hearing Shun was compassionate to his brother Xiang __ __ ❷❸ he knew he would be able to put the people first. Therefore, he treated the blind man's son with tremendous filial piety. Next, he acted as Yao's minister with tremendous devotion. Yao abdicated the empire and conferred it, facing south [he] ruled the empire and was very gentlemanly. Therefore, Yao's abdication of the state ❷❹ to Shun was like this. . . .

This passage begins with a contrast of "the way" (道 *dao*) versus "the rule" (王 *wang*) and "the actions" (行 *xing*) of Yao and Shun. "The way" involves abdication, it is said to be the flourishing of sagacity, and in the third paragraph of the quotation it is said to be the utmost in righteousness. We can understand this as fitting with righteousness being related to the broader social sphere of the state and being in contrast to the smaller social sphere of humanity and the family. If a person abdicates the throne in favor of another more worthy than his son, the power of the family is eclipsed and the concerns of the state are given priority. Such a system favors the state in that the best person is found for the position.

Yao and Shun's method for ruling or acting relates to the family and is associated with humanity. The relationship between humanity and the family is clear in that this type of government includes being filial and fraternal, but not elevating the outstanding. Throughout the previously quoted passage, contrasts are drawn between humane aristocracy and righteous meritocracy. For example, loving one's family is being filial and humane, but elevating the outstanding is abdicating and being righteous. Also, "Loving the family one forgets the outstanding; you are humane but not righteous. Elevating the outstanding distances one from the family; you are righteous but not humane." 愛親忘賢，仁而未義也。尊賢遺親，義而未仁也。[15] Humanity and righteousness each represent a method of

ruling that relies on different and potentially competing methods. The relationship between righteousness and meritocracy
is clear, but it seems strange to think that Yao and Shun's
method of ruling could be aristocratic. Aristocracy is a system
whereby power is passed within a family, and Yao clearly did
not follow this.

The question remains, then, if righteousness relates to a
meritocracy and humanity is a contrasting system that relies
on the family, how can humane government be understood?
·Dynastic legends tell us that meritocracy in early China was
quickly replaced by a system where the right to rule was passed
from father to son. The only possible explanation of humane
government during times prior to the change is that it relates to
governing through aristocracy. Aristocracy must remain a part
of government under a ruler such as Yao, despite his son not
inheriting the throne, because of the importance of balance.
Each mention of humanity in "Tang Yu zhidao" is paired with a
parallel instance of righteousness, indicating that these are two
competing sides needing to be balanced. Only a sage can accomplish this, but achieving this hybrid is the ideal government
since it combines the power of an aristocracy with the fairness
of a meritocracy.

The other side of this issue is that individuals, such as both
Yao and Shun, were said to have mastered this system. That
is to say, humanity and righteousness are not simply elements
of a faceless bureaucracy; they represent the actions of specific
people. Individuals are supposed to act with humanity and righteousness, and the two are to be in harmony despite relating
to separate parts of the society, either the state or the family.
That means that the whole point of balancing humanity and
righteousness in the workings of government on the macro scale
is to enable the same to flourish in the actions of the individual
people on the micro scale.

In Guodian texts, royal succession is not the only area in
which meritocracy and aristocracy should be harmonized. "The
Five Aspects of Conduct" relies on an identical methodology to

describe how a legal case should be judged. This broadens the issue of harmonization from one that is being related primarily to succession issues to one that incorporates the daily activities of government. The text states that righteousness would result in the admonishment (簡 *jian*) of one guilty of a great and rare crime, but humanity would result in leniency (匿 *ni*) for a lesser and more common crime. "The Five Aspects of Conduct" treats humanity as a concept applicable to a smaller social sphere, the family, and relates righteousness to broader considerations, such as would be relevant to the state. This is analogous to the view of succession seen in "Tang Yu zhidao," but it places greater emphasis on the role of the individual. In "The Five Aspects of Conduct," a legal case requires the judge to balance both concerns in making a decision. Ultimately, the government is working toward a harmonious balance in society by correcting the excesses of criminals.

In "The Five Aspects of Conduct," admonishment is a public reprimand and is in contrast to being lenient to someone in private. The following are a few examples of *jian* in received texts. *Analects* 5.22 and *Mencius* 7B.37 have almost identical quotations on the subject. The *Mencius* states, "When Confucius was in Chen[16] he said 'Why not go home? Our young men at home are undisciplined in their ambition.'"[17] 孔子在陳曰。盍歸乎來。[18] 吾黨之士狂簡。[19] Another negative connotation of *jian* can be found in *Mencius* 4B.27: "He showed me scant courtesy."[20] 是簡驩也。[21] Further along in the same passage, we see: "Ziao thought I was showing him scant courtesy"[22] 子敖以我為簡。[23]

These examples of *jian* in received texts share an interesting commonality with the recently excavated "Five Aspects of Conduct." In both types of texts, *jian* pertains to behavior that is unacceptable in public. In "The Five Aspects of Conduct," it is a more severe violation as it relates to a contravention of righteousness that could result in execution. In the examples from received texts, the term is milder in that it refers to uncouth behavior with no indication that it would be a capital offense.

The following is an example of how to treat two types of legal cases in "The Five Aspects of Conduct":

> Admonishment as a term is like remonstrating ❸❾ that can only be applied to the great and rare [cases]. Leniency as a term is like being lenient for minor crimes[24] that can be applied to lesser and more common[25] [cases]. Admonishment is the method of righteousness. Leniency ❹⓿ is the method of humanity. That which is hard is the method of righteousness, while that which is soft is the method of humanity. "He was neither violent nor hasty neither hard nor soft." This summarizes what I am referring to ❹❶.■ [26]

> 簡之為言猶　練❸❾也，大而晏者也。匿之為言也猶匿匿也，小而輇者也。簡，義之方也。匿，❹⓿　仁之方也。剛，[27]　義之方。柔，仁之方也。『不強不絿，[28]　不剛不柔，』此之謂也。❹❶■ [29]

This quotation juxtaposes leniency, softness, and humanity with admonishment, hardness, and righteousness as was discussed in chapter 3. These two sides relate to contrasting situations, the punishment of serious versus minor crimes. Since the ideal of government is to avoid cleaving to either side, harmonization of the two must be obtained. This is reinforced by the quotation from *The Odes* that states that one should be "neither hard nor soft." Hard and soft are linked to humanity and righteousness, respectively, so we must assume the author is *not* implying that we should have a total absence of humanity and righteousness. Rather, this should be read as an admonition to avoid extremes and seek a harmonization of the two sides.

In addition to "The Five Aspects of Conduct" and "Tang Yu zhidao," several other Guodian texts contain fleeting reflections of humanity and righteousness constituting the two sides of family and state harmonization. The excerpts provided in the following properly demonstrate the breadth of this trend. In "Yu Cong One" 語叢一, we see: "Being thick in humanity and thin in righteousness you are familial but do not elevate [the outstanding]. Being thick in righteousness and thin in humanity you elevate [the outstanding] but are not familial." 7:2 (厚於仁, 薄)於義, 親而不尊。厚於義, 薄於仁, 尊而不親.[30] "Zun de yi" 尊德義 states, "Humanity can be familial, righteousness can elevate [the outstanding]." 3. 仁為可親也, 義為可尊也. . .[31] It is interesting that we see consistent tension between the practice of humanity and righteousness.

"Liu de" 六德 section 7:2 also follows the same trend of state and family harmonization, but the context is the proper expression in mourning. Funerals in early China were a religious occasion where family responsibility always trumped duties to the state. Even a sovereign was not exempt from the responsibility of carrying out the proper mourning rituals.[32] The following passage explains the boundaries:

Humanity is family; righteousness is state. The rites and music are shared. The inner establishes the father, son, and ❷❻ husband. The outer establishes the ruler, minister and married women. The coarsest hemp cloth mourning attire and cane are for the father, for the ruler it is the same. The second degree of mourning attire ❷❼ of male hemp with hemmed borders is for elder and younger brothers, for the wife it is the same. For distant relatives you bare the left arm and remove the cap, for friends ❷❽ it is the same. For your father you cut off relations with the ruler, for the ruler you do not cut off relations with your father. For your older and younger brother you cut off relations with your wife, for your wife you do not cut off relations with your older and younger brother. For ❷❾ your clan you enfeeble your friends, for your friends you do not enfeeble your clan. People have six virtues, and three relations that are unceasing. In family ❸⓿ administration, humanity hides righteousness; in state administration, righteousness cuts off humanity.

■仁, 内也。義, 外也。禮樂, 共也。内立父、子、❷❻夫也, 外立君、臣、婦也。疏斬布絰杖, 為父也, 為君亦然。疏衰❷❼齊牡麻絰, 為昆弟也, 為妻亦然。袒免, 為宗族也, 為朋友❷❽亦然。為父絕君, 不為君絕父。為昆弟絕妻, 不為妻絕昆弟。為❷❾宗族疾[33] 朋友, 不為朋友疾宗族。人有六德, 三親不斷。門内❸⓿之治恩掩義, 門外之治義斬恩.[34]

This passage makes use of vocabulary familiar from descriptions of mourning activities in the *Book of Rites* and *Yili*. The regulations themselves are not particularly novel, but the context provided by Guodian provides a new and valuable interpretation. The "Liu de," like "The Five Aspects of Conduct" and "Tang Yu zhidao," reflects a political philosophy that values a harmonization of state and family.

Although harmony is important, the potential for conflict is also obvious in the passage from "Liu de." Depending on the situation, either humanity or righteousness will be trumped by the other. This duality and simultaneous struggle for harmony can be seen as omnipresent from a diachronic perspective—a religious commitment that spans one's entire life. It can also be seen as pervasive in that it spans a wide group of social structures including family, friends, and even political relations. The diachronic side is clear in the persistent importance of harmony from our youngest familial interactions with siblings and parents right through the mourning rituals of the deceased. There is continuity across time, since the paradigms we rely on for our interactions with others are ingrained in us from youth and then remain with us to guide us in our later life. In fact, the diachronic characteristic provides the key to achieving harmony. The "Liu de" instructs us that family and state administration rely on separate principles, humanity and righteousness. These are discussed as a social system that seems to be in constant conflict with various friends, relatives, and political associates constantly snubbing each other. However, by knowing that the rules of engagement are such that I must give preference to my father before my ruler, the system can be worked out over time. The details of this balancing were discussed further in chapter 1 of this book.

Received Texts

One text that discusses unity laced with a hint of harmonizing meritocracy and an aristocracy is the *Book of Rites*.

Despite the text being difficult to date,[35] the "Li yun" 禮運 chapter contains the famous passage known as the Grand Unity.[36] This text describes a utopian society where the tension between public and private has disappeared. The result is that priorities for individual families do not interfere with those of the state. Harmonizing these conflicting concerns is obviously important. One conclusion that might be drawn from the statement "Thus men did not love their parents only…"[37] is that the family is being eclipsed by the state. However, the key term in this phrase is the word "only" (獨 *du*). The text is not instructing us not to love our parents, or that such love should be even equal or subordinate to other priorities. Instead, it is advising us that we should apply the love of our own parents to the love of others. In recently excavated texts, we can see a similar line of thinking, since familial love is the basis for governing humanely.

At this point, we should mention an opposing perspective, that early Chinese texts do not advocate governance by a hybrid system combining the strengths of both a meritocracy and an aristocracy. The late A. C. Graham cited the Mohists as the earliest to support the idea of promoting and rewarding the outstanding, which he believed Mencius resisted, except in unusual situations. Graham felt that Xunzi was actually the first Confucian to embrace this idea.[38] Although it was published after Graham's death, Guodian confirms that if you accept the category of Confucian, you can find texts sympathetic to Confucian ideas that were espousing meritocratic ideas far earlier than previously assumed. However, this does not eliminate the possibility that Mohists were the first to propose these ideas. The important difference is that based on Guodian, it now seems Mozi also saw the value of at times emphasizing the family instead of the outstanding.

Two important passages in the *Mozi* deal with state-family relations. The more famous exploration of the subject is in the chapter "Elevating the Outstanding" 尚賢 where righteousness is emphasized, but "Moderation in Funerals" 節葬 provides an interesting contrast by advocating government based on humanity. These passages show that the *Mozi* continues the trend of using the terms "righteousness" and "humanity" to discuss the way to govern the state and its families. The following is from "Moderation in Funerals":

> Mo Tzu said: The humane[39] man in planning for the welfare of the empire is no different from a filial son planning for the welfare of his parents is he? Now when a filial son plans for the welfare of his parents, what is it he aims at? If his parents are poor, we seeks to enrich them; if the members of the family are few, he seeks to increase their number; if the family is in disorder, he seeks to bring it to order. In his efforts he may in time find his strength prove insufficient, his wealth inadequate, and his wisdom wanting. And yet so long as he has unused strength, untried schemes, and unrealized prospects for benefit, he dares not cease working for the welfare of his parents. The same is true of the humane man planning for the welfare of the world. If the people of the world are poor, he seeks to enrich them; if they are few, he seeks to increase their number; and if they are in disorder, he seeks to bring them to order. In his efforts he may in time find his strength prove insufficient, his wealth inadequate, and his wisdom wanting. And yet so long as he has unused strength, untried schemes, and unrealized prospects for benefit, he dares not cease working for the welfare of the world. It is by seeking these three aims that the humane man plans for the welfare of the world.[40]

子墨子言曰。仁者之為天下度也。辟之。無以異乎孝子之為親度也。今孝子之為親度也。將奈何哉。曰。親貧則從事乎富之。人民寡則從事乎眾之。眾亂則從事乎治之。當其於此也。亦有力不足財不贍。智不智。然後已矣。無敢舍餘力隱謀遺利。而不為親為之者矣。若三務者。孝子之為親度也。既若此矣。雖仁者之為天下度亦猶此也。曰。天下貧則從事乎富之。人民寡則從事乎眾之。眾而亂則從事乎治之。當其於此。亦有利不足。財不贍。智不智。然後已矣。無敢舍餘力。隱謀遺利。而不為天下為之者矣若三務者。此仁者之為天下度也。[41]

This quotation includes parallel sections that show that the way to govern the family through being filial provides a solid basis for governing the state with humanity. It is surprising to see that humanity can be used for governing the empire. "Filial" 孝 and "humane" 仁 are two important terms that tie the sections together and form a bridge between family and government.

The three areas that filial and humane actions address are poverty, lack of population, and disorder. That disorder is included is interesting, since this system of governing through humanity is what we have termed aristocracy in Guodian. Aristocracy is the opposite of meritocracy, a system of promotion that is inherently disruptive, since it drives social mobility.

This quotation fits into the larger argument presented in "Moderation in Funerals" that discusses the ideal way in which society functioned in antiquity. Mozi states that the way society operates in his day is unlike the preceding quotation, where humanity and acting filial formed the basis for planning for the welfare of the world. Instead, Mozi sees the society of his day as misunderstanding the role of family-based morality, since it has been corrupted through being channeled into the production of elaborate funerals. The current trend in his day of ostentatious funerals turns humanity and acting filial into dysfunctional practices that lead to bankruptcy and social harm.

In the *Mozi*, we do not find an explicit discussion of balancing humane and righteous government. "Moderation in Funerals" makes no mention of righteousness, and the following quotation from "Elevating the Outstanding" does not mention humanity. It is by combining these two chapters of *Mozi* that balancing family and state becomes pivotal to good governance. The standard by which people are judged for inclusion in government in the chapter "Moderation in Funerals" continues to be the moral principles learned from the family, but these principles must be applied to the empire as a whole.

Mozi describes the second side of government in "Elevating the Outstanding," where he advocates specifically nonfamilial solutions to government.[42] What is meant by "Elevating the Outstanding" is that one should disregard family connections when deciding who should be employed or rewarded by a government. This chapter advocates a meritocracy, which is in contrast to the family-based moral calculus of "Moderation in Funerals." It is important to note that righteousness remains the central term for this discussion of meritocracy:

> Therefore, when the sage kings of ancient times administered their states, they announced: "The unrighteous shall not be enriched, the unrighteous shall not be exalted, the unrighteous shall be no kin to us, the unrighteous shall not be our intimates!" When the rich and exalted men of the kingdom heard this, they all began to deliberate among themselves, saying, "We have trusted in our wealth and exalted position, but now the lord promotes the righteous without caring whether they are poor or humble. We too, then, must become righteous." Likewise the kin of the ruler began to deliberate, saying, "We have trusted in the bond of kinship, but now the lord promotes the righteous without caring how distant the relationship. We too, then, must become righteous." Those who were intimate with the ruler deliberated, saying, "We have trusted in the intimacy we enjoyed, but now the lord promotes the righteous without caring how far removed they may have been from him until now. We too, then, must become righteous." And when those who were far removed from the ruler heard it, they also deliberated, saying, "We used to believe that, since we were so far removed from the ruler, we had nothing to trust in. But now the lord promotes the righteous without caring how far removed they may be. We too, then, must become righteous." So the vassals of distant and outlying areas, as well as the noblemen's sons serving in the palace, the multitudes of the capital, and the peasants of the four borders, in time came to hear of this, and all strove to become righteous.[43]

是故古者聖王之為政也。言曰。不義不富。不義不貴。不義不親。不義不近。是以國之富貴人聞之。皆退而謀曰。始我所恃者。富貴也。今上舉義不辟貧賤。然則我不可不為義。親者聞之。亦退而謀曰。始我所恃者親也。今上舉義不辟疏。然則我不可不為義。近者聞之。亦退而謀曰。始我所恃者近也。今上舉義不辟遠。然則我不可不為義。遠

者聞之。亦退而謀曰。我始以遠為無恃。今上舉義不辟遠。然則我不
可不為義。逮至遠鄙郊外之臣。門庭庶子。國中之眾。四鄙之萌人聞
之。皆競為義。[44]

This passage describes government where promotions should be
decided without consideration of wealth, familial relationships,
or intimacy. Instead, righteousness is the yardstick by which
one selects people for government service. Family ties have no
bearing on the assessment of righteousness, and promotions in
the country are based on the morality of an individual with no
reference to his family. The stated impact is that everyone in
the empire would desire to develop their morality so that they
could be promoted. Clearly, this chapter advocates a meritocracy based purely on morality. However, since "Moderation in
Funerals" advocates government based on morals derived from
the family, Mozi appears to recognize two sides to a society, one
where it is important to consider values derived from the family and one where these concerns are absent. These two positions would seem incommensurable were it not for passages in
Mencius, Xunzi, and previously mentioned Guodian texts that
contain similarly divided characteristics. The difference is that
the *Mozi* does not discuss the two methods in a single passage.

The analysis of the *Mozi* provided in the previous few pages
is contrary to what one would conclude from a reading of the
Mozi that looks to homogenize the unique elements that make
each passage distinct. These two passages at first blush appear
to be outliers. The beginning of "Moderation in Funerals" not
only contradicts "Elevating the Outstanding" but also is at odds
with other chapters such as "Universal Love." Mozi repeatedly
states his opposition to the family as a viable building block for
harmonious interpersonal relations on a larger state level.

It would be tempting to dismiss the beginning of "Moderation
in Funerals" as a manuscript error resulting from several bamboo strips of a Confucian text being accidentally mixed into
the *Mozi*. In light of Guodian, however, we must consider the
possibility that these conflicting perspectives on humanity

and righteousness are distant intellectual relatives of "Tang Yu zhidao" and "The Five aspects of Conduct."

Since Mohism is so harshly attacked in *Mencius* 3B.9, 7A.26, and 7B.26, it is surprising to find a similar understanding of the relationship between the state and its families in these two texts. Graham has observed that the principle Mozi is best known for, "Concern for Everyone" (兼愛 *jianai*), is derived from Confucius's "one thread." He supports this by citing *Mencius* 3A.5, where Yizhi 夷之, a Mohist, states that a love without gradations begins with caring for our own family members. The Mohist also agrees that Confucians are correct in praising rulers who acted as though caring for a newborn baby.[45] Therefore, family as a shared source of moral understanding between the *Mencius* and *Mozi* should not be dismissed, but instead seen as an important area of common ground.

Mencius

Having established the importance of differing perspectives on meritocracy and aristocracy in "Tang Yu zhidao" and in the *Mozi*, we turn our attention to analyzing the position of Mencius on this issue. In the *Mencius*, we see a cluster of passages in the Wan Zhang chapter 萬章 that discuss elevating the outstanding in the context of ancient sages.[46] Passages such as 5B.3 and 5B.6 in the second half of the chapter praise the elevation of the outstanding. The "A" section of the chapter tends to present an opposing perspective, since the elevation of the outstanding is criticized, such as in 5A.6. We begin with 5B.3, which discusses the value of friendship. The following is from the end of the passage, where Shun visits Yao and they become friends:

> Shun went to see the emperor, who placed his son-in-law in a separate mansion. He entertained Shun but also allowed himself to be entertained in return. This is an example of an Emperor making friends with a common man.

"For an inferior to show deference to a superior is known as 'honouring the honoured'; for a superior to show deference to an inferior is known as 'elevating the outstanding'.[47] These two derive, in fact, from the same principle."[48]

舜尚見帝。帝館甥於貳室。亦饗舜。迭為賓主。是天子而友匹夫也。
用下敬上。謂之貴貴。用上敬下。謂之尊賢。貴貴尊賢。其義一也。[49]

In this passage, Mencius expresses support for meritocracy by praising the elevation of the outstanding. Elevating an outstanding person in this quotation flattens the normally hierarchical relationship between emperor and commoner, allowing talented people to be discovered. It is interesting to compare this with "Tang Yu zhidao," a text that describes a meritocracy as but one way to govern that needs to be balanced with aristocratic methods. There is an interest in balancing a binary pair of concepts in 5B.3, but in this case, the important factors are the greater powers of the ruler and the lesser powers of the common person.

Mencius 5B.6 is similarly concerned with the relationship between superior and inferior positions. The passage begins with a discussion of hierarchical relationships and concludes with a description of elevating the outstanding in the case of Yao and Shun:

. . . In Zisi's view, to make him bob up and down rendering thanks for the gifts of meat for the tripod was hardly the right way to take care of a gentleman. In the case of Yao, he sent his nine sons to serve Shun and gave him his two daughters as wives. After this, the hundred officials provided Shun with cattle and sheep and granaries for his use while he worked in the fields. And then Yao raised Shun to high office. Hence the phrase, "elevating the outstanding[50] by kings and dukes."[51]

子思以為鼎肉。使己僕僕爾亟拜也。非養君子之道也。堯之於舜也。
使其子九男事之。二女女焉。百官牛羊倉廩備。以養舜於畎畝之中。
後舉而加諸上位。故曰王公之尊賢者也。[52]

The first similarity between this quotation and 5B.3 is that both passages describe elevating one who is outstanding in entirely positive terms. The benefit of using merit to select people for office is clear; the country is strengthened by having someone as capable as Shun as the ruler. There is no mention of a condition where one would not proceed with raising someone up who was particularly talented, quite the opposite of the message in passage 5A.6.

Despite the previous passages' praise of the idea of elevating one who is outstanding, other parts of the *Mencius*, particularly the first half of the Wan Zhang chapter, describe limitations to meritocracy. The clearest statement of this appears in 5A.6, which begins with a question by Wan Zhang: "'It is said by some that virtue declined with Yu who chose his own son to succeed him, instead of an outstanding man. Is this true?'"[53] 萬章問曰。人有言。至於禹而德衰。不傳於賢而傳於子。有諸。[54] Mencius disagrees with Wan Zhang but concludes the passage with the following:

> A common man who comes to possess the Empire must not only have the virtue of a Shun or a Yu but also the recommendation of an Emperor. That is why Confucius never possessed the Empire. On the other hand, he who inherits the Empire is only put aside by Heaven if he is like Jie or Zhou. That is why Yi, Yi Yin and the Duke of Zhou never came to possess the Empire. . . . That the Duke of Zhou never came to possess the empire is similar to the case of Yi in Xia and that of Yi Yin in Yin. Confucius said, "In Tang and Yu succession was through abdication, while in Xia, Yin and Zhou it was hereditary. The basic principle was the same."[55]

> 匹夫而有天下者。德必若舜禹。而又有天子薦之者。故仲尼不有天下。繼世以有天下。天之所廢。必若桀紂者也。故益伊尹周公不有天下。. . . 周公之不有天下。猶益之於夏伊尹之於殷也。孔子曰。唐虞禪。夏后殷周繼。其義一也。[56]

Mencius describes how some of the most outstanding people in antiquity never became emperors, since they were never recommended for the job. Mencius feels that the dual requirement of talent plus recommendation is why great people such as Confucius and the Duke of Zhou never became emperors. A system that excludes monumentally talented people is clearly not a meritocracy. Instead, the passage describes several situations when hereditary concerns were the primary consideration for rulership.

Mencius states that as long as the person who inherits the throne is not among the worst villains of the world such as a Jie or a Zhou, heaven will not intervene to remove him from power. This so limits the importance of individual merit that this criterion becomes unrelated to the selection of an emperor in all but the most extreme of cases. We can see that 5A.6 is describing an aristocracy, since it values lineage far more than merit.

It might seem that Mencius is somewhat dissatisfied with aristocracy, since it prevented Confucius and other men he held in enormous esteem from being rulers. However, there are two indications in 5A.6 that Mencius sees aristocracy as positive. First, he concludes with a quotation from Confucius stating that "the basic principle was the same" 其義一也 between hereditary succession and abdication. Prior to the discovery of "Tang Yu zhidao" and "The Five Aspects of Conduct," this passage was difficult to understand. Surely, abdication and hereditary transmission are pure opposites. Now that we have excavated manuscripts that explain a harmonization of state and family as unifying, we can translate the phrase as "the basic principle is unity" 其義一也. Each solution to succession has advantages and disadvantages that must be unified. Consistent in both systems is harmonious unification.

The second indication is at the beginning of 5A.6 when Wang Chang asks if virtue declined when Yu broke with meritocracy and allowed his own son to be his successor. Mencius replies that virtue did not decline when this occurred. He explains that heaven decides if the country should be ruled by an outstanding individual or a son. Since Mencius does not see shortcomings in either system, 5A.6 provides a cogent argument for balancing aristocratic and meritocratic methods in government.

However, the lineage that Mencius values is more than a mere bloodline. It is also connected to heaven, since the ruler is the recipient of Heaven's Mandate (天命 *tianming*).[57] Mencius's emphasis on receiving a recommendation is thus an indication of the importance of heaven, not the power of individual rulers. Heaven's value system is often not concerned with merit, since blood descendants of rulers with the mandate are given preference over people of greater capacity but who lack a royal lineage.

Support for aristocracy is scattered through the first half of the Wan Zhang chapter but is strangely absent in the second half. This difference in attitudes about the importance of royal blood is illustrated by the following example from the second half of the chapter, 5B.9. When King Xuan of Qi 齊宣王 asked: "'What about ministers of royal blood?' [Mencius replied] ❻ If the prince made serious mistakes, they would remonstrate with him, but if repeated remonstrations fell on deaf ears, they would depose him.' The King blenched at this."[58] 請問貴戚之卿。曰。君有大過則諫。反覆之而不聽。則易位。王勃然變乎色。[59] This strong support of meritocratic ideas in the latter half of the Wan Zhang chapter is significantly different from the aristocratic themes in the first half.

When faced with these contradictory views on government, there are three choices. We could conclude that Mencius is in favor of aristocratic government, meritocratic government, or some sort of hybrid of the two. Prior to the discovery of texts at Guodian, scholars had no cogent reason to consider the hybrid explanation. However, having shown support for the hybrid model in "Tang Yu zhidao," the contradictory views of Mencius and Mozi begin to look as if they are part of a trend. Next, we will examine Xunzi, who also oscillates between the support of meritocracy and aristocracy. This appears within a single paragraph that seems to indicate further support for a hybrid ideal in government.

Xunzi

Xunzi discusses government by aristocracy and meritocracy in two important passages. The first is in the "Rectifying Theses," wherein Xunzi is adamant that abdication never occurred in ancient times. He believes that being set apart from other humans, the Son of Heaven could never abdicate. In 18.5A he states, "In accord with popular opinion, persuaders offer the thesis: 'Yao and Shun abdicated and yielded their thrones.' This is not so."[60] 世俗之為說者曰。堯舜擅讓。是不然。[61] In the sections divided as 18.5B and C, Xunzi continues to oppose what he terms the "popular opinion" that rulers abdicate at death, or in the event of old age and infirmity. Since there could only ever be one true ruler, essentially nothing has changed during the transition. Xunzi feels this is different from abdication; when one ruler dies, another simply takes over. For a meritocracy to include the sovereign, abdication is essential. Thus, at first blush, the "Rectifying Theses" appears to be supporting government through aristocracy and nothing more. A closer analysis of 18.5B will demonstrate that this chapter actually supports a hybrid government of meritocracy and aristocracy.

Passage 18.5B begins by stating that even at death a ruler does not abdicate, making it impossible to raise a talented replacement to the throne. Following this, there is a list of what a ruler does that sets him apart from others. This list is interesting in that its content is strongly meritocratic. For example, Xunzi describes a sage's actions using the phrase[62] "filled offices by measuring his capacity"[63] 量能而授官。[64] Xunzi also states, "Given the situation in which there is no sage among his descendants, but there is one among the Three Dukes, then the empire will turn to him naturally as though he were restoring and reviving it."[65] 聖不在後子而在三公。則天下如歸。猶復而振之矣。[66] This passage contains an unmistakable encapsulation of a hybrid meritocracy/aristocracy. It is aristocratic, since preference is given to descendants in succession questions,[67] but meritocratic in that a talented person outside the direct line of descent is acceptable.

In the *Xunzi*, succession does not directly involve heaven. This is different from the *Mencius* and is indicative of a generally different view of the role of heaven between the two authors. Heaven is directly involved in human affairs in the *Mencius*, while the *Xunzi* adopts a more mechanistic view. An example from the *Xunzi* is: "Whoever strengthens the base and spends in moderation, heaven can not impoverish. Whoever completes the nourishment [sc. of the people] and moves in accordance with the seasons, Heaven can not cause to be ill." 彊本而節用，則天不能貧，養備而動時，則天不能病.[68] This example is mechanistic as heaven reacts to human behavior, but is not capricious or personally involved. As such, heaven serves as an unwavering model for humans but is not threatened by evil tyrants or enhanced by sage rulers.[69] Xunzi is not defending the status of heaven by objecting to abdication. Instead, he is arguing for the importance of a powerful ruler. By eliminating the possibility of abdicating in favor of one more talented, it seems Xunzi is hoping that the ruler will be able to govern more effectively. Not feeling the pressure to contend for his position, a ruler could have greater latitude when carrying out his main responsibility, which, according to 18.5B, includes the correct assignment of ranks and offices.

Another chapter in which Xunzi discusses the question of succession is "On the Regulations of a King" 王制篇. Here he argues that one's position in government should not be related to bloodline, even if one is a direct descendant of the king:

> Someone inquired of me about the technique of government. I replied: Promote the outstanding[70] and capable without regard to seniority; dismiss the unfit and incapable without hesitation; execute the principal evildoers without trying first to instruct them; and transform the common lot of men without trying first to rectify them.

> Although the distinctions between social classes have not yet been fixed, there will still be [such basic distinctions as] primary and secondary. Although they be the descendants of kings and dukes

or knights and grand officers, if they are incapable of devotedly observing the requirements of ritual and moral principles, they should be relegated to the position of commoners. Although they be the descendants of commoners, if they accumulate culture and study, rectify their character and conduct, and are capable of devotedly observing the requirements of ritual principles and justice, they should be brought to the ranks of a prime minister, knight or grand officer. . . . This may be described as "Heaven's Power"—such is the government of the True King.[71]

請問為政。曰。賢能不待次而舉。罷不能不待須而廢。元惡不待教而誅。中庸民不待政而化。分未定也。則有昭繆。[72] 雖王公士大夫之子孫。不能屬於禮義。則歸之庶人。雖庶人之子孫也。積文學。正身行。能屬於禮義。則歸之卿相士大夫. . . . 夫是之謂天德。王者之政也[73]

This passage holds that even common people should be elevated to high positions in the state if they are talented. Similarly, people of noble birth who lack the ability to follow principles of morality should be demoted to the position of a commoner. All that is lacking from this quotation is the specific inclusion of kings in the range of positions open to commoners for promotion. However, the general thrust of the chapter is to argue that kings must strive to become true kings and that lineage is unrelated to morality.

If we view the process of social mobility propounded in "On the Regulations of a King" in the context of the chapter "Man's Nature Is Evil" 性惡篇, we see that there should be no limits to how far a common person might go if he cultivates morality. "Small man, noble man—it was never so that one could not become the other; but they do not become each other, not because they can not, but because they can not be forced. Thus it is like this that a person in the street can become Yu."[74] 小人君子者。未嘗不可以相為也。然而不相為者。可以而不可使也。故塗之人可以為禹則然。[75] This quotation explains Xunzi's belief that if the royal household fails to produce a suitable heir, it is acceptable to look elsewhere for a replacement.

Graham has a different perspective on the elevation of the outstanding in early China. He states that in no school of thought did the concept of elevating the outstanding include the ruler.[76] The first half of Wan Zhang in the *Mencius* and the *Xunzi's* "Rectifying Theses" express serious reservations about abdication, which seems to have contributed to Graham's perspective. However, both philosophers express contrasting views, such as *Mencius* 5B.3 and 5B.6, and *Xunzi's* "On the Regulations of a King" and "Man's Nature Is Evil." Graham's approach to *Mencius* and *Xunzi* is to find a middle ground that can roughly accommodate the range of views expressed on elevating the outstanding. This is an understandable methodology, since the Guodian texts had not been published when Graham was formulating his perspective. With the addition of recently excavated manuscripts from Guodian, it becomes evident that pre-Qin texts embraced a harmonization of aristocratic and meritocratic government methods that includes elevating the outstanding to rulership positions. As a result, Graham's perspective on the elevation of the outstanding is likely incorrect.

Xunzi believes that rulers should be selected based on a mix of meritocratic and aristocratic concerns. When meritocratic, it cannot involve abdication per se but would simply be a transfer of rule from one outstanding king to the next. *Mencius* 5A.6 also agrees that preference should be given to hereditary lines over a replacement coming from outside the family. However, Mencius proposes only minimal standards for those eligible based on hereditary transmission. For Mencius, a search for a nonhereditary ruler would occur only in the dire situation of a tyrant or horrible villain being in line to the throne.[77]

Xunzi argues that rulers should be sages, which can be seen as a more stringent requirement for rulership. Mencius only requires that the hereditary replacement be better than the level of the worst tyrants in history. David Nivison believes that the abdication of the king of Yan to Zhizi is a factor in Mencius's treatment of this subject in the "Wan Zhang" chapter.[78] Since Xunzi is writing after Mencius, the king of Yan could also be a factor in his "Rectifying Theses." Despite Xunzi being opposed to abdication, his standards for those eligible for hereditary transmission are surprisingly much higher than those of Mencius. This seems to be a contributing factor to Graham calling Xunzi the first Confucian to embrace the elevation of the outstanding.[79]

Conclusion

"Tang Yu zhidao" and "The Five Aspects of Conduct" assert that the most important function of government is to assist in the harmonization of state and family relations. These texts see the relationship between these two entities—the family and the collection of families that ultimately constitute the state—as being inherently problematic; they are conflicting social groupings. The tension between these social groupings is particularly apparent when selecting a successor for government service and when deciding a legal case. Both of these situations require a choice with a single result: selection or rejection, punishment or forgiveness. However, these texts posit an interesting third solution. State and family disharmony can be overcome by developing a hybrid government that employs both meritocratic and aristocratic methods. The latter emphasize rulership that is based on and beneficial to the family. The former emphasize meritocratic methods that promote talented individuals for the good of the state.[80]

A contrary perspective can be found in the work of Mark Edward Lewis. He provides "Works on Political Methods," a list that includes the *Book of Lord Shang* 商君書, the *Han Feizi* 韓非子, and *Guanzi* 官子 in his chapter "Warring States Political History" in *The Cambridge History of Ancient China*.[81] In a subsequent section of Lewis's chapter, entitled "Scholars and the State," he writes, "Unlike kings, reforming ministers, commanders, and persuader/diplomats, the scholars were neither indispensable elements of the new state structure nor active participants in the political world, but they evolved in close relation with the states of the period."[82] He continues by clarifying his category of scholars as comprising Confucians and Mohists. Of Confucius, he says, "He held only low office and played no role in the politics of the period."[83] While there is no doubt that this statement is a completely accurate description of political philosophy in early China during certain periods and in certain places, there are also important exceptions, such as Guodian.[84] Guodian texts were found in the grave of a man who taught the heir apparent to the throne, and these texts see political decisions as related to ideas connected to what others classify as Confucian, Mohist, and Laozi.

Prior to the Guodian discovery, it was believed that within an individual received text, such as the *Mozi*, *Mencius*, or *Xunzi*, one was obligated to search for a stable position on key philosophical issues. Texts then would cleave to one form of succession, either hereditary or selecting the most skilled person for the job. It was natural to consider them separate systems as none of the received texts discussed exactly how those two forms of succession interrelated. The impact of Guodian on scholarship is that we should no longer force coherence upon our analyses of complex religious and philosophical systems. With the discovery of "Tang Yu zhidao," "The Five Aspects of Conduct," and other recently excavated texts from Guodian, we now have a body of work that discusses the harmonization of meritocratic and aristocratic forms of succession. Instead of two competing forms of succession, it now seems that governments would ideally build on the strengths of both systems to harmonize state and family relations. This changes how we understand the foundational era of Chinese government—the transitions from Yao to Shun to Yu. There was no monumental shift from meritocracy to aristocracy from the perspective of Guodian, since both sides were simply focused on the same goal, harmonizing the state and family.

Appendix: Guodian Version of "The Five Aspects of Conduct"

1. The five aspects of conduct are: When humanity forms within [your heart] it is called virtuous conduct. If [humanity] is not formed within it is called a mere act. When righteousness forms within [your heart] it is called virtuous ❶ conduct. If [righteousness] is not formed within it is called a mere act. When ritual forms within [your heart] it is called virtuous ❷ conduct. If [ritual] is not formed within it is called a mere act. When wisdom forms within [your heart] it is called virtuous conduct. If it is not formed within it is called a mere act. When sagacity forms within [your heart] it is called virtuous ❸ conduct. If [sagacity] is not formed within it is called a mere act. ■

1. 行五: 仁¹形²於內謂之德之行, 不形於內, 謂之行。義形於內, 謂之德之❶行, 不形於內謂之行。禮形於內, 謂之德之行, 不形於內謂之 ❷ (行。智形) 於內, 謂之德之行, 不形於內謂之行。聖形於內, 謂之德❸之行, 不行於內謂之行。³■

2. There are five aspects of virtuous conduct, that, when united,⁴ are called virtue itself. When only four of these actions are united it is called being adept [at virtue. Adeptness is the way of humans ❹ while virtue is the way of heaven. If a noble man's⁵ inner heart lacks concern, then he will lose his inner heart's wisdom. If his inner heart lacks wisdom, his inner heart will lack ❺ happiness. If his inner heart lacks happiness, he will not be at ease. Not being at ease he will not be musical and without music he will lack virtue. ■ ⁶

2. 德之行五和，謂之德，四行和，謂之善。善，人❹道也。德，天道也。君子無中心之憂則無中心之智。無中心之智則無中心 ❺（之悅。無中心之悅，則不）安。不安，則不樂。不樂，則無德。∎

3. If someone forms the five aspects of conduct within his inner heart and at the appropriate time practices them ❻ he is said to be a noble man. When a gentleman has his goals set on the way of a noble man he is said to have the goals of a gentleman. Being adept [at virtue] but not practicing it, you will not make progress.[7] Being virtuous but lacking ❼ a goal your [virtue] will not be completed. Being wise but not thinking you will not comprehend. Thinking without essence, you will not have keen insight. Thinking without extension, you will not comprehend. Thinking without lightness, [the five aspects of conduct] will not be formed. Not being formed you will not be at ease. Not being at ease you will not be musical, not being musical ❽ you will lack virtue. ∎

3. 五行皆形於內，時行❻ 之，謂之君（子）。士有志於君子道，謂之之志士。善弗為無近，德弗 ❼ 志不成，智弗思不得。思不精不察，思不長 [不得，思不輕][8] 不形。不形不安，不安不樂，不樂 ❽ 無德。∎

4. Not being humane your thoughts will not be essential. Not being wise your thoughts will not be extended. No humanity and no wisdom: "When I do not see my lord, my sorrowful heart ❾ cannot be agitated."[9] Now that I have seen him, my heart cannot be happy.[10] "And I have seen him and I have observed him my heart will be ❶❶ happy."[11] This is what the preceding quotation means. If you are not humane, your thoughts will not be essential. If you are not sagacious, your thoughts will not be light. No humanity and no sagacity: ❶❶ "While we do not see our husbands, our hearts must not be full of grief. Let us but see our husbands and our hearts will not rest." ∎ [12]

4. 不仁，思不能精。不智，思不能長。不仁不智。「未見君子，憂心 ❾ 不能惙惙; 既見君子，心不能悅; 亦既見之，亦既觀之，我心則 ❶❶（悅），」此之謂（也。不）仁，思不能精。不聖，思不能輕。不仁不聖。❶❶「未見君子，憂心不能忡忡; 既見君子，心不能降。」∎

5. Humane thoughts: [they] are essential; being essential ❶❷ you will have keen insight; having keen insight you will be at ease; being at ease you will be gentle; being gentle you will be happy; being happy your demeanor is pleasant; having a pleasant demeanor you can be intimate; being intimate you will be loving; loving your countenance will be jade-like; having a jade-like countenance you will be formed; being formed you will be humane. ■ ❶❸

5. 仁之思也精。精❶❷則察，察則安，安則溫，溫則悅，悅則戚，戚則親，親則愛，愛則玉色，玉色則形。形則仁。■ ❶❸

6. Wise thoughts: [they] are extended; having extended [your thoughts] you will comprehend; once you comprehend you will not forget; not forgetting you will have keen vision; having keen vision you will be able to perceive an outstanding person; being able to perceive an outstanding person you will have a jade-like[13] countenance; having a jade-like countenance you will be formed; being formed you will be ❶❹ wise. ■

6. 智之思也長，長則得，得則不忘，不忘則明。明則見賢人，見賢人則玉色，玉色則形，形❶❹則智。■

7. Sagacious thoughts: [they] are light; being light they form, forming they will not be neglected, not neglecting you will have keen hearing;[14] having keen hearing you will hear the way of the noble man; hearing the way of the noble man you will be like jade sounds; being like jade sounds you will be formed; being formed you will be ❶❺ sagacious. ■

7. 聖之思也輕，輕則形，形則不忘，不忘則聰。聰，則聞君子道，聞君子道則玉音，玉音則形，形❶❺則聖。■

8. "A good person, a noble man, his manner is unified."[15] Only after you are able to unify [your manner] can you be a noble man. Then you are always concerned about your uniqueness[16]. ■ ❶❻

8. 「淑人君子，其儀宜一也。」 能為一，然後能為君子。[君子] 慎其獨也。■ ❶❻

9. "I looked until I could no longer see her and cried like rain."[17] "Only when you are able to display your wings unevenly"[18] do you understand the utmost sadness. A noble man is concerned about his ❶❼ uniqueness.■

9.「(瞻望弗及)，泣涕如雨。」能「差池其羽，」然後能至袁。君子慎其❶❼(獨也。■)

10. Regarding a noble man's being adept [at virtue], there is something that he takes as the beginning and something that he takes as the end. Regarding a noble man being virtuous, ❶❽ there is something that he takes as the beginning but nothing that he takes as the end. One who has a bronze [bell] voice and jade vibrancy is a virtuous one.

10. (君)子之為善也，有與始，有與終也。君子之為德也，❶❽ (有與始，有與) 終也。[19] 金聲而玉振之，有德者也。■

11. A bronze [bell] voice is adept [at virtue] while jade vibrancy is sagacious. Being adept [at virtue] is the way of humans ❶❾ while being virtuous is the way of heaven. Only those who have virtue, can have a bronze [bell] voice and jade vibrancy. Not having keen hearing you will lack keen vision; not having keen vision you will lack sagacity; no sagacity no ❷⓿ wisdom; no wisdom no humanity; without humanity you will not be at peace; without peace you will not be musical; without music you will lack virtue. ■

11. 金聲，善也。玉音，聖也。善，人❶❾ 道也。德，天 (道也)。唯有德者，然後能金聲而玉振之。不聰不明，[不明不聖]，不聖不 ❷⓿ 智，不智不仁，不仁不安，不安不樂，不樂無德。■

12. If you are not open to change[20] you will not be happy; if you are not happy you will not have a pleasant demeanor; if you do not have a pleasant demeanor you will not be intimate; if you are not intimate, you will not love; if you do not love you will not be humane.

12. 不變不悅，不悅不戚，不戚不親，不親不愛，不愛不仁。■

13. If you are not upright you will not be steadfast; not being steadfast, you will not be courageous; not being courageous ❷❶ you will not admonish; not admonishing you will not act [appropriately]; not acting [appropriately], you will not be righteous. ■

13. 不直不肆，²¹不肆不果，不果❷❶不簡，不簡不行，不行不義。■

14. If you do not keep the appropriate distance you will not be reverent; if you are not reverent, you will not be stern; if you are not stern you will not show honor; if you do not show honor you will not be polite; if you are not polite you will not [follow the] rites.■

14. 不遠不敬，不敬不嚴，不嚴不尊，不尊不恭，不恭不禮。■

15. One who has never ❷❷ heard the way of the noble man, is said not to have keen hearing. One who has never seen an outstanding person, is said not to have keen vision. If you hear the way of the noble man but do not know ❷❸ it is the way of the noble man this is called not being sagely. If you see an outstanding person but you do not know he has virtue, this is called not being wise.■ ❷❹

15. 未嘗❷❷ 聞君子道，謂之不聰。未嘗見賢人，謂之不明。聞君子道而不知❷❸其君子道也，謂之不聖。見賢人而不知其有德也，謂之不智。■❷❹

16. Seeing something and knowing it is wisdom; hearing something and knowing it is sagacity. Illustrating the illustrious is wisdom and the dread of majesty is sagacity. "Illustration of illustrious [virtue] is required below and the dread of majesty ❷❺ is on high."²² This is what is meant.■

16. 見而知之，智也。聞而知之，聖也。明明，智也，赫赫，聖也。「明明在下，赫赫 ❷❺ 在上，」此之謂也。■

17. Hearing the way of the noble man is having keen hearing; hearing something and knowing it is sagacity. Sages know the way of heaven ❷❻. Knowing something and putting it into

practice is righteousness. Practicing something with the appropriate timing is virtue. Recognizing an outstanding person is having keen vision. Recognizing something and ❷❼ knowing it is wisdom. Knowing and being at peace is humanity. Being at peace and reverential is [following the] rites. Where sageness, wisdom, ritual and music are born is the harmonious combination of the five ❷❽ aspects of conduct. Being unified you are musical. If there is music there is virtue and a state and its families can arise. King Wen's appearance was like this. "King Wen ❷❾ was on high and shone brightly upon all under heaven."[23] This is what is meant by the above quote.■

17. 聞君子道，聰也。聞而知之，聖也。聖人知天❷❻道也。知而行之，義也。行之而時德也。見賢人，明也。見而知之，❷❼ 智也。知而安之，仁也。安而敬之，禮也。聖，知禮樂之所由生也，五 ❷❽ (行之所和) 也。和則樂，樂則有德，有德則邦家興。文王之示也如此。「文❷❾ (王在上，於昭) 於天，」此之謂也。■

18. Recognizing something and knowing it is wisdom. Knowing and being at peace is humanity. Being at peace ❸⓿ and practicing it, you are righteous. Practicing it and being reverential [is to follow] the rites. Humanity, righteousness and the rites are what emerge when you unify the four aspects of conduct. Having harmonized ❸❶ them you can bring them together; when together you are adept [at virtue].

18.   見而知之，智也。知而安之，仁也。安❸⓿而行之，義也。行而敬之，禮。仁義，禮所由生也。四行之所和也，和❸❶則同。同則善。■

19. Your appearance and countenance are mild and changeable.[24] When using your inner heart to interact with others, you will be happy. When your inner heart is happy, and you influence ❸❷ your brothers' behavior you have a pleasant demeanor. Having a pleasant demeanor and living up to your words you are intimate. Being intimate and affectionate you will be loving. Loving your father and extending this to love others you are humane.

19. 顏色容貌溫變也。以其中心與人交，悅也。中心悅旃，遷 ²⁵ ❸❷ 於兄弟，戚也。戚而信之，親 [也]。親而篤之，愛也。愛父，其繼愛人，仁也。■

20. When your inner heart ❸❸ distinguishes and is appropriately put into practice you are upright. If you are upright and attain you are steadfast. If you are steadfast and are not intimidated by those who are strong and powerful you are courageous. You should not ❸❹ allow lesser concerns to jeopardize greater concerns, thus you admonish. If there is a serious crime with a capital punishment, this is called acting [correctly]. Venerating the noble, those with rank, and elevating the outstanding, you are righteous. ■❸❺

20. 中心❸❸辯然，而正行之，直也。直而遂之，肆也。肆而不畏強禦，果也。不❸❹以小道害大道，簡也。有大罪而大誅之，行也。貴貴，其等尊賢，義也。■❸❺

21. When using your external heart to interact with others you [maintain the appropriate] distance. [Maintaining the appropriate] distance and being stern, is reverence. Being reverent, but not [overly] frugal or regulated this is stern. Being stern and having awe ❸❻ you venerate. Venerating, but not being arrogant, you can revere. Revering and widely interacting with others is [to act in accordance with] the rites. ■

21. 以其外心與人交，遠也。遠而莊之敬也。敬而不懈，嚴也。嚴而畏❸❻之，尊也。尊而不驕，恭也。恭而博交，禮也。■

22. Without admonishment you cannot act [appropriately]. Not being lenient you cannot have insight into the way ❸❼. Meting out a capital punishment for a serious crime is admonishment. Issuing a pardon for an insignificant crime is being lenient. Not ❸❽ meting out a capital punishment for a serious crime is not acting [properly]. Not issuing a pardon for an insignificant crime you cannot have keen insight into the way.

22. 不簡，不行。不匿，不辯[37]於道。有大罪而大誅之，簡也。有小罪而赦之，匿也。有大罪而弗[38]大誅也，不行也。有小罪而弗赦也，不辯於道也。■

23. Admonishment as a term is like remonstrating [39] that can only be applied to the great and rare [cases]. Leniency as a term is like being lenient for minor crimes that can be applied to lesser and more common [cases]. Admonishment is the method of righteousness. Leniency [40] is the method of humanity. That which is hard is the method of righteousness, while that which is soft is the method of humanity. "He was neither violent nor hasty neither hard nor soft."[26] This summarizes what I am referring to [41].■

23. 簡之為言也，猶練 [27][39]也，大而晏者也。匿之為言也猶匿匿也，小而軫者也。簡，義之方也。匿，[40]仁之方也。強，義之方。柔，仁之方也。「不強不絿，不剛不柔，」此之謂[41]也。■ [28]

24. A noble man puts the great parts together. Those who are able to progress become nobles,[29] those who cannot cease where they dwell. For the case of grave [42] and rare crimes, the noble man adopts [admonishment]. In the case of minor and common crimes, he adopts [leniency].

When one without morality is able to achieve the way of the noble man he is called an outstanding person. When you know a noble [43] man and recruit him, this is called respecting the outstanding. When you know [a noble man] and assign him duties, this is called respecting an outstanding person. The latter is a gentleman respecting an outstanding person.■[44]

24. 君子集大成。能進之為君子，弗能進之，各止於其裏。大而[42]晏者，能有取焉。小而軫者，能有取焉。胥儦儦 [30]達諸君子道，謂之賢。君[43]子知而舉之，謂之尊賢。知而事之謂之尊賢者也［。前，王公之尊賢者也］；[31] 後，士之尊賢者也。■

25. Ears, eyes, nose, mouth, hands and feet are the six that the mind employs. If the mind says yes none dare not say yes.[32] If it [says to] agree, none dare disagree. If it [says to] [45] advance

none dare not advance. If it [says to] withdraw none dare not withdraw. If it [says to] go deep none dare not go deep. If it [says to] go shallow, none dare not go shallow. When there is harmony there is equality; when there is equality there is adeptness [at virtue]. ■❹❻

25. 耳目鼻口手足六者，心之役也。心曰唯莫敢不唯；若莫敢不諾；❹❺進莫敢不進；後莫敢不後；深莫敢不深；淺莫敢不淺。和則同　同則善。■❹❻

26. When you see something and understand it is called advancement. When you understand something from a metaphor it is called getting closer. When you understand something from a parable this is called making progress. ❹❼ Knowing something from minute signs is heavenly. "Shangdi is with you, have no doubts in your heart."[33] That is the case referred to here. ■

26.目而知之，謂之進。喻而知之謂之進之，譬而知之謂之進之，❹❼幾而知之，天也。「上帝臨汝，毋貳爾心，」此之謂也。■

27. What greatly bestows upon humans is heaven. Close relations are what are bestowed upon all of its people.■

27. 天施諸其人，天也。 [34] 其❹❽人施諸人，狎也。■

28. Those that hear the way and are happy are those that like humanity. Those that hear the way and are awed by it are those who are fond of ❹❾ righteousness. Those who hear the way and are reverent are those who are fond of the rites. Those who hear the way and are musical are those who like virtue.■ ❺⓿

28. 聞道而悅者，好仁者也。 聞道而畏者，好❹❾義者也。 聞道而恭者，好禮者也。聞道而樂者，好德者也。■❺⓿

Notes

Introduction

1. This town is in Jingmen municipality (荊門市), Shayang district (沙洋区), Sifang county (四方鄉).

2. That bamboo strips are still not seen as being as valuable as other items from tombs can be seen in the example of the famous Shanghai Museum. The museum has several rooms full of bronze vessels right next to the main entrance. However, as of the summer of 2006, the only bamboo strips displayed are on an upper floor in a single unimpressive case.

3. For excellent introductions to the state of Chu, which controlled the region when Guodian was closed, see Constance A. Cook and John Major, eds. *Defining Chu: Image and Reality in Ancient China* (Honolulu: University of Hawai'i Press, 1999); Edward L. Shaughnessy, *Rewriting Early Chinese Texts* (Albany: State University of New York Press, 2006).

4. Wu Hung, "Art and Architecture of the Warring States Period," in *Cambridge History of Ancient China: From the Origins of Civilization to 221 B.C.*, ed. Michael Loewe and Edward L. Shaughnessy (Cambridge: Cambridge University Press, 1999), 708.

5. Brackets indicate interpolations; parentheses are for lacunae.

6. Unless otherwise noted, translations are my own. The main transcription of ancient script into modern characters used in this book is by Li Ling, but many other sources have been consulted, and their differing transcriptions will be noted at length. Li Ling 李零, *Guodian Chujian Jiaoduji* 郭店楚簡校讀記 (Beijing: Beijing University Press, 2002), 78.

7. Dale M. Hilty, Rick L. Morgan, and Joan E. Burns, "King and Hunt Revisited: Dimensions of Religious Involvement," *Journal for the Scientific Study of Religion* 23, 3 (1984): 252–66; Christopher G. Ellison, Jason D. Boardman, David R. Williams, and James S. Jackson, "Religious Involvement, Stress, and Mental Health: Findings from the 1995 Detroit Area Study," *Social Forces* 80, 1 (2001): 215–49.

8. Harold S. Himmelfarb, "Measuring Religious Involvement," *Social Forces* 53, 4 (1975): 606–18.

9. This is based on an inscription on the base of a cup that has been transcribed as either "Crown Prince's Teacher" 東宮之師 or "Crown Prince's Cup" 東宮之杯. Questions over this transcription raise important doubts about the source of this claim. Liu Zuxin, "An Overview of Tomb Number One at Jingmen Guodian," in *The Guodian Laozi: Proceedings of the International Conference, Dartmouth College, May 1998*, ed. Sarah Allan and Crispin Williams (Berkeley: The Society for the Study of Early China and Institute of East Asian Studies, University of California, 2000), 29.

10. For a picture of the Guodian weapons, see Hubeisheng Jingmenshi Bowuguan 湖北省荊門市博物館, "Jingmen Guodian yihao Chumu" 荊門郭店—號楚墓, *Wenwu* 7 (1997): 40. The weapons at Mawangdui are described here: Hunansheng Bowuguan 湖南省博物館, "Changsha Mawangdui er san hao Han mu fajue jianbao" 長沙馬王堆二三號漢墓發掘簡報, *Wenwu* 7 (1974): 39–48, 63.

11. From the Han era, the term *jia* 家 is the "ism" in the schools of Confucianism, Daoism, and Legalism 法家. This term produced a series of labels that might not be accurate reflections of the constituent members of these schools. This phenomenon has been discussed by Willard Peterson, among others. The result of these "isms" has been that works with significant philosophical differences such as the *Analects* and *Mencius* have been grouped under the single umbrella of Confucianism. Despite this, we should be clear that this systematizing is not necessarily even a true reflection of Han era scholarship. Daniel Gardner points out that the commentarial tradition that arose as an important project of the Han is a process that illustrates the *changing* meanings and understandings of a text over time. Therefore, while Han scholarship might have been interpreted as narrowing and systematizing in later times, this is not necessarily an accurate reading of the era. Mark Csikszentmihalyi has a detailed discussion of the way that the school issue relates to "The Five Aspects of Conduct" in particular. One of the earliest studies in English that I am aware of is

by Herrlee Creel. Willard J. Peterson, "Squares and Circles: Mapping the History of Chinese Thought," *Journal of the History of Ideas* 49, 1 (1988): 47–60; Daniel K. Gardner, "Confucian Commentary and Chinese Intellectual History," *Journal of Asian Studies* 57, 2 (1998): 397–422; Mark Csikszentmihalyi, *Material Virtue: Ethics and Body in Early China* (Leiden: Brill, 2004), 13–58, passim 22–32; Herrlee Glessner Creel, "Sinism—A Clarification," *Journal of the History of Ideas* 10, 1 (1949): 135–40.

12. This study is treating Guodian texts as the starting point for comparison with received texts, and righteousness has been selected as the translation for *yi* 義. While there are other translations that could work in other instances, "The Five Aspects of Conduct" is different for connecting *yi* with *jian* 簡 (admonishment) and in turn *dazhu* 大誅 (heavy or capital punishment). Because *yi* relates to the broader society, where it is often called upon to respond to injustice, righteousness seemed the best choice. "Without admonishment you cannot act [appropriately]. Not being lenient you cannot have insight into the way ❸❼. Meting out a capital punishment for a serious crime is admonishment." 不簡，不行。不匿，不辯 ❸❼ 於道。有大罪而大誅之，簡也。 Li Ling, *Guodian Chujian Jiaoduji*, 78–80. Numbers in black rings indicate the ends of bamboo strips, so ❸❼ indicates the end of the thirty-seventh strip of the text. For images of the strips, see *Guodian Chumu zhujian* 郭店楚墓竹簡 (Beijing: Wenwu, 1998).

13. The connection is actually more than just shared vocabulary, as the specific philosophical connotations of humanity as a family-based ethical principle is one of the important creations of the *Analects*, such as can be seen in passage 1:2, where being filial is the root of humanity. Pang Pu takes this as being combined with the rites in the *Analects* to form a dual concern for internal and external sources of moral cultivation, which shifts to an emphasis on the internal side in subsequent generations. He then categorizes Guodian as emphasizing the internal side. I will discuss the reasons I disagree with this categorization in chapter 2. See Pang Pu 龐樸, "Kongmeng zhijian—Guodian Chujian zhong de rujia xinxing shuo" 孔孟之間—郭店楚簡中的儒家心性說 in *Guodian Chujian yanjiu. Zhongguo zhexue* 20 (1999): 23–25.

14. Wei Qipeng 魏启鹏, Li Xueqin 李學勤, Liang Tao 梁涛, Jiang Guanghui 姜廣輝, Li Jinglin 李景林, Liao Mingchun 廖名春, and Zhang Weihong 張衛紅, for example, all believe that this text was written by Zisi 子思, which has come to be termed the School of Zisi, Mencius, and "The Five Aspects of Conduct" 思孟五行學派. This school is seen

as merely a subset of Confucianism, which limits our ability to understand why a text like "The Five Aspects of Conduct" would be consistently buried alongside the *Laozi*. Wei Qipeng 魏启鹏, "Jianbo 'Wuxing' Jianshi" 簡帛《五行》箋釋, Chutu wenxian yizhu yanxi congshu P010. (Taipei: Wanjuanlou, 2000), 149–70; Li Xueqin 李學勤, "Jingmen Guodian Chujianzhong de Zisizi" 荆門郭店楚簡中的子思子, *Guodian Chujian yanjiu. Zhongguo zhexue* 20 (1999): 75–80; Liang Tao 梁濤, "Xunzi dui Simeng 'Wuxing shuo' de Pipan" 荀子對思孟"五行"說的批判, *Chinese Culture Research* (2001 Summer): 40–46; Jiang Guanghui 姜廣輝, "Guodian Chujian yu Zisizi—Jian Tan Guodian Chujian De Sixiang Shi YiYi" 郭店楚簡與子思子兼談郭店楚簡的思想史意義, *Guodian Chujian Yanjiu. Zhongguo zhexue* 20 郭店楚簡研究《中國哲學》中國哲學第二十輯 (1999), 81–92; Li Jinglin 李景林, "Boshu 'Wuxing' Shendu Xiaoyi" 帛書《五行》慎獨說小議, *Renwen Zazhi* 6 (2003): 23–27; Liao Mingchun 廖名春, "Guodian Chujian Rujia Zhuzuo Kao" 郭店楚簡儒家著作考, *Kongzi Yanjiu* 3 (1998): 69–83; Zhang Weihong 張衛紅, "'Shilun Wuxing' de chengde jinlu" 試論《五行》的成德進路, *Shihezi Daxue Xuebao Zhexue Shehui Kexue Bao* 3.4 (2003): 22–30.

15. Other problems will be discussed in detail in chapter 2, where it will be shown that Mencius uses humanity and righteousness differently from "The Five Aspects of Conduct."

16. The closure of the Mawangdui tomb in 168 B.C.E. occurs closest to the time of Sima Tan (d. 110 B.C.E.). However, even Tan has been shown to be more interested in syncretism than dividing and separating philosophers. Kidder Smith, "Sima Tan and the Invention of Daoism, 'Legalism,' *et cetera*," *Journal of Asian Studies* 62, 1 (2003): 129–56.

17. One important exception is of course Liao Mingchun, who has analyzed the shape of the strips and calligraphy to conclude that it is likely that "The Five Aspects of Conduct" and Black Robes were copied by the same individual. Liao Mingchun, "Guodian Chujian Rujia Zhuzuo Kao," 82–83.

18. In this book, heaven will be used to translate (天 *tian*) despite the obvious unwanted freight that comes along with a term with inescapable Judeo-Christian connotations.

19. This is apparent from *Mencius* 7A.1.

20. See *Mencius* 6A.8.

21. There are several places where this idea can be found in the Guodian "Five Aspects of Conduct," but the clearest expression can be found on strip 25.

22. Donald Harper argues that the systematic pairing of yin and yang does not appear during the Warring States. This should eliminate the possibility that the observation of an entirely separate set of binary opposites in Guodian has anything to do with yin and yang. In addition, Ikeda Tomohisa argues that the Five Aspects 五行 document found in Guodian and Mawangdui is unrelated to the identically titled concept of the Five Phases 五行 of metal, wood, water, fire, and earth 金，木，水，火，土 that becomes important in the Han. Donald Harper, "Warring States Natural Philosophy and Occult Thought," in *Cambridge History of Ancient China*, ed. Michael Loewe and Edward Shaughnessy (Cambridge: Cambridge University Press, 1999), 860–66; Ikeda Tomohisa 池田知久, *Maôtai kanbo hakusho gogyôhen kenkyû* 馬王堆漢墓帛書五行篇研究 (Tokyo: Kyûko, 1993), 85–88.

Chapter One

1. Russell Arben Fox, "Confucian and Communitarian Responses to Liberal Democracy," *Review of Politics* 59, 3 (1997): 561–92.

2. Li Ling, *Guodian Chujian Jiaoduji*, 78.

3. James Legge, *The Chinese Classics*, vol. 4, *The She King* 詩經 vol. 4 (Hong Kong, 1871.; repr., Taipei: Jinxue, 1968), 23–24; Ruan Yuan 阮元 (1764–1849), *Mao shi zhengyi* 毛詩正義, in *Shisanjing Zhushu* 十三經注書 (1815; repr., Taipei: Yiwen, 1960), 52.

4. Li Ling, *Guodian Chujian Jiaoduji*, 78. See also Jeffrey Riegel, "Eros, Introversion, and the Beginnings of Shijing Commentary," *Harvard Journal of Asiatic Studies* 57.1 (1997): 143–177.

5. Michael Puett, "The Ethics of Responding Properly: The Notion of *Qíng* 情 in Early Chinese Thought," in *Love and Emotions in Traditional Chinese Literature*, ed. Halvor Eifring (Leiden: Brill, 2004), 179.

6. The importance of this difference is discussed at the end of chapter 2.

7. Li Ling, *Guodian Chujian Jiaoduji*, 80.

8. Li Ling, *Guodian Chujian Jiaoduji*, 95.

9. Li Ling, *Guodian Chujian Jiaoduji*, 95.

10. Li Ling, *Guodian Chujian Jiaoduji*, 95.

11. Jiang Guanghui disagrees with this and feels the text only endorses abdication. This one-sided view continues in his assessment

of Xunzi, who he feels only criticizes abdication. Jiang Guanghui, "Guodian Chujian yu Zisizi," 82.

12. Understanding these transformations from majority to minority also requires considering what criteria are being used for comparison. From the perspective of benefit, abdication is advantageous for the government as a whole, since talented people will be employed but detrimental to the single individual lineage of the royal house. In this situation, the government is the majority and the family is the minority. When considering power, however, the situation is reversed as the royal house commands more authority than a single talented individual who then would be seen as the minority. These transformations are related, though, since both situations involve the impact of humanity and righteousness when practiced in society.

13. I am of course playing devil's advocate here. Treating conflicting morals as having equal value is different from treating conflicting people as having equal value only if you divorce these morals from the social context abundantly apparent in The Five Aspects of Conduct."

14. Yu Ying-Shih also discusses the belief that the deceased could become hungry and even commit murder in early China. He translates the Mawangdui letter to the bureaucracy of the underworld as "On the twenty fourth day, second month, twelfth year [of Emperor Wen's reign, 168 B.C.] Household Assistant Fen to the lang-chung 郎中 in charge of the dead: A list of mortuary objects is herewith forwarded to you. Upon receiving this document, please memorialize without delay to the Lord of the Grave (chu-tsang chun 主藏君)." Yu Ying-Shih, "'O Soul, Come Back!': A Study in the Changing Conceptions of the Soul and Afterlife in Pre-Buddhist China," *Harvard Journal of Asiatic Studies* 47, 2 (1987): 363–95.

15. The most significant of the transformations that the tomb context causes us to bear mentioning is of course the transformation from life to death. It would seem, then, that after death, the text would continue to advocate moral cultivation and its spread among those encountered in the netherworld, but again, details regarding this are not present in the texts.

16. Li Ling, *Guodian Chujian Jiaoduji*, 78. The Guodian edition contains paragraph markers that are represented by a box "■" here and elsewhere.

17. Li Ling, *Guodian Chujian Jiaoduji*, 78.

18. This interpolation is based on the Mawangdui version.

19. Li Ling, *Guodian Chujian Jiaoduji*, 78.

20. D. C. Lau, trans., *Mencius: A Bilingual Edition*, rev. ed. (Hong Kong: Chinese University Press, 2003), 251.

21. Jiao Xun 焦循 (1763–1820), *Mengzi zhengyi* 孟子正義, in *Zhuzi Jicheng*諸子集成 (Beijing: Zhonghua, 1996), 6A.8, 456.

22. Ikeda notes that the *Shuowen Jiezi*《說文解字》 defines "wei" 唯 as "nuo" 諾. Because both of these characters appear one after another here, the meaning of "wei" should be understood as yes or showing agreement. Ikeda Tomohisa, *Maôtai kanbo hakusho gogyôhen kenkyû*, 481 n. 6; Jiang Renjie 蔣人傑, *Shuowen Jiezi Jizhu* 說文解字集注, vol. 1 (Shanghai: Guji, 1996), 256.

23. At first, the *Analects* might seem similar to the *Mencius* in that there are passages where self-cultivation is an exceedingly difficult process. Proper action is described as very difficult in 4:6, where acting with humanity for a single day is as though a Herculean task. In the fist four books of the *Analects*, however, such descriptions are rare. More common are passages that describe cultivation as having tremendous positive power. In 1:2, decline is said to be impossible as long as morals are firmly established at home. Rather than seeing cultivation as a difficult process, 1:1 states that learning and its maintenance through timely practice is pleasurable.

There is not a similar positive view of the society that one might encounter. Instead, there is a clear indication that one's talent might not be recognized by others in 1:16. In addition, it is important to recognize that there are examples of those who failed to realize morality completely. Passage 2:7 discusses people who are called filial, yet have failed to understand what true filial actions entail.

Describing moral cultivation in the *Analects* as a process that is unlike the struggles of Mencius does not mean that it does not extend through one's life and is thus easy. Examples of cultivation being a lifelong process abound. In 2:4, it is seen as a process that builds even through the age of seventy. The *Analects* even hopes that the impact of our morality will continue to influence those who know us after we die. In 4:20, this impact is said to last three years in the case of good sons.

24. For a thorough treatment of this in transmitted sources, see Sarah Allan, *The Heir and the Sage Dynastic Legends in Early China* (San Francisco: Chinese Materials Center, 1981).

25. See chapter 2 for further details on the internal versus external sorites.

26. Paragraph 13, strips 21–22.

27. Paragraph 25, strip 45.

Chapter Two

1. Portions of this chapter and the translation in the appendix appeared in a modified form in Kenneth Holloway, "'The Five Aspects of Conduct': Introduction and Translation," *Journal of the Royal Asiatic Society* 15.2 (2005): 179–98.

2. See translation in the appendix of this book, where strip numbers appear in black circles.

3. It specifically refers to relations among brothers, and loving one's father.

4. This is important as "The Five Aspects of Conduct" manages to see criminal conduct as an avenue for the individual to apply self-cultivation to the society as a whole in that the implementation of punishment requires understanding humanity and righteousness. It might be possible to construct an argument that 13.18 is implying a broader context of self-cultivation by considering the context provided in *Analects* 1.2, where the family serves to establish morals that are then applied elsewhere. However, it is tenuous at best to argue that these two passages necessarily share the same perspective on the inner workings of human relations and that 1.2 must necessarily relate to 13.18. *Analects* 1.2 appears later in the section entitled "*Analects*." 13:18, "The Duke of She told Confucius, 'In my country there is an upright man named Gong. When his father stole a sheep, he bore witness against him.' Confucius said, 'The upright men in my community are different from this. The father conceals the misconduct of the son and the son conceals the misconduct of the father. Uprightness is to be found in this.'" Wing-tsit Chan, *A Source Book in Chinese Philosophy* (Princeton, N.J.: Princeton University Press, 1963), 41. 葉公語孔子曰：「吾黨有直躬者，其父攘羊，而子證之。」孔子曰：。「吾黨之直者異於是：父為子隱，子為父隱，直在其中矣。」Cheng Shude程樹德 (1877–1944), *Lunyu jishi* 論語集釋 (Beijing: Zhonghua, 1990), 922–24; Liu Baonan劉寶楠 (1791–1855), *Lunyu zhengyi* 論語正義, in *Zhuzi Jicheng* 諸子集成 (Beijing: Zhonghua, 1996), 291.

5. *Nei* 內and *wai* 外 have been translated "family" and "state" instead of "inner" and "outer" to reflect the context of the subsequent sentences that are contrasting family and state obligations.

6. Li Ling, *Guodian Chujian Jiaoduji*, 131–32.

7. This is at the end of paragraph 19. Li Ling, *Guodian Chujian Jiaoduji*, 80.

8. This is the end of paragraph 20. Li Ling, *Guodian Chujian Jiaoduji*, 80.

9. *Lunyu jishi*, 13; *Lunyu zhengyi*, 4.

10. In exploring what this root entails, we must begin by answering what it means to be filial. The densest concentration of passages on this subject is in *Analects* 2:5–8. These passages include a variety of ways in which a child should tend to the needs of a parent. This includes basic sustenance with a measure of reverence (2:7), ensuring parents are free from concern (2:6), as well as both parents and children avoiding unnecessary discord (2:5, 8). This last point is clearly one that must be tempered by occasional chiding on the part of the child when the parent commits an error (4:18). For a related discussion of the importance of family in state affairs, see Roger T. Ames and David L. Hall, trans. *Focusing the Familiar: A Translation and Philosophical Interpretation of the* Zhongyong (Honolulu: University of Hawai'i Press, 2001), 38–40.

11. One might suppose that this broader application of humanity is accomplished through the learning of righteousness, but this passage contains no such reference. A thorough treatment of this subject can be found in Chong Kim-chong, "The Practice of Jen," *Philosophy East and West* 49.3 (1999): 298–316. Interestingly, Shun Kwong-loi's treatment of humanity in the *Analects* focuses much less on passage 1:2, as he is much more interested in examining the relationship between humanity and the rites. Shun Kwong-loi, "*Jen* and *Li* in the *Analects*," *Philosophy East and West* 43.3 (1993): 457–79.

12. Lau, trans., *Mencius*, 291–93.

13. *Mengzi zhengyi* 7A.15, 530.

14. Lau uses Wade-Giles instead of pinyin.

15. Lau, trans., *Mencius*, 243.

16. *Mengzi zhengyi* 6A.4, 437–38.

17. For a further discussion of this, see Irene Bloom, "Mencian Arguments on Human Nature (*Jen-hsing*)," *Philosophy East and West* 44.1 (1994): 33–34.

18. The term that is translated "love" is actually the adverbial form of the noun "family."

19. This is the same character that is elsewhere translated "Righteousness."

20. Lau, trans., *Mencius*, 115.

21. *Mengzi zhengyi* 3A.4, 226.

22. This is the same character that is elsewhere translated "Righteousness."

23. Lau, trans., *Mencius*, 169.

24. *Mengzi zhengyi* 4A.27, 313.

25. See for example *Mencius* 1A.1, 4B.19, 2B.2, 3B.4, 3B.9, 6A.1, 6A.8, 6A.17, and 6B.4.

26. This is the same character that is elsewhere translated "Righteousness."

27. Lau, trans., *Mencius*, 167.

28. *Mengzi zhengyi* 4A.20, 309.

29. According to Chong, this is at least as early as Zhuxi. Chong Kim-chong, "The Practice of Jen," 299.

30. Chong Kim-chong, "The Practice of Jen," 298.

31. See Pian Yuqian 駢宇騫 and Duan Shuan 段書安, *Ben shiji yilai chutu jianbo gaishu*本世紀以來出土簡帛概述 (Taipei: Wanjuanlou, 1999), 32–42. For a discussion of an earlier but much shorter silk text recovered from looters, see Li Ling and Constance A. Cook, "Translation of the Chu Silk Manuscript," in *Defining Chu: Image and Reality in Ancient China*, ed. Constance A. Cook and John S. Major (Honolulu: University of Hawaii Press, 1999), 171–76.

32. Jingmen Shi Bowuguan 荊門市博物館, "Jingmen Guodian yihao Chumu"荊門郭店一號楚墓, *Wenwu* 7 (1997): 35–48.

33. Pang Pu 龐樸, *Boshu Wuxingpian Yanjiu* 帛書五行篇研究, (Jinan: Qilu, 1980).

34. Pang Pu 龐樸, "Gumu xinzhi—Mandu Guodian Chujian" 古墓新知-漫讀郭店楚簡, *Guoji ruxue lianhehui jianbao* 2 (1998); reprinted in *Dushu* 9 (1998); *Guodian Chumu yanjiu, Zhongguo* zhexue 20 (1999): 8; and Pang Pu et al, *Gumu xinzhi* 古墓新知, Chutu sixiang wenwu yu wenxian yanjiu congshu 10 (Taipei: Taiwan guji, 2002), 1–6. Also as "Gumu xinzhi: Guodian Chujian de jiazhi" 古墓新知: 郭店楚簡的價值 in *Jingmen Zhiye shu Xueyuan xuebao* 2 (2003): 1–5; "New Information from an Old Tomb: Reading the Guodian Bamboo Strips," *Contemporary Chinese Thought* 32.1 (2000): 43–49.

35. This perspective is supported by Kidder Smith in his analysis of categories of schools in the *Shiji* 史記. Smith, "Sima Tan and the Invention of Daoism, 'Legalism,' et cetera."

36. Li Ling, *Guodian Chujian Jiaoduji*, 130–38.

37. Guo Qiyong 郭齊勇, "Guodian Rujia Jian De Yiyi Yu Jiazhi" 郭店儒家簡的意義與價值, *Hubei Daxue Xuebao Zhexue shehui Kexue Ban* 2 (1999): 4–6.

38. My decision to translate this term as "essence" is based on the work of A. C. Graham, Michael Puett, and Ding Sixin all of whom question the meaning of emotion for *qing* 情 in pre-Han texts. *Xunzi*

is one point where the term begins to have some emotional elements, but it is not until the Song dynasty that the term really begins to mean "emotion." A. C. Graham, "The Background of the Mencian Theory of Human Nature," *Tsing Hua Journal of Chinese Studies*, n.s., 6 I.2 (1967), reprinted in Graham, *Studies in Chinese Philosophy and Philosophical Literature* (Albany: State University of New York Press, 1990), 59–65; Ding Sixin丁四新, "On the Implications of 'Qing' in Guodian Slips," *Modern Philosophy* 04 (2003): 61–68; Puett, "The Ethics of Responding Properly."

39. Li Ling, *Guodian Chujian Jiaoduji*, 105.

40. Pang Pu, "Kong Meng zhijian," 28.

41. Paul Goldin finds similarities in the understanding of *xing* 性 and *dao* 道in the *Xunzi* and Guodian manuscripts such as "Xing zi ming chu" and "Cheng zhi wen zhi" 成之聞之. Paul Rakita Goldin, "Xunzi in the Light of the Guodian Manuscripts," *Early China* 25 (2000): 123–24.

42. The Classic is virtually identical between the two editions. The Explanation, as the name suggests, provides explanations for virtually every passage of the Classic.

43. Li Xueqin, "Jingmen Guodian Chujianzhong de Zisizi," 77.

44. Ikeda Tomohisa 池田知久, "Guodian Chujian 'Wuxing' Yanjiu" 郭店楚簡《五行》研究Guodian Jian Yu Ruxue Yanjiu" 郭店楚簡《五行》研究郭店簡與儒學研究, *Zhongguo zhexue* 21 中國哲學 (2000): 98–99.

45. This is the section that begins, "Not having keen hearing you lack keen vision, no sagacity no ❷❶ wisdom . . ." (不聰不明,不聖不智, . . .) and runs to the end of paragraph 11. These characters are then placed prior to the start of paragraph 15.

46. This section begins, "Your appearance and countenance are mild and changeable" 顏色容貌溫變也, and runs from the top of strip 32 through bottom of strip 37.

47. Pang Pu 龐樸, "Zhubo 'Wuxing' Pian Bijiao" 竹帛《五行》篇比較, *Guodian Chumu yanjiu. Zhongguo zhexue* 20 (1999): 221–27.

48. Ikeda Tomohisa, *Maôtai kanbo hakusho gogyôhen kenkyû*, 171.

49. Li Ling, *Guodian Chujian Jiaoduji*, 78.

50. Liao Mingchun廖名春, "Jingmen Guodian Chujian yu Xianqin Ruxue" 荊門郭店楚簡與先秦儒學, *Guodian Chujian yanjiu. Zhongguo zhexue* 20 (1999): 46.

51. Line 199 of the Mawangdui silk scroll.

52. Line 281 of the Mawangdui silk scroll.

53. In the Guodian edition, the first character of the paragraph reads, "What greatly bestows upon humans is heaven (大施(者→諸)其人, 天也)." The first sentence of the Mawangdui text reads: "It is heaven that gives rise to heaven's people 天生諸其人天也." While the first two characters differ between these versions, the important question is should the first character be "great 大" or "heaven 天"? The difference in modern Chinese is one stroke, but in the Guodian edition it is written with two heavy strokes 夵. Some instances of the character for "great" in the Guodian text are the same as in modern Chinese 大. Clearly, this character is lacking the two top strokes that would make it "heaven." However, the example of the character "great" that appears on strip 42 is slightly different:夫. This second instance of "great" shows that the horizontal stroke in the modern character can be written with a slightly downward concaved shape in the Guodian script. There are two instances of the character "heaven" on strip 48, which provide an excellent comparison. The first and second instances are also written this way: 夵. Here, the strokes in "heaven" that are repeated in "great" can curve downward slightly. Therefore, it seems that from a calligraphic perspective there is no reason to substitute the character "heaven" for the character "great" in the first character of paragraph 27. Despite this, it is possible for two brushstrokes to be missing in a handwritten text; as a result, most editions follow the Mawangdui version.

54. Zisi is believed to have been Confucius's grandson and the founder of the school where Mencius received his education. Fung Yu-lan, *History of Chinese Philosophy*, vol. 1 (Princeton, N.J.: Princeton University Press, 1952; repr., 1983), 107.

55. Jiang Guanghui provides citations beginning with the *Hanshu Yiwenzhi* 漢書藝文志, where Zisi is listed as an author. Unfortunately, we have no idea what these texts were aside from their titles. Jiang Guanghui, "Guodian Chujian yu Zisizi," 82.

56. See note 14 of the introduction for a list of scholars.

57. Exact dates unknown.

58. Wang Xianqian王先謙 (1842–1918), *Xunzi Jijie* 荀子集解, in *Zhuzi Jicheng*諸子集成 (Beijing: Zhonghua, 1996), "Fei Shier Zi" 非十二字, 59.

59. Pang Pu, "Simeng Wuxing xinkao" 思孟五行新考, in *Zhubo Wuxing pian jiaozhu ji yanjiu* (Taipei: Wanjuanlou, 2000), 133–43.

60. This is John Knoblock's translation of what I translate as "The Five Aspects of Conduct." John Knoblock, Xunzi: *A Translation and*

Study of the Complete Work, vol. 1 (Stanford, Calif.: Stanford University Press, 1988), 224.

61. The text states that it is Ziyou, but there is disagreement as to the accuracy of this. Knoblock, *Xunzi*, 1:303 n. 50.

62. An anonymous reader for the *Journal of the Royal Asiatic Society* pointed out, and I agree, that it is surprising that Knoblock translates this as "offends against Zisi and Mencius." It seems Xunzi is criticizing Zisi and Mencius, so it should read, "the offenses of Zisi and Mencius." Knoblock, *Xunzi*, 1:224.

63. *Xunzi Jijie*, "Fei Shier Zi," 59–60.

64. Jiang Guanghui, "Guodian Chujian yu Zisisizi," 82. I do not believe that "Tang Yu zhidao" is advocating abdication as the text is actually in favor of government that incorporates the advantages of meritocracy (inherent in abdication) with aristocracy, which is established by hereditary transmission. A transcription of the text is available here: Li Ling, *Guodian Chujian Jiaoduji*, 95–99.

65. Pang Pu, "Simeng Wuxing Kao."

66. Liu Yameng, "Three Issues in the Argumentative Conception of Early Chinese Discourse," *Philosophy East and West* 46.1 (1996): 33.

67. Li Xueqin李學勤, "Cong Jianbo Yiji 'Wuxing' Tandao 'Daxue'" 從簡帛佚籍《五行》談到《大學》, *Kongzi yanjiu* 孔子研究 (March 1998): 50–51.

68. He relies on the following dates: Confucius 551–479, Zengzi 505–436, Zisi 483–402, Mencius 390–305. He states that he previously thought that Shizi may have lived during Mencius's time but now believes he lived around 450 B.C.E. Li Xueqin, "Cong Jianbo Yiji 'Wuxing' Tandao 'Daxue,'" 50.

69. Liang Tao梁濤, "Guodian Chujian Yu 'Zhongyong'" 郭店楚簡與《中庸》, *Gongan Taida Lishixuebao* 25.6 (2000): 32.

70. Liang Tao, "Guodian Chujian Yu 'Zhongyong,'" 33–34.

71. Liao Mingchun, "Guodian Chujian Rujia Zhuzuo Kao," 73, 82–83.

72. Lau, trans., *Mencius*, 271.

73. *Mengzi zhengyi* 6B.6, 489.

74. Liang Tao quotes the following: "Therefore, after Confucius and Mozi, the Confucians split into eight and the Mohists split into three." 故孔墨之後。儒分為八。墨離為三。 Liang Tao 梁濤, "Simeng Xuepai Kaoshu" 思孟學派考述, *Zhongguo zhexueshi* 3 (2002): 28; Wang Xianshen 王先慎 (1859–1922), *Hanfeizi Jijie* 韓非子集解, in *Zhuzi Jicheng*諸子集成 (Beijing: Zhonghua, 1996), "Xianxue" 顯學, 351.

75. Pang Pu, "Kong Meng Zhi Jian," 22.

76. *Hanfeizi Jijie*, 351.

77. In fact, this is not attested to in traditional commentaries. Pang Pu, "Simeng Wuxing Kao."

78. Liang Qichao 梁啓超, "Yinyang Wuxing Shuo Zhi Laili" 陰陽五行說之來歷, *Yinbingshi Wenji* 飲冰室文集 Vol. 7.36 (Taipei: Chung Hwa Book Company, 1970), 47–64.

79. James Legge, *The Chinese Classics*, vol. 3, *The Shoo King*尚書 (Hong Kong, 1865; repr., Taipei: Jinxue, 1968), 153; Ruan Yuan阮元 (1764–1849), *Shang shu zhengyi* 尚書正義, in *Shisanjing Zhushu*十三經注書 (1815; repr., Taipei: Yiwen, 1960), "The Speech at Kan" 尚書甘誓, 98.

80. This is evident in *Mencius* 7A.1.

81. As examples, he cites Xunzi荀子，"Zhengming" 正名and "Jiebi" 解蔽.

82. Ikeda Tomohisa 池田知久, "Mawangdui Hanmu Boshu 'Wuxingpian' Suojiande Shenxin Wenti" 馬王堆漢墓帛書《五行篇》所見的身心問題, *Daojia Wenhua Yanjiu* 道家文化研究3 (1999): 349–59.

83. Ikeda Tomohisa, "Mawangdui Hanmu Boshu 'Wuxingpian' Suojiande Shenxin Wenti"; Pang Pu, "Simeng Wuxing Kao."

84. Jon Moline, "Aristotle, Eubulides and the Sorites," *Mind*, n.s., 78.311 (1969): 393–407.

85. Michael Tye, "Sorites Paradoxes and the Semantics of Vagueness," *Philosophical Perspectives* 8 (1994): 189–206; Terence Horgan, "Vagueness and the Forced-March Sorites Paradox," *Philosophical Perspectives* 8 (1994): 159–88.

86. Hebei Sheng wen wu yan jiu suo Dingzhou Han mu zhu jian zheng li xiao zu河北省文物研究所定州漢墓竹簡整理小組, *Dingzhou Han mu zhu jian Lun yu* 定州漢墓竹簡論語 (Beijing: Wenwu, 1997).

87. *Odes* quotations can be found in paragraphs 4, 8, 9, 16, 17, 23, and 26. There are no *Analects* quotations.

Chapter Three

1. A similar issue of religious sentiment being involved in the bridging of individuals is introduced in the concept of fiduciary communities by Tu Weiming. See Tu Weiming, *Centrality and Commonality: An Essay on Confucian Religiousness*. A revised and enlarged edition of *Centrality and Commonality: An Essay on Chung-yung* (Albany: State University of New York Press, 1989).

2. Li Ling, *Guodian Chujian Jiaoduji*, 79.

3. Li Ling, *Guodian Chujian Jiaoduji*, 78.

4. Li Ling, *Guodian Chujian Jiaoduji*, 79.

5. Scott Cook, "Consummate Artistry and Moral Virtuosity: The 'Wu xing' 五行 Essay and Its Aesthetic Implications," *Chinese Literature: Essays, Articles, Reviews* 22 (2000): 124 n. 26.

6. The following paragraphs refer to either bronze or jade sound or appearance: 5, 6, 7, 10, and 11.

7. Two important approaches to tackling such a broad project can be seen in the philosophical approach of Chad Hansen and the historical scholarship of Michael Puett. In *A Daoist Theory of Chinese Thought*, for example, Hansen sought to create a single hypothesis that could bring together schools of thought described as disparate in the Han dynasty. While overcoming Han divisions is also an important part of my work, Hansen's grand narrative approach obscured important ways that even single texts can include a range of perspectives. A contrasting methodology can be seen in Puett's *The Ambivalence of Creation*, where a discussion of innovation and artifice anchors his analysis of diverse texts. This brings important nuance to his work that is particularly important when he covers broad periods such as the Warring States. Chad Hansen, *A Daoist Theory of Chinese Thought: A Philosophical Interpretation* (New York: Oxford University Press, 1992); Michael Puett, *The Ambivalence of Creation: Debates Concerning Innovation and Artifice in Early China* (Stanford, Calif: Stanford University Press, 2001), 39–91.

8. See the analytical methodology section at the end of chapter 2 of this book.

9. Since the first lines of the text define the five aspects as humanity, righteousness, the rites, wisdom, and sagacity, reference to harmonizing four or five aspects is self-inclusive of the harmonizing elements of sagacity or wisdom.

10. Li Ling, *Guodian Chujian Jiaoduji*, 79.

11. Li Ling, *Guodian Chujian Jiaoduji*, 78.

12. Li Ling, *Guodian Chujian Jiaoduji*, 79.

13. Mark Csikszentmihalyi argues that *Analects* 2:7 and 2:8 show an interesting similarity to "The Five Aspects of Conduct." Passage 2:7 advises people that acting in a filial manner involves more than providing nourishment to one's parents; it is also important to be reverent. Analects 2:8 follows a similar theme in that facial expression or demeanor is described as being filial instead of simply providing the best portions

of food and wine. The important difference remains that the concept of acting in a filial manner is *not* discussed as something that is specifically embodied prior to practice. Csikszentmihalyi, *Material Virtue*, 67–69.

14. Li Ling, *Guodian Chujian Jiaoduji*, 79.

15. *Mengzi zhengyi*, 2A.6, 139.

16. *Mengzi zhengyi*, 6A.15, 467–70.

17. Alan K. L. Chan, "A Matter of Taste: *Qi* (Vital Energy) and the Tending of the Heart (*Xin*) in *Mencius* 2A2," in *Mencius: Contexts and Interpretations*, ed. Alan K. L. Chan (Honolulu: University of Hawai'i Press, 2002), 46.

18. *Mengzi zhengyi*, 2A.2, 114.

19. Chan, "A Matter of Taste."

20. This quotation appears in Chan, "A Matter of Taste," 60. Compare with Lau, trans., *Mencius*, 63.

21. *Mengzi zhengyi*, 2A.2, 123.

22. Chan, "A Matter of Taste," 60–61.

23. This unity is the result of cultivation, but without cultivation, there is a split between the mind and the sensory organs. Ikeda Tomohisa feels that this is a similarity between "The Five Aspects of Conduct" and the *Xunzi* in that there is a perceived split between the mind and the body. Ikeda Tomohisa, "Mawangdui Hanmu Boshu 'Wuxingpian,'" 349–59.

24. For example, paragraph 10 of "The Five Aspects of Conduct" states, "Regarding a noble man's being adept [at virtue], there is something that he takes as the beginning and something that he takes as the end. Regarding a noble man being virtuous, ❶❽ there is something that he takes as the beginning but nothing that he takes as the end." (君)子之為善也，有與始，有與終也。君子之為德也，❶❽ (有與始，有與) 終也。Li Ling, *Guodian Chujian Jiaoduji*, 79.

25. There are two important recent studies on the *Odes*: Mark Laurent Asselin, "The Lu-School Reading of 'Guanju' as Preserved in an Eastern Han fu," *Journal of the American Oriental Society* 117, 3 (1997): 427–43; Haun Saussy, "Repetition, Rhyme, and Exchange in the *Book of Odes*," *Harvard Journal of Asiatic Studies* 57.2 (1997): 519–42.

26. 聰 is translated "keen hearing" to highlight the contrast with 明 "keen sight" that is dominant in this text.

27. *Mao shi zhengyi*, 271; Legge, *The She King*, 222–23.

28. My decision to translate this as "concerned about your uniqueness" instead of "cautious when alone" is indebted to Ames and Hall *Focusing the Familiar*, 118–19 n. 10.

29. *Mao shi zhengyi*, 77–78; Legge, *The She King*, 42–43.

30. *Mao shi zhengyi*, 77–78; Legge, *The She King*, 42–43.

31. These are *yan* 晏 (grave crimes) (Mawangdui version: *han* 罕), which relate to righteousness, and *zhen* 軫 (minor crimes), which relate to humanity.

32. Such as in paragraph 2: "There are five aspects of virtuous conduct, that, when united, are called virtue itself. When only four of these actions are united it is called being adept [at virtue]." 德之行五和，謂之德，四行和，謂之善。Li Ling, *Guodian Chujian Jiaoduji*, 78.

33. Li Ling, *Guodian Chujian Jiaoduji*, 79.

34. Li Ling, *Guodian Chujian Jiaoduji*, 79.

35. Lau also also mentions the connection between this passage and "The Five Aspects of Conduct." Lau, trans., *Mencius*, 218–19.

36. *Mengzi zhengyi*, 5B.1, 397–98.

37. This can also be seen in *Xunzi's* 荀子 "Yibing" 議兵, where "bronze tone" is a ritual sound that signals a military to withdraw. *Xunzi Jijie*, "Yibing," 184.

38. Li Ling's transcription reads "[有與始，有與]," but this lacuna is being corrected based on the Mawangdui version, which both Ikeda Tomohisa and Pang Pu transcribe as "有與始，無與." Li Ling, *Guodian Chujian Jiaoduji*, 79; Pang Pu, *Boshu Wuxingpian Yanjiu*, 34; Ikeda Tomohisa, *Maôtai kanbo hakusho gogyôhen kenkyû*, 234–37.

39. Li Ling, *Guodian Chujian Jiaoduji*, 79.

40. For a detailed discussion of commentaries on *Mencius* 5B.1 as well as other received texts, see Csikszentmihalyi, *Material Virtue*, chap. 4.

41. Lau, trans., *Mencius*, 287.

42. *Mengzi zhengyi*, 7A.1, 517.

43. It should be mentioned of course that this chapter is looking at the *Mencius* through the lens of "The Five Aspects of Conduct," since 7A.1 does not explicitly associate heaven with the infinite, as I will later argue is the case in paragraphs 9 and 10 of "The Five Aspects of Conduct."

44. Li Ling, *Guodian Chujian Jiaoduji*, 79.

Chapter Four

1. These characters can also be romanized as "Dayi shengshui" following Wei Qipeng, who points out that pre-Qin texts do not distinguish *da* 大 and *tai* 太. Wei Qipeng, *Chujian Laozi jianshi* 楚簡《老

子》束釋 Chutu wenxian yizhu yanxi congshu P003 (Taipei: Wanjuan-lou, 1999), 89.

2. D. C. Lau, "The Treatment of Opposites in 'Lao Tzu,'" *Bulletin of the School of Oriental and African Studies* 21.1/3 (1958): 344–60.

3. James Legge, *Li Ki Book of Rites*, vol. 27 (Oxford: Clarendon, 1885; repr., Delhi: Motilal Banarsidass, 1966), 364–66.

4. Ruan Yuan阮元 (1764–1849), *Li ji zhengyi* 禮記正義, in *Shisan-jing Zhushu* 十三經注書 (1815; repr., Taipei: Yiwen, 1960), "Li Yun" 禮運 413.

5. A. C. Graham, *Disputers of the Tao: Philosophical Argument in Ancient China* (La Salle, Ill.: Open Court, 1989), 298.

6. Hsiao Kung-chuan, *A History of Chinese Political Thought*, vol. 1, *From the Beginnings to the Sixth Century A.D.*, trans. F. W. Mote (Princeton, N.J.: Princeton University Press, 1979), 124–42.

7. One early example of this is Li Ling. In volume 17 of *Daojia Wenhua Yanjiu*, he divides the Guodian texts into two groups. The three selections from the *Laozi*老子, "Taiyi shengshui" 太—生水, and "Yucong Four" 語叢四 are grouped as philosophically Daoist and Dao-ist Military Strategy Schools (道家和道家陰謀派的文獻). "Ziyi" 緇衣, "The Five Aspects of Conduct" 五行, "Lumugong wen Zisi" 魯穆公問子思, "Qiongda Yishi" 窮達以時, "Tang Yu zhidao" 唐虞之道, "Zhongxin zhi dao" 忠信之道, "Xingzi ming chu" 性自命出, "Chengzhi wenzhi" 成之聞之, "Liu de"六德, "Zun de yi" 尊德義, and "Yucong" 語叢Three, One, and Two are described as philosophically Confucian (如傢文獻). Li Ling, "Guodian Chujian Jiaoduji" 郭店楚簡校讀記, *Daojia Wenhua Yanjiu* 17 (1999): 455–542.

8. Robert G. Henricks, *Lao Tzu's Tao Te Ching* (New York: Columbia University Press, 2000), 12–13.

9. Gu Jiegang 顧頡剛, "Shanrang Chuanshuo Qiyu Mojia Kao" 禪讓傳說起於墨家考 *Gushi Bian*, 7B (repr., Shanghai: Guji, 1982), 30–33.

10. A9 refers to Robert Henricks's numbering system for Guodian texts; (2) refers to the traditional chapter number in transmitted editions of the *Laozi*. For an explanation of this numbering system, see Henricks, *Lao Tzu's Tao Te Ching*, 6–8.

11. Henricks, *Lao Tzu's Tao Te Ching*, 50.

12. Wei Qipeng, *Chujian Laozi jianshi*, 16.

13. See Henricks, *Lao Tzu's Tao Te Ching*, 28.

14. Benjamin Schwartz, "The Thought of the *Tao-te-ching*," in *Lao-tzu and the Tao-te-ching*, ed. Livia Kohn and Michael LaFargue (Albany: State University of New York Press, 1998), 201.

15. Although he has very different reasons for believing so, D. C. Lau agrees with the idea that there must be some sort of distinction maintained among terms in the *Laozi*. See Lau, "The Treatment of Opposites in 'Lao Tzu,'" 350.

16. Mark Csikszentmihalyi, "Mystical and Apophatic Discourse in the *Laozi*," in *Religious and Philosophical Aspects of the Laozi*, ed. Mark Csikszentmihalyi and Philip J. Ivanhoe (Albany: State University of New York Press, 1999), 33–58.

17. Jane Geaney, *On the Epistemology of the Senses in Early Chinese Thought* (Honolulu: University of Hawai'i Press, 2002), 153.

18. Henricks, *Lao Tzu's Tao Te Ching*, 34.

19. Wei Qipeng, *Chujian Laozi jianshi*, 6.

20. Schwartz "The Thought of the Tao-te-ching," 200.

21. Henricks, *Lao Tzu's Tao Te Ching*, 42.

22. Wei Qipeng, *Chujian Laozi jianshi*, 11, 65.

23. Henricks, *Lao Tzu's Tao Te Ching*, 72.

24. Wei Qipeng, *Chujian Laozi jianshi*, 32.

25. Schwartz, "The Thought of the Tao-te-ching," 201.

26. Translation changed from Henricks, *Lao Tzu's Tao Te Ching*, 108.

27. These last characters (其德乃慱（溥）普) are interpolated from the MWD edition. Wei Qipeng, *Chujian Laozi jianshi*, 54–55.

28. Normally, when discussing the cosmogony in the *Laozi*, we would expect reference to chapter 42, which appears in the received version as well as the Mawangdui silk version. Moss Roberts translates the passage as "The number one of the Way was born. A duad from this monad formed. The duad next a triad made; The triad bred the myriad." 道生一，一生二，二生三，三生萬物。Moss Roberts, *Laozi Dao De Jing: The Book of the Way* (Berkeley: University of California Press, 2001), 116; Gao Ming高明, *Boshu Laozi jiaozhu* 帛書老子校注 (Beijing: Zhonghua, 1996), 29. In addition, it is important to note that Xing Wen cites Li Xueqin's 李學勤1998 Wenwu 文物 article as the original source for the theory that "Taiyi shengshui" is an interpretation of *Laozi* 42. Xing Wen 邢文, "Lun Guodian *Laozi* yu jinben *Laozi* bu shu yixi—Chujian *Taiyi shengshui* ji qi yiyi" 論郭店《老子》與今本《老子》不屬一係—楚簡《太一生水》及其意義, *Guodian Chujian yanjiu Zhongguo zhexue* 20 (1999): 179.

29. Translation adapted from Henricks, *Lao Tzu's Tao Te Ching*, 108–10.

30. These characters (以家 觀) are interpolated from the MWD edition. Wei Qipeng, *Chujian Laozi jianshi*, 54–55.

31. A15 (56) also has the phrase "He closes the holes, Blocks the Gates," 閉其兌, 塞其門 implying the greater importance of this type of cultivation. Henricks, *Lao Tzu's Tao Te Ching*, 65–67, 102–4.

32. Wei Qipeng, *Chujian Laozi jianshi*, 51.

33. Henricks, *Lao Tzu's Tao Te Ching*, 165–67.

34. Henricks, *Lao Tzu's Tao Te Ching*, 123.

35. Wei Qipeng, *Chujian Laozi jianshi*, 69.

36. The Guodian texts were of course not available when his article was written. Lau, "The Treatment of Opposites in 'Lao Tzu,'" 350.

37. Xing Wen, "Lun Guodian *Laozi* yu jinben *Laozi* bu shu yixi—Chujian *Taiyi shengshui* ji qi yiyi," 165–86.

38. Henricks, *Lao Tzu's Tao Te Ching*, 123–26.

39. Wei Qipeng, *Chujian Laozi jianshi*, 69.

40. Liang Tao argues that this latter part, where virtue is not formed within and one is merely acting, still represents a part of virtue. Central to his argument is what is likely a copy error on strip 4 of the text, where it states that if sagacity is not formed within, it is still virtuous conduct. The problem with this is that elsewhere in the text, sagacity is described as a lofty virtue, but it still relates to forming all virtues within our bodies. A second problem is that in the Mawangdui version, the copy error is not present, which is why I believe that what we are seeing is merely a scribal error. Liang Tao 梁濤, "Jianbo Wuxing xintan: Jianlun Wuxing zai sixiangshi zhong de diwei" 簡帛《五行》新探: 兼論《五行》在思想史中的地位, *Kongzi yanjiu* 5 (2002): 39–51; reprinted in Pang Pu et al., *Gumu xinzhi*, 191–217.

41. This style of argument is prominent in another early text, the *Great Learning* 大學. The ensuing divergent interpretations of the phrase "investigation of things" 格物in neo-Confucianism should serve as a caution to us in approaching sorites in "The Five Aspects of Conduct."

42. I call them double sorites, since each word that appears in paragraphs 12 through 14 is repeated in the same order in paragraphs 19 through 21 of the Guodian edition.

43. The terms *yuse, yuyin, jingsheng,* and *yuzhen* 玉色, 玉音, 金聲, and 玉晨 appear to have a similar meaning in this text. They roughly represent an external manifestation of a person's internal virtue. *Yuse* is found in the "Yuzao" 玉藻chapter of the *Book of Rites*. All other citations I found for these terms are later. *Li ji zhengyi*, "Yuzao" 玉藻, 569.

44. 聰 is translated "keen hearing" to highlight the contrast with 明 "keen sight" that is dominant in this text.

45. These three paragraphs contain the only epanaleptical sorites in the text.

46. The exact structure of this sentence is repeated five times for each of the other virtues, with only the first character of each sentence being changed so that they cover each of the virtues.

47. The final commonality between the paragraphs is one that is present only between the paragraphs that discuss sagacity and wisdom. Both of these paragraphs link sensory acuity with sagacity and wisdom.

48. The MWD version uses the character 逃 *zhi* instead of 肆 *si*. In explanation 11 of the MWD version, *zhi* appears as follows: "One who excels is one who completes." 逃者終之者也. Ikeda Tomohisa, *Maôtai kanbo hakusho gogyôhen kenkyû*, 259.

49. See paragraph 23 of the Guodian edition.

50. Guodian edition paragraph 23.

51. Guodian edition paragraph 19.

52. Guodian edition paragraph 20.

53. Regarding the distinction between the internal and external heart, the Mawangdui edition is not particularly helpful. It provides general advice about how to be a good person in explaining each of the three instances of "internal" and "external" heart that appear. Therefore, based on clues provided by the text itself, we cannot be sure exactly what is meant by internal and external heart.

54. Similarly, "humanity," "sagacity," and "wisdom" are not equally related in the epanaleptical sorites. Here, sagacity and wisdom are more closely related because they involve, respectively, visual and auditory acuity. We can see this as further evidence that humanity is given unique status in the text.

55. This issue of lesser concerns being the basis of greater concerns receives a great deal of attention in the Explanation portion of the Mawangdui text, but this is more relevant to issues raised exclusively in the Explanation. For an article that discusses this subject, see Riegel, "Eros, Introversion, and the Beginnings of Shijing Commentary," 143–177.

56. Guodian edition paragraph 23.

57. Li Ling, *Guodian Chujian Jiaoduji*, 95.

58. Li Ling, *Guodian Chujian Jiaoduji*, 95.

59. Li Ling, *Guodian Chujian Jiaoduji*, 95.

Chapter Five

1. By family, I refer to the Confucian concept of the family as a basic building block for the state as seen in a range of texts from *Analects* 1:2 to the *Great Learning*. "Family" is used instead of "lineage" in much of this chapter to remain faithful to the political philosophy being discussed. For interesting but early analysis of the changing role of the family, see Hsu Cho-yun, Ancient China in Transition: An Analysis of Social Mobility 722–222 BC (Stanford, Calif.: Stanford University Press, 1965).

2. Tu Wei-ming has argued that pre-Han Confucian governments tended to be more sensitive to the needs of the people and were less inclined to force a top-down hierarchy. This respect of the rights of the people and acceptance of dissent would make sense in a system that believes in balancing meritocratic and aristocratic methods of government. Tu Wei-ming, "Probing the 'Three Bonds' and 'Five Relationships,'" in *Confucianism and the Family*, ed. Walter H. Slote and George A. De Vos (Albany: State University of New York Press, 1998), 121–136.

3. For a thorough discussion of variant characters, see Ri Jōri 李承律, "Kakuten sokan 'Tō Gu no michi' yakuchū" 郭店楚簡『唐虞之道』譯注, *Kakuten sokan no Kenkyū* 郭店楚簡の思想史研究 (Tōkyō: Daitō Bunka Daigaku Daigakuin Jimukyoku, 1999–2004), 52–104.

4. The Wenwu edition has *jun* 均 "even," but this does not seem to fit the parallel context. *Guodian Chumu zhujian*, 157.

5. Wenwu has *gong* 躬 (personally); an alternate translation would be "embody humanity." *Guodian Chumu zhujian*, 157.

6. Wenwu has the descendantless character 㐤, which it states means *shi* 始 (start). This would change the translation to "start by making the body upright . . ." *Guodian Chumu zhujian*, 159 n. 6.

7. Wenwu has *jiao* 教 (teaching), which it states should be read as *taixue* 太學 "grand learning." *Guodian Chumu zhujian*, 159 n. 8.

8. Ri Jōri notes that "Zun de yi" 尊德義 and "Liu de" 六德 have this character transcribed as *gui* 㐤, a variant of *gui* 歸 (return). Ri Jōri, "Kakuten sokan 'Tō Gu no michi' yakuchū," 61 n. 21.

9. Wenwu transcribes this character as fang 方 (method). The picture of the strip it provides on page 39 shows the *fang* character at the top. Li Ling's transcription is supported by the addition of two strokes at the bottom of the character that are very close to the right side of *shi* 施 (use). The character has been translated as "method,"

which could fit either transcription. *Guodian Chumu zhujian*, 39, 157; Li Ling, *Guodian Chujian Jiaoduji*, 95–99.

10. The Wenwu edition has *cheng* 成 (complete) but notes that Qiu Xigui裘錫圭 believes it should be *jie*皆 (all), which is what is followed here. *Guodian Chumu zhujian*, 157, 159 n. 11.

11. *Gumang* 瞽盲 (blind) here and later appear in the Wenwu edition as *gusou* 瞽叟 (blind old man) as is found in the received texts of the *Mozi* and *Lüshi Chunqiu* describing Shun's blind father. Li Ling has *gumang*瞽盲 (blind), which also refers to Shun's father. *Guodian Chumu zhujian*, 157; Li Ling, *Guodian Chujian Jiaoduji*, 95–99.

12. The Wenwu edition transcribes both instances of this character as *yi* 弋 (branch/support), which in meaning is similar to *dai*戴 (revere/support). *Guodian Chumu zhujian*, 157.

13. Li Ling, *Guodian Chujian Jiaoduji*, 95–99.

14. *Tian xia* 天下 (all under the firmament) is translated as "state" to reflect the political tone of the text.

15. Jiang Guanghui's assessment of "Tang Yu zhidao" does not seem to account for this passage; he views the text as only endorsing abdication. This one-sided view continues in his assessment of Xunzi, who he feels only criticizes abdication. Jiang Guanghui, "Guodian Chujian yu Zisizi," 82.

16. Wade-Giles is used, but I have changed it to pinyin for the sake of consistency; all subsequent instances have also been changed.

17. Lau, trans., *Mencius*, 327.

18. In the *Analects*, these four characters are "Go back! Go back!" 歸與! 歸與! Yang Shuda 楊樹達 (1885–1956), *Lunyu shu zheng* 論語疏證 (Beijing: Kexue, 1955), 92.

19. *Mengzi zhengyi* 7B.37, 602.

20. Lau, trans., *Mencius*, 183.

21. *Mengzi zhengyi*, 349.

22. Lau, trans., *Mencius*, 183.

23. *Mengzi zhengyi*, 350.

24. Pang Pu states that the second *ni* (匿) should be pronounced *te* 慝, meaning "depraved" or "to do evil." In this case, due to the previous context, it should refer to a *xiaozui* 小罪. Thus it means to be lenient for minor crimes. The evidence he cites for this meaning is Xunzi's "Yuelunpian" 樂論篇and "Tianlunpian" 天論篇, where commentators argue in both cases that *ni* 匿 should be te慝. Pang Pu, *Boshu Wuxingpian Yanjiu*, 56 n. 5.

25. Ikeda and Pang Pu agree that *yan* 晏 should mean "rare" and that *zhen* 軫 should be a contrasting term such as "common." Ikeda Tomohisa, *Maôtai kanbo hakusho gogyôhen kenkyû*, 425–26 nn. 14–15; Pang Pu 龐樸, *Zhubo "Wuxing" pian jiaozhu ji yanjiu* 竹帛《五行》篇校注及研究, Chutu wenxian yizhu yanxi congshu (Taipei: Wanjuanlou, 2000), 71 nn. 1, 3.

26. This translation is based on the received ode translated by James Legge, "He was neither violent nor remiss neither hard nor soft" 不競不絿不剛不柔. Legge treats *qiu* 絿(urgent) as meaning *huan*緩 (remiss or slow). However, the *Mao shi zhengyi* notes that *qiu* 絿 should be *ji*急 (in haste), which is why this translation was altered. The Mawangdui version of *The Five Aspects of Conduct* reads, "Neither forcing nor stopping neither hard nor soft" 不勮不救不剛不柔. Legge, *The She King*, 641; *Mao shi zhengyi*, 802; Ikeda Tomohisa, *Maôtai kanbo hakusho gogyôhen kenkyû*, 419.

27. Li Ling transcribes *gang* 剛 (hard) as *qiang* 強 (strong) here and in the quotation that follows from the *Book of Odes*. In both cases, I follow the original Wenwu transcription of "hard," which is also followed by Ikeda Tomohisa. Finally, the Mawangdui version also uses "hard" instead of "strong." Li Ling, *Guodian Chujian Jiaoduji*, 78–80; *Guodian Chumu zhujian*, 151, 154 n. 55; Ikeda Tomohisa, *Maôtai kanbo hakusho gogyôhen kenkyû*, 419; Ikeda Tomohisa 池田知久, "Kakuten sobo chikukan gogyō yakuchū" 郭店楚墓竹簡 "五行" 譯注, *Kakuten Sokan no shisōshi teki* kenkyū (Tōkyō : Tōkyō Daigaku Bungakubu Chūgoku Shisō Bunkagaku Kenkyūsitsu, 1999), 42.

28. *Guodian Chumu zhujian* transcribes this as *qiu* 梂, which is defined in the *Shuowen Jiezi* 說文解字 as *lishi* 櫟實 (acorn). Jiang Renjie, *Shuowen Jiezi Jizhu*, 2:1162; *Guodian Chumu zhujian*, 157–60.

29. Li Ling, *Guodian Chujian Jiaoduji*, 80.

30. Li Ling, *Guodian Chujian Jiaoduji*, 160.

31. Li Ling, *Guodian Chujian Jiaoduji*, 139.

32. Nivison shows that certain problems with the early Zhou chronology can be attributed to two start dates for a reign that is likely the result of the ruler being in mourning. David S. Nivison, "The Dates of Western Chou," *Harvard Journal of Asiatic Studies* 43.2 (1983): 481–580.

33. In the Wenwu edition, Qiu Xigui notes that this should be *sha* 殺, which he defines as *shengjian* 省减 (economize). In the next sentence he also has "humanity" instead of "kindness." *Guodian Chumu zhujian*, 190 n. 21–2.

34. Li Ling, *Guodian Chujian Jiaoduji*, 131–32.

35. The relevance of this text to a discussion of Warring States texts is questioned by Graham, who believes this text dates from the Han. Graham, *Disputers of the Tao*, 298. Hsiao Kung-chuan has an extensive treatment of the subject and concludes that Qian Mu錢穆 and others who date the "Li Yun" as Han are overzealous, and that their views are an outgrowth of the 1920s and 1930s movement to doubt antiquity. Hsiao instead argues that the ideas of the Grand Unity can be justified as Confucian and need not be seen as Mohist, Huang-Lao, or anything else. Hsiao Kung-chuan, *History of Chinese Political Thought*, 1:124–42. As can be seen from the treatment of "Tang Yu zhidao" in previous pages, the Grand Unity seems very Confucian in light of recently excavated texts.

36. This quotation in full can be found in chapter 4 of this book.

37. Translation here from Legge, *Li Ki Book of Rites*, 364–66.

38. Graham, *Disputers of the Tao*, 45–47. See also Hsiao Kung-chuan, *History of Chinese Political Thought*, 250–57. Jiang Guanghui feels Xunzi opposes abdication, but he does discuss "On the Regulations of a King" 王制篇 and "Man's Nature Is Evil" 性惡篇, where Xunzi advocates ideas that are related to meritocratic lines of reasoning. Jiang Guanghui, "Guodian Chujian yu Zisizi," 82.

39. Here and in subsequent instances, Watson uses "benevolent" instead of "humane." Burton Watson, trans., *Mo Tzu Basic Writings* (New York: Columbia University Press, 1966), 65.

40. Watson, *Mo Tzu Basic Writings*, 65.

41. Sun Yirang 孫詒讓 (1848–1908), *Mozi Jiangu* 墨子閒詁, in *Zhuzi Jicheng* 諸子集成 (Beijing: Zhonghua, 1996), "Jie Zang Xia" 節葬下 104–5.

42. A diversity of views might seem natural in the *Mozi*, since the Mohists had split into three branches that disagreed with each other by the early Han. If we were to suppose, then, that the differing perspectives are the result of texts being written by separate branches, this would simply mean that within the general category of Mohist perspectives, groups conceived of government either as being modeled on the family or as a strict meritocracy. For a discussion of divergent trends in the *Mozi*, see Erik W. Maeder, "Some Observations on the Composition of the 'Core Chapters' of the *Mozi*," *Early China* 17 (1992): 27–82.

43. Watson, *Mo Tzu Basic Writings*, 19–20.

44. *Mozi Jiangu*, "Shang Xian Shang" 尚賢上, 25–26.

45. Graham, *Disputers of the Tao*, 41–45.

46. There are other examples in addition to the Wan Zhang occurrences. For example, 6B.7 supports the idea of elevating the outstanding but does not discuss sage kings, humanity, or righteousness. In addition, 2A.5 is entirely devoted to the positive effects that elevating the outstanding has on the empire. These include being seen as a parent by the common people.

47. The original translation has "honoring the good and wise" for "elevating the outstanding." It has been changed to fit the translation used elsewhere in this book.

48. Lau is correct in translating *yi* 義 as "principle" here, but it is a specific type of principle that pertains to the relationship between superior and inferior, greater with lesser. Lau, trans., *Mencius*, 225. Here are two examples: In 5B.6, Wan Zhang is talking with Mencius: "'But if the ruler gives him rice,' said Wan Zhang, 'would he accept it?' 'Yes.' 'On what principle does he accept it?'" Lau, trans., *Mencius*, 231 萬章曰。君餽之粟。則受之乎。曰。受之。受之何義也。*Mengzi zhengyi*, 5B.6, 419–20. *Mencius* 5B.7 states, "May I ask on what grounds does one refuse to meet feudal lords?" Lau, trans., *Mencius*, 233. 敢問不見諸侯。何義也。 *Mengzi zhengyi*, 5B.7, 424. Therefore, the meaning of *Yi* continues to relate to concerns with state and family similar to the meaning of righteousness discussed elsewhere in this chapter.

49. *Mengzi zhengyi*, 5B.3, 410–11.

50. The original translation has "the honoring of the good and wise" for "elevating the outstanding."

51. Lau, trans., *Mencius*, 233.

52. *Mengzi zhengyi*, 5B.6, 423–24.

53. Lau has "virtuous man" instead of "outstanding man" Lau, trans., *Mencius*, 207.

54. *Mengzi zhengyi*, 5A.6, 381.

55. Lau, trans., *Mencius*, 209.

56. *Mengzi zhengyi*, 5A.6, 383–85.

57. See, for example, *Mencius* 5A.5.

58. Lau, trans., *Mencius*, 237.

59. *Mengzi zhengyi*, 5B.9, 429–30.

60. John Knoblock, *Xunzi: A Translation and Study of the Complete Works*, vol. 3. (Stanford, Calif.: Stanford University Press, 1994), 39.

61. *Xunzi Jijie*, "Zheng Lun Pian" 正論篇, 221.

62. This phrase also appears in the "The Teachings of the Ru" 儒效 and "On the Way of the Lord" 君道 chapters of *Xunzi*. Interestingly, it

also appears twice in "The Prince and His Ministers" 君臣上 chapter of the *Guanzi* 管子.

63. Knoblock, *Xunzi*, 3:40.

64. *Xunzi Jijie*, 221.

65. Knoblock, *Xunzi*, 3:40.

66. *Xunzi Jijie*, 222.

67. It could be argued that requiring the absence of sages among the descendants of a king prior to turning to a sage from among the Three Dukes is implying that all things being equal, a sage in the royal family is still preferable to a sage found elsewhere. However, this could simply be a practical consideration. If there is a situation where there are two sages in the empire, one who is a direct descendant and one who is not, bestowing the position upon a descendant would result in less political tension than giving it to one who is not a relative.

68. Paul Rakita Goldin, *Rituals of the Way: The Philosophy of Xunzi* (Chicago: Open Court, 1999), 50.

69. This can be seen in the following: "The course of Heaven is constant; it is not preserved by Yao and is not destroyed by Jie" 天行有常: 不為堯存, 不為桀亡, Liang Shuren 梁叔任, *Xunzi yue zhu* 荀子約注 (Taibei: Shijie, 1966), 220.

70. The original translation has "worthy."

71. John Knoblock, *Xunzi: A Translation and Study of the Complete Works*, vol. 2. (Stanford, Calif.: Stanford University Press, 1990), 94.

72. Yang Liang 楊倞 notes that this character should be *mu* 穆 and explains, "Father is in the zhao position and son in the mu position (in the ancestral temple). Governing should distinguish, before titles are set, distinctions should be made. Make the outstanding at the front; those who are not should follow. In this way zhao and mu differentiate"; 父昭子穆。言為政當分未定之時則為之分別，使賢者居上，不肖居下，如昭穆之分別然; *Xunzi yue zhu*, 99. Knoblock's translation of distinction between social classes could be questioned; from the perspective of Yang's note, at least, the passage refers to moral and/or generational distinctions.

73. *Xunzi Jijie*, 94.

74. Goldin, *Rituals of the Way*, 8.

75. *Xunzi Jijie*, 296.

76. Graham has a section entitled "Criticism of Hereditary Monarchy" where he treats this subject at some length. Graham, *Disputers of the Tao*, 292–99.

77. For example, see *Mencius* 5A.6.

78. David Nivison, "Mengzi as Philosopher of History," in *Mencius: Contexts and Interpretations*, ed. Alan K. L. Chan (Honolulu: University of Hawai'i Press, 2002), 294–98.

79. Graham, *Disputers of the Tao*, 45.

80. Scott Cook holds a very different perspective on the role of government in Guodian texts. He argues that a core concern of these manuscripts is a critique of coercive measures involving punishment. Black Robes is central to his argument, a text also known from the received tradition where the ideal is the persuasion of the populace by a moral leader. While this perspective is an accurate assessment of Black Robes, "The Five Aspects of Conduct" and "Tang Yu zhidao" are more interested in a unified society. In addition, we can see in "The Five Aspects of Conduct" that coercion by punishment is not deemed problematic. Scott Cook, "The Debate over Coercive Rulership and the 'Human Way': Recently Excavated Warring States Texts," *Harvard Journal of Asiatic Studies* 64.2 (2004): 399–440.

81. Lewis notes that this category is derived from the Han bibliographies that list these works as *fajia* 發家 (Legalist). As such, we could consider the category simply a faithful translation of a term from Chinese sources. However, the chapter describes the impact of other potential candidates for inclusion in political philosophy such as Confucians and Mohists as inconsequential, since he feels that they were not really participants in the political process. Mark Edward Lewis, "Warring States: Political History," in *The Cambridge History of Ancient China: From the Origins of Civilization to 221 B.C.*, ed. Michael Loewe and Edward Shaughnessy (Cambridge: Cambridge University Press, 1999), 589.

82. Lewis, "Warring States," 641.

83. Lewis, "Warring States," 641.

84. By exceptions I do not mean to imply that these constitute either a majority or a minority; such a distinction seems beyond our ability to determine reliably with excavated sources, which reflect only a fraction of the original corpus of material.

Appendix

1. This character 仁 is in Guodian written with the characters for body (身 *shen*) above the character heart (心 *xin*). Virtue, on the other

hand (德 *de*) is written with straight (直 *zhi*) above the character for heart. *Guodian Chumu zhujian*, 147.

2. The character for form (形 xing) is written as mold (型xing). *Guodian Chumu zhujian*, 147.

3. This transcription follows the Mawangdui version. In Guodian, it states, "When sagacity forms within [your heart] it is called virtuous conduct. If [sagacity] is not formed within it is called virtuous conduct." 聖形於內, 謂之德之行, 不行於內謂之行。 The high degree of parallelism between wisdom and sagacity seems to justify following the Mawangdui (MWD) version here. See, for example, the consistency between the fifth through seventh paragraphs below. *Guodian Chumu zhujian*, 147.

4. See chapter 1 for a discussion of the importance of unity and harmony in the text.

5. See the section entitled "The Rhetoric of Self-Cultivation" in chapter 3 for a discussion of the term "noble man."

6. The MWD version contains the following line that is absent here from the Guodian version. It repeats the line in Guodian with the character for sagacity substituted for the character for wisdom: "If a noble man's inner heart lacks concern, his inner heart will lack sagacity. If his inner heart lacks sagacity, his inner heart will lack happiness. If his inner heart lacks happiness, he will not be at ease. Not being at ease he is not musical and without music he will lack virtue." 君子無中心之憂, 則無中心之聖。 無中心之聖, 則無中心之說。 無中心之說, 則不安。 不安則不樂。 不樂則無德。Ikeda Tomohisa, *Maôtai kanbo hakusho gogyôhen kenkyû*, 171.

7. Literally, it means you will not get closer.

8. This interpolation is based on the MWD version. The characters for essence and extension are repeated in the beginning of the fifth and sixth paragraphs on humanity and wisdom. The third term, "lightness," which is included in MWD, seems appropriate, since it appears at the start of the seventh paragraph on sagacity that parallels the fifth and sixth. For further discussion of these parallels, see chapter 4 of this book.

9. The GD version reads: "未見君子憂心不能惙惙既見君子心不能悦 亦既見之亦既觀之我心則⊠." The last character is likely 悦 based on the MWD version and the received *Book of Odes*. However, the first part of the quotation is significantly different and a deliberate misquotation. The received *Book of Odes* reads: "When I do not see my lord, my sorrowful heart is agitated." Legge, *The She King*, 23. 未見君子憂心惙惙亦

既見止亦既觀之我心則悦 *Mao Shi Zhengyi*, 52. This means that without humanity and wisdom, your heart does not respond appropriately. This same passage can be found in the *Hanshi Waizhuan* 韓詩外傳 "Confucius said, 'The superior man has three worries: That he does not know—can he not but worry? That he knows but does not study [what he knows]—can he not but worry? That he studies but does not practice what he has studied—can he not but worry?' The Ode says, 'When I have not yet seen the superior man, My sorrowful heart is very sad.'" James Robert Hightower, trans., *Han Shih wai chuan: Han Ying's Illustrations of the Didactic Application of the Classic of Songs* (Cambridge, Mass.: Harvard University Press, 1952), 26. 孔子曰: "君子有三憂。弗知, 可無憂與? 知而不學, 可無憂與? 學而不行, 可無憂與? "《詩》曰: "未見君子憂心惙惙." *Hanshi Waizhuan* 韓詩外傳, in Sibu Congkan. vol. 4 四部叢刊初篇縮本第四 (Taibei: Shangwu, 1967), 6.

10. The MWD version includes the characters *Shiyue* 詩曰 prior to this quotation.

11. There is no misquotation here. *Mao Shi Zhengyi*, 52; Legge, *The She King*, 23–24.

12. This sentence is adapted from "While we do not see our husbands, our hearts must be full of grief. Let us but see our husbands and our hearts will rest." Legge, *The She King*, 264. 未見君子, 憂心忡忡; 既見君子, 我心則降。*Mao Shi Zhengyi*, 168. This quotation is a reversal of the correct response your heart should have in such a situation.

13. See chapter 4, note 43 for a discussion of jade.

14. 聰 is translated "keen hearing" to highlight the contrast with 明 "keen sight" that is dominant in this text.

15. *Mao Shi Zhengyi*, 271; Legge, *The She King*, 4:222–23.

16. My decision to translate this as "concerned about your uniqueness" instead of "cautious when alone" is indebted to the Ames and Hall *Focusing the Familiar*, 118–19 n. 10.

17. *Mao Shi Zhengyi*, 77–78; Legge, *The She King*, 4:42–43.

18. *Mao Shi Zhengyi*, 77–78; Legge, *The She King*, 4:42–43.

19. Since this interpolation is based on the MWD edition, my translation reflects the decision by Pang Pu and Ikeda Tomohisa that this should read 無與終 "nothing he takes as the end." Li Ling's transcription reads "there is a beginning and *something* he takes as the end" [有與始, 有與], but this lacuna is being corrected based on the Mawangdui version, which both Ikeda Tomohisa and Pang Pu transcribe as "有與始, 無與終." Pang Pu, *Boshu Wuxingpian Yanjiu*, 34;

Ikeda Tomohisa, *Maôtai kanbo hakusho gogyôhen kenkyû*, 234–37; Li Ling, *Guodian Chujian Jiaoduji*, 79.

20. The MWD explanation states that this means, "doing your best" (勉 *mian*). Wei Qipeng, "Jianbo 'Wuxing' Jianshih," 27.

21. The MWD version uses the character 迣 *zhi* instead of 肆 *si*. There is much debate over how to transcribe this character, and others do not use *si*. However, while the debate continues, all we really have to assist us is the MWD version. In explanation 11 of the MWD version, *zhi* appears as follows: "One who excels is one who completes." 迣者終之者也. Ikeda Tomohisa, *Maôtai kanbo hakusho gogyôhen kenkyû*, 259.

22. *Mao Shi Zhengyi*, 236; James Legge, *The She King*, 4:432.

23. *Mao Shi Zhengyi*, 235; James Legge, *The She King*, 4:427.

24. "Changeable" here could be related to paragraph 12 above.

25. MWD has "your inner heart is happy; you influence your brothers' behavior" 中心說 (悅) 焉, 遷于兄弟. However, since *zhan* 旃 is a contraction of *zhiyan* 之焉 it does not change the translation. The character *zhan* 遷 could also be transcribed *qian*, but they are interchangeable by the Han dynasty. *Guodian Chumu zhujian*, 153 n. 40.

26. See chapter 5, n. 26 for details on the translation of this quotation from the *Odes*.

27. Wei Qipeng feels that *lian* 練should be *jian* 諫and cites the *Zhouli* "Diguan" "Shuguan" 《周禮. 地官. 序官》where the note states that *jian* 諫means "to make upright having the justice of execution" 正有誅殺之義. Wei Qipeng, "Jianbo 'Wuxing' Jianshi," 44–45. In the MWD version, the character 賀: "Congratulations" appears, but Ikeda says that the character should be *heng* 衡, balance or scale. Ikeda Tomohisa, *Maôtai kanbo hakusho gogyôhen kenkyû*, 419–21.

28. For epigraphic issues related to this paragraph, see chapter 5, notes 24–28.

29. Ikeda cites various sources for the phrase "cease where they dwell." First is "humanity has neighbours, righteousness has gates . . ." 仁有里 義有門 . . . *Xunzi Jijie*, "Dalüe Pian" 大略篇, 324. He also lists "In neighbourhoods, humanity is best. If you select not to dwell in a humane (neighborhood) how can you be considered wise?" 里仁為美 擇不處仁, 焉得知. *Lunyu Zhengyi*, 4.1, 74; Ikeda Tomohisa, *Maôtai kanbo hakusho gogyôhen kenkyû*, 450 n. 8. This line from *Analects* 4.1 is also quoted in *Mencius* 2A.7.

30. Li Ling notes that *lülü* 儢儢 means one who does not exert effort in Xunzi. Pang Pu transcribes these characters as *lülü* 繥繥, which

he says could refer to 索盧參 Sulu Shen, a thief mentioned in the *Lüshi chunqiu* 呂氏春秋 who deserved punishment but went on to become an important scholar. Either way, it implies one who has risen from low moral status. Li Ling, *Guodian Chujian Jiaoduji,* 81; Pang Pu, *Zhubo "Wuxing" Pian Jiaozhu Ji Yanjiu,* 74.

31. This is based on the MWD version, which reads: "前, 王公之尊賢者也. 後, 士之尊賢者也."

32. See chapter 1, n. 22.

33. Translation is based on James Legge. Legge, *The She King,* 4:463; *Mao Shi Zhengyi,* 236.

34. See chapter 2, n. 53 for a detailed discussion of epigraphic issues related to this passage.

Bibliography

A regularly updated bibliography of Guodian materials can be found at http://www.paulrgoldin.com. Modern sources have not been separated into Chinese-language and Western-language sources because there are authors who publish in more than one language. Characters are provided only when authors publish in non-Western languages.

Modern Sources

Allan, Sarah. *The Heir and the Sage Dynastic Legends in Early China.* San Francisco: Chinese Materials Center, 1981.

Allan, Sarah, and Crispin Williams, eds. *The Guodian Laozi: Proceedings of the International Conference, Dartmouth College, May 1998.* Berkeley, The Society for the Study of Early China and Institute of East Asian Studies, University of California, 2000.

Allinson, Robert E. "The Debate between Mencius and Hsün-tzu: Contemporary Applications." *Journal of Chinese Philosophy* 25.1 (1998): 31–49.

Ames, Roger T., and David L. Hall, trans. *Focusing the Familiar: A Translation and Philosophical Interpretation of the* Zhongyong. Honolulu: University of Hawai'i Press, 2001.

Asselin, Mark Laurent. "The Lu-School Reading of 'Guanju' as Reserved in an Eastern Han fu." *Journal of the American Oriental Society* 117.3 (1997): 427–43.

Barnard, Noel. *The Ch'u Silk Manuscript*. Canberra: Australian National University, 1973.

Behuniak, James. "Nivison and the 'Problem' in Xunzi's Ethics." *Philosophy East and West* 50.1 (2000): 97–110.

———. "Poem as Proposition in the *Analects*: A Whiteheadian Reading of a Confucian Sensibility." *Asian Philosophy* 8.3 (1998): 191–202.

Berthrong, John H. *Transformations of the Confucian Way*. Boulder, Colo.: Westview, 1998.

Bilsky, Lester James. *The State Religion of Ancient China*. 2 vols. Taipei: Oriental Cultural Service for] the Chinese Association for Folklore, 1975.

Blanford, Yumiko F. "Discovery of Lost Eloquence: New Insight from the Mawangdui 'Zhanguo Zonghengjia Shu.'" *Journal of the American Oriental Society* 114.1 (1994): 77–82.

Bloom, Irene. "Human Nature and Biological Nature in Mencius." *Philosophy East and West* 47.1 (1997): 21–32.

———. "Mencian Arguments on Human Nature (*Jen-hsing*)." *Philosophy East and West* 44.1 (1994): 19–53.

Bodde, Derk. "Harmony and Conflict in Chinese Philosophy." In *Studies in Chinese Thought*, ed/ Arthur F. Wright, 19–80. Midway reprint. Chicago: University of Chicago Press, 1953.

Boltz, William G. "The Fourth-Century B.C. Guodiann Manuscripts from Chuu and the Composition of the Laotzyy." *Journal of the American Oriental Society* 119.4 (1999): 590–608.

Boodberg, Peter. "The Semasiology of Some Primary Confucian Concepts." *Philosophy East and West* 2 (1953): 317–32.

Brooks, E. Bruce, and A. Taeko Brooks. *The Original Analects: Sayings of Confucius and His Successors*. New York: Columbia University Press, 1998.

Cai, Zhongde 蔡仲德. "Guodian Chujian Rujia Yuelun Shitan" 郭店楚簡儒家樂論試探. *Kongzi Yanjiu* 孔子研究 3 (2000): 44–49.

Chan, Alan K. L. "Confucian Ethics and the Critique of Ideology." *Asian Philosophy* 10.3 (2000): 245–61.

———. "A Matter of Taste: *Qi* (Vital Energy) and the Tending of the Heart (*Xin*) in *Mencius* 2A2." In Alan K. L. Chan, 42–71.

———. ed. *Mencius: Contexts and Interpretations*. Honolulu: University of Hawai'i Press, 2002.

Chan, See Yee. "Disputes on the One Thread of Chung-Shu." *Journal of Chinese Philosophy* 26.2 (1999): 165–86.

Chan, Sin Yee. "Gender and Relationship Roles in the *Analects* and the *Mencius*." *Asian Philosophy* 10.2 (2000): 115–32.

Chan, Wing-tsit. *A Source Book in Chinese Philosophy*. Princeton, N.J.: Princeton University Press, 1963.

Chen, Fubin 陳福濱, et al., eds. *Ben shiji chutu sixiang wenxian yu Zhongguo gudian zhexue yanjiu lunwen chi* 本世紀出土思想文獻與中國古典哲學研究論文集. 2 vols. Taipei: Fujen Daxue, 1999.

Chen, Lai 陳來."Rujia Xipu Zhi Chongjian Yu Shiliao Kunjing Zhi Tupo—Guodian Chujian Rushu Yu Xianqin Ruxue Yanjiu" 儒家系譜之重建與史料困境之突破—郭店楚簡儒書與先秦儒學研究. *Guodian Chujian Guoji Xueshu Yantaohui Lunwenji* 郭店楚簡國際學術研討會論文集, 562–70.

Chen, Ligui 陳麗桂. "Cong Guodian Zhujian 'Wuxing' Jianshi Boshu 'Wuxing' Shuowen Dui Jingwen De Yiwei Qingkuang" 從郭店竹簡《五行》檢視帛書《五行》說文對經文依違情況. In Chen Fubin et al., 1:173–98.

Chen, Ming 陳明. "'Tang Yu zhidao' Yu Zaoqi Rujia De Shehui Linian" 《唐虞之道》與早期儒家的社會理念. *Guodian Chujian yanjiu. Zhongguo zhexue* 20 郭店楚簡研究《中國哲學》中國哲學第二十輯 (1999): 243–62.

Chen, Ning 陳寧. "Confucius' View of Fate (*Ming*)." *Journal of Chinese Philosophy* 24.3 (1997): 323–59.

———. "Guodian Chumu Zhujian Zhong De Rujia Jenxing Yanlun Chutan" 《郭店楚墓竹簡》中的儒家人性言論初探. *Zhongguo zhexueshi* 中國哲學史 4 (1998): 39–46.

Chong, Kim Chong. "Confucius's Virtue Ethics: *Li, Yi, Wen,* and *Chih* in the *Analects*." *Journal of Chinese Philosophy* 25.1 (1998): 101–30.

———. "The Practice of Jen." *Philosophy East and West* 49.3 (1999): 298–316.

Connery, Christopher Leigh. *The Empire of the Text: Writing and Authority in Early Imperial China*. Lanham, Md.: Rowman and Littlefield, 1998.

Cook, Constance A., and John S. Major, eds. *Defining Chu: Image and Reality in Ancient China*. Honolulu: University of Hawai'i Press, 1999.

Cook, Scott [i.e., Gu, Shikao, q.v.]. "Consummate Artistry and Moral Virtuosity: The 'Wuxing' 五行 Essay and Its Aesthetic Implications." *Chinese Literature: Essays, Articles, Reviews* 22 (2000): 113–46.

———. "The Debate over Coercive Rulership and the 'Human Way': Recently Excavated Warring States Texts." *Harvard Journal of Asiatic Studies* 64.2 (2004): 399–440.

————. "Xun Zi on Ritual and Music." *Monumenta Serica* 45 (1997): 1–38.

Creel, Herrlee G. *Confucius and the Chinese Way*. New York: Harper and Row, 1949.

————. "Sinism–A Clarification." *Journal of the History of Ideas* 10, 1 (1949): 135–40.

Csikszentmihalyi, Mark. *Material Virtue: Ethics and the Body in Early China*. Leiden: Brill, 2004.

————. "Mysticism and Apophatic Discourse in the Laozi." In Csikszentmihalyi and Ivanhoe, 33–58.

————. and Philip J. Ivanhoe, eds. *Religious and PhilosophicalAspects of the Laozi*. Albany: State University of New York Press, 1999.

Cua, A. S. *Ethical Argumentation: A Study in Hsün Tzu's Moral Epistemology*. Honolulu: University of Hawai'i Press, 1985.

Cui, Yongdong 崔永東. "Guodian Chujian Zhong De Fanzui Yufang Sixiang Chutan" 郭店楚簡中的犯罪預防思想初探. Guodian Chujian Guoji Xueshu Yantaohui Lunwenji郭店楚簡國際學術研討會論文集, 423–28.

Ding Sixin丁四新. "On the Implications of 'Qing' in Guodian Slips." *Modern Philosophy* 04 (2003) 61–68.

Du, Weiming 杜維明 [i.e., Tu Wei-ming, q.v.]. "Guodian Chujian yu Xianqin Ru Dao Sixiang De Chongxin Dingwei" 郭店楚簡與先秦儒道思想的重新定位. *Guodian Chujian Yanjiu. Zhongguo zhexue* 20郭店楚簡研究《中國哲學》中國哲學第二十輯(1999): 1–6.

Dubs, Homer H. "Did Confucius Study the Book of Changes?" *T'oung Pao* 24 (1927): 82–90.

————. "Mencius and Sün-dz on Human Nature." *Philosophy East and West* 6 (1956): 213–22.

————. trans. *The Works of Hsüntze*. London, Arthur Probsthain, 1928.

Eifring, Halvor, ed. *Love and Emotions in Traditional Chinese Literature*. Sinica Leidensia 63. Leiden: Brill, 2004.

Ellison, Christopher G., Jason D. Boardman, David R. Williams, and James S. Jackson. "Religious Involvement, Stress, and Mental Health: Findings from the 1995 Detroit Area Study." *Social Forces* 80.1 (2001): 215–49.

Eno, Robert. *The Confucian Creation of Heaven: Philosophy and the Defense of Ritual Mastery*. Albany: State University of New York Press, 1990.

Fang, Ming 方銘. "Kongzi Jinshan Jinmei de Shenmei Lixiang Xinlun" 孔子盡善盡美的審美理想新論. In Yao, Xiaoou et al., 117–28.

Fehl, Noah Edward. *Li: Rites and Propriety in Literature and Life*. Hong Kong: Chinese University, 1971.

Fingarette, Herbert. *Confucius: The Secular as Sacred*. New York: Harper and Row, 1972.

Fox, Russell Arben. "Confucian and Communitarian Responses to Liberal Democracy." *Review of Politics* 59.3 (1997): 561–92.

Fung, Yu-lan. *History of Chinese Philosophy*. Vol. 1. 1952. Reprint, Princeton, N.J.: Princeton University Press, 1983.

———. *History of Chinese Philosophy*. Vol. 2. 1953. Reprint, Princeton: Princeton University Press, 1983.

Gao, Ming 高明. *Boshu Laozi jiaozhu* 帛書老子校注. Beijing: Zhonghua, 1996.

Gardner, Daniel K. "Confucian Commentary and Chinese Intellectual History." *Journal of Asian Studies* 57.2 (1998): 397–422.

Geaney, Jane. *On the Epistemology of the Senses in Early Chinese Thought*. Honolulu: University of Hawai'i Press, 2002.

Goldin, Paul Rakita. *Rituals of the Way: The Philosophy of Xunzi*. Chicago.: Open Court, 1999.

———. "Xunzi in the Light of the Guodian Manuscripts." *Early China* 25 (2000): 123–24.

Gong, Jianping 龔建平. "Guodian Chujian Zhong de Rujia Liyueh Sixiang shulue" 郭店楚簡中的儒家禮樂思想述略. *Guodian Chujian Guoji Xueshu Yantaohui Lunwenji* 郭店楚簡國際學術研討會論文集, 149–54.

———. "Guodian Jian yu Liji Erti" 郭店簡與禮記二題. *Wuhan Daxue Xuebao (Zheshe ban)* 5 (1999): 34–37.

Graham, A. C. "The Background of the Mencian Theory of Human Nature." *Tsing Hua Journal of Chinese Studies*, n.s., 6 I.2 (1967). Reprinted in Graham, *Studies in Chinese Philosophy*, 59–65.

———. *Disputers of the Tao: Philosophical Argument in Ancient China*. La Salle, Ill.: Open Court, 1989.

———. *Studies in Chinese Philosophy and Philosophical Literature*. Albany: State University of New York Press, 1990.

Gu, Jiegang 顧頡剛. "Shanrang Chuanshuo Qiyu Mojia Kao" 禪讓傳説起於墨家考. *Gushi Bian*, 7B. Reprint, Shanghai: Guji, 1982.

Gu, Shikao 顧史考 [i.e., Scott Cook, q.v.]. "Guodian Chujian Rujia yishu de Pailie Tiaocheng Chuyi Erhshan Ze" 郭店楚簡儒家逸書的排列調整芻議二三則. *Zhongguo dianji yu wenhua* 中國典籍與文化 6 (2000), 208–216.

———. "Guodian Chujian Rujia yishu yu qi dui Taiwan Ruxue SiMeng Chuantong de Yiyi" 郭店楚簡儒家逸書與其對臺灣儒學思孟傳統的意義. *Dier jie Taiwan Ruxue Guoji Xueshu Yantaohui* 第二屆臺灣儒學國際學術研討會 Tainan: Guoli Chenggong Daxue Wenxuexi, 1999, 169–211.

Guo, Lihua 郭梨華. "Jian Bo 'Wuxing' de liyueh kaoshu" 簡、帛《五行》的禮樂考述. In Chen Fubin et al., 2:511–47.

———. "Zhujian 'Wuxing' de 'Wuxing' Yanjiu" 竹簡《五行》的 "五行" 研究. *Guodian Chujian Guoji Xueshu Yantaohui Lunwenji* 郭店楚簡國際學術研討會論文集, 249–60.

Guo, Qiyong 郭齊勇. "Guodian Rujia Jian De Yiyi Yu Jiazhi" 郭店儒家簡的意義與價值. *Hubei Daxue Xuebao (Zhexue shehui Kexue Ban)* 2 (1999): 4–6.

———. "Guodian Rujia jian yu Mengzi xinxing lun" 郭店儒家簡與孟子心性論. *Wuhan Daxue xuebao (Zheshe Ban)* 5 (1999): 24–28.

———. "Zailun 'Wuxing' yu 'Shengzhi'" 再論五行與聖智 *Zhongguo zhexueshi* 3 (2001): 20–26.

Guodian Chumu zhujian 郭店楚墓竹簡. Beijing: Wenwu, 1998.

Guodian Chujian guoji xueshu yantaohui lunwenji 郭店楚簡國際學術研討會論文集. Ed. Wuhan Daxue Zhongguo Wenhua Yanjiuyuan. Renwen luncong. Wuhan: Hubei renmin, 2000.

Hall, David L., and Roger T. Ames. *Thinking from the Han: Self, Truth, and Transcendence in Chinese and Western Culture*. Albany: State University of New York Press, 1998.

———. *Thinking through Confucius*. Albany: State University of New York Press, 1987.

Han, Xing 韓星. "Guodian Chujian Rujia Tiandao Guan Shulue" 郭店楚簡儒家天道觀述略. *Xibei Daxue Xuebao: Zheshe Ban* 西北大學學報:哲社版 2 (2000): 46–49.

Hansen, Chad. *A Daoist Theory of Chinese Thought: A Philosophical Interpretation. New York, Oxford University Press, 1992.*

———. *Language and Logic in Ancient China.* Ann Arbor, University of Michigan Press 1983.

Hardy, Grant. *Worlds of Bronze and Bamboo: Sima Qian's Conquest of History*. New York: Columbia University Press, 1999.

Harper, Donald. "Warring States Natural Philosophy and Occult Thought." In Loewe and Shaughnessy, 813–84.

He, Linyi 何琳儀. *Zhanguo Guwen Zidian* 戰國古文字典 Beijing: Zhonghua Shuju 中華書局, 1998.

Hebei Sheng wen wu yan jiu suo Dingzhou Han mu zhu jian zheng li xiao zu 河北省文物研究所定州漢墓竹簡整理小組. *Dingzhou Han mu zhu jian Lun yu* 定州漢墓竹簡論語. Beijing: Wenwu, 1997.

Henricks, Robert G. *Lao Tzu's Tao Te Ching*. New York: Columbia University Press, 2000.

Hightower, James Robert, trans. *Han Shih wai chuan: Han Ying's Illustrations of the Didactic Application of the Classic of Songs*. Cambridge, Mass.: Harvard University Press, 1952.

Hilty, Dale M., Rick L. Morgan, and Joan E. Burns. "King and Hunt Revisited: Dimensions of Religious Involvement." *Journal for the Scientific Study of Religion* 23.3 (1984): 252–66.

Himmelfarb, Harold S. "Measuring Religious Involvement." *Social Forces* 53.4 (1975): 606–18.

Holloway, Kenneth W. "'The Five Aspects of Conduct': Introduction and Translation." *Journal of the Royal Asiatic Society* 15.2 (2005): 179–98.

Holzman, Donald. "Confucius and Ancient Chinese Literary Criticism." In *Chinese Approaches to Literature from Confucius to Liang Ch'i-ch'ao*, ed. Adele Austin Rickett, 21–41. Princeton, N.J.: Princeton University Press, 1978.

———. "The Place of Filial Piety in Ancient China." *Journal of the American Oriental Society* 118.2 (1998): 185–99.

Horgan, Terence. "Vagueness and the Forced-March Sorites Paradox." *Philosophical Perspectives* 8 (1994): 159–88.

Hsiao, Kung-chuan. *A History of Chinese Political Thought*. Vol. 1, *From the Beginnings to the Sixth Century A.D.* Trans. F. W. Mote. Princeton, N.J.: Princeton University Press, 1979.

Hsu, Cho-yun. *Ancient China in Transition: An Analysis of Social Mobility 722–222 BC*. Stanford, Calif.: Stanford University Press, 1965.

Hubeisheng Jingmenshi Bowuguan 湖北省荊門市博物館. "Jingmen Guodian yihao Chumu" 荊門郭店一號楚墓. *Wenwu*文物 7 (1997): 35–48.

Hunansheng Bowuguan 湖南省博物館. "Changsha Mawangdui er san hao Han mu fajue jianbao" 長沙馬王堆二三號漢墓發掘簡報. *Wenwu* 文物7 (1974): 39–63.

Ikeda, Tomohisa 池田知久. "Guodian Chujian 'Wuxing' Yanjiu" 郭店楚簡《五行》研究 Guodian Jian Yu Ruxue Yanjiu郭店簡與儒學研究. *Zhongguo zhexue* 21 《中國哲學》第二十一輯 (2000): 92–133.

———. "Kakuten sobo chikukan gogyō yakuchū" 郭店楚墓竹簡 "五行" 譯注. *Kakuten Sokan no shisōshi teki* kenkyū. Tōkyō: Tōkyō

Daigaku Bungakubu Chūgoku Shisō Bunkagaku Kenkyūsitsu, 1999.

———. "Kakuten Sokan 'Gogyō' no Kenkyū" 郭店楚簡《五行》の研究. *Guodian Chujian Guoji Xueshu Yantaohui Lunwenji*郭店楚簡國際學術研討會論文集, 210–39.

———. *Maôtai kanbo hakusho gogyôhen kenkyû* 馬王堆漢墓帛書五行篇研究. Tokyo: Kyūko, 1993.

———. "Mawangdui Hanmu Boshu 'Wuxingpian' Suojiande Shenxin Wenti." 馬王堆漢墓帛書《五行篇》所見的身心問題. *Daojia Wenhua Yanjiu* 道家文化研究3 (1999): 349–59.

Im, Manyul. "Emotional Control and Virtue in the *Mencius*." *Philosophy East and West* 49.1 (1999): 1–14.

Ivanhoe, Philip J., ed. *Chinese Language, Thought, and Culture: Nivison and His Critics*. Chicago: Open Court, 1996.

———. *Confucian Moral Self Cultivation*. New York: Peter Lang, 1993.

———. *Ethics in the Confucian Tradition: The Thought of Mencius and Wang Yang-ming*. Atlanta: Scholars Press, 1990.

———. "A Happy Symmetry: Xunzi's Ethical Thought." *Journal of the American Academy of Religion* 59.2 (1991): 309–22.

———. "Human Nature and Moral Understanding in Xunzi." *International Philosophical Quarterly* 34.2 (1994): 167–76.

———. "A Question of Faith: A New Interpretation of *Mencius* 2B.13." *Early China* 13 (1988): 153–65.

———. "Reweaving the 'One Thread' of the Analects." *Philosophy East and West* 40.1 (1990): 17–33.

———. "Thinking and Learning in Early Confucianism." *Journal of Chinese Philosophy* 17.4 (1990): 473–94.

Jensen, Lionel. *Manufacturing Confucianism: Chinese Traditions and Universal Civilization*. Durham, N.C.: Duke University Press, 1997.

Jiang, Guanghui姜廣輝. "Guodian Chujian yu Yuandian Ruxue—Guonei Xueshujie Guanyu Guodian Chujian De Yanjiu (i)" 郭店楚簡與原典儒學—國內學術界關於郭店楚簡的研究（一）. *Shupin* 書品 1999.1. Reprinted in *Guodian jian yu Ruxue yanjiu* 郭店簡與儒學研究. *Zhongguo zhexue* 21 《中國哲學》第二十一輯(2000): 263–73.

———. "Guodian Chujian yu Zisizi—Jian Tan Guodian Chujian De SixiangShiYiYi"郭店楚簡與《子思子》—兼談郭店楚簡的思想史意義. *Zhexue Yanjiu* 哲學研究 7 (1998): 56–61. Reprinted in *Guodian Chujian Yanjiu. Zhongguo zhexue* 20 郭店楚簡研究《中國哲學》中國哲學第二十輯(1999): 81–92.

———. "Guodian Yihao Mu Muzhu Shi Shei?" 郭店一號墓墓主是誰? *Guodian Chujian Yanjiu. Zhongguo zhexue* 20郭店楚簡研究《中國哲學》中國哲學第二十輯(1999): 397–99.

Jiang, Renjie蔣人傑. *Shuowen Jiezi Jizhu* 說文解字集注. 3 vols. Shanghai: Guji, 1996.

Jiang, Xinyan. "Mencius on Human Nature and Courage." *Journal of Chinese Philosophy* 24.3 (1997): 265–89.

Jingmen Shi Bowuguan 荊門市博物館. *Guodian Chumu zhujian* 郭店楚墓竹簡. Beijing: Wenwu, 1998.

———. "Jingmen Guodian yihao Chumu" 荊門郭店一號楚墓. *Wenwu* 7 (1997): 35–48.

Karlgren, Bernhard. *Glosses on the Book of Songs*. Göteborg: Elanders, 1964.

Kline, T. C., III, and Philip J. Ivanhoe, eds. *Virtue, Nature, and Moral Agency in the* Xunzi. Indianapolis: Hackett, 2000.

Knapp, Keith. "The *Ru* Interpretation of *Xiao*." *Early China* 20 (1995): 195–222.

Knechtges, David R. "Riddles as Poetry: The 'Fu' Chapter of the *Hsün-tzu*." *Wen-lin: Studies in the Chinese Humanities* 2 (1989): 1–31.

Knoblock, John, trans. *Xunzi: A Translation and Study of the Complete Works*. 3 vols. Stanford, Calif.: Stanford University Press, 1988–94.

Kohn, Livia, and Michael LaFargue, eds. *Lao-tzu and the Tao-te-ching*. Albany: State University of New York Press, 1998.

Kroll, J. L. "Disputation in Ancient Chinese Culture." *Early China* 11/12 (1985–87): 118–45.

Lau, D. C. *Mencius*. 2 vols. Hong Kong: Chinese University Press, 1984.

———. trans. *Mencius: A Bilingual Edition*. Rev. ed. Hong Kong: Chinese University Press, 2003.

———. "On Mencius' Use of the Method of Analogy in Argument." *Asia Major* 10 (1963): 173–94.

———. "Some Notes on the *Mencius*." *Asia Major* 15.1 (1969): 62–81.

———. "Theories of Human Nature in *Mencius* and *Shyuntzyy*." *Bulletin of the School of Oriental and African Studies* 15.3 (1953): 541–65.

———. "The Treatment of Opposites in 'Lao Tzu.'" *Bulletin of the School of Oriental and African Studies* 21.1/3 (1958): 344–60.

Legge, James. *The Chinese Classics*. Vol. 4, *The She King* 詩經. Hong Kong: 1871. Reprint, Taipei: Jinxue, 1968.

———. *The Chinese Classics*. Vol. 3, *The Shoo King* 尚書. Hong Kong: 1865. Reprint, Taipei: Jinxue, 1968.

———. *Li Ki Book of Rites*. Vol. 27. Oxford: Clarendon, 1885. Reprint, Delhi: Motilal Banarsidass, 1966.

Lenk, Hans, and Gregor Paul, eds. *Epistemological Issues in Classical Chinese Philosophy*. Albany: State University of New York Press, 1993.

Lewis, Mark Edward. "Warring States: Political History." In Loewe and Shaughnessy, 587–650.

———. *Writing and Authority in Early China*. Albany: State University of New York Press, 1999.

Li, Cunshan李存山. "Cong jianben 'Wushing' dao Boshu 'Wuxing'" 從簡本《五行》到帛書《五行》. *Guodian Chujian guoji xueshu yantaohui lunwenji* 郭店楚簡國際學術研討會論文集, 240–48.

———. "Xianqin Rujia De Zhengzhi Lunli Jiaokeshu—Du Chu-Jian 'Zhongxin Zhi Dao' ji Qita" 先秦儒家的政治倫理教科書—讀楚簡《忠信之道》及其他. *Zhongguo wenhua yanjiu* 中國文化研究 22 (1998): 20–26. Reprinted as "Du Chujian 'Zhongxin zhi dao' ji Qita" 讀楚簡《忠信之道》及其他 in *Guodian Chujian Yanjiu. Zhongguo zhexue* 20 郭店楚簡研究《中國哲學》中國哲學第二十輯 (1999): 263–78.

Li, Jinglin 李景林. "Boshu 'Wuxing' Shendu Xiaoyi" 帛書《五行》慎獨說小議. *Renwen Zazhi*人文雜志 6 (2003): 23–27.

———. "Cong Guodian Jian Kan Simeng Xuepai De Xing Yu Tiandao Lun—Jiantan Guodian Jian Rujialei Zhuzuo De Xuepai Guishu Wenti" 從郭店簡看思孟學派的性與天道論—兼談郭店簡儒家類著作的學派歸屬問題. *Guodian Chujian Guoji Xueshu Yantaohui Lunwenji* 郭店楚簡國際學術研討會論文集, 625–35.

Li, Ling 李零. "An Archaeological Study of Taiyi (Grand One) Worship." *Early Medieval China* 2 (1995–96): 1–39.

———. "The Formulaic Structure of Chu Divinatory Bamboo Slips." *Early China* 15 (1990): 71–86.

———. "Guodian Chujian Jiaoduji." 郭店楚簡校讀記 *Daojia Wenhua Yanjiu* 道家文化研究17 (1999): 455–542.

———. *Guodian Chujian Jiaoduji* 郭店楚簡校讀記. Rev. ed. Beijing: Beijing University Press, 2002.

Li, Ling, and Constance A. Cook. "Translation of the Chu Silk Manuscript." In Cook and Major, 171–76.

Li, Shuyou. "On Characteristics of Human Beings in Ancient Chinese Philosophy." *Journal of Chinese Philosophy* 15.3 (1988): 221–54.

Li, Xueqin 李學勤. "Basic Considerations on the Commentaries of the Silk Manuscript *Book of Changes*." *Early China* 20 (1995): 367–80.

———. "The Confucian Texts from Guodian Tomb Number One: Their Date and Significance." In Allan and Williams, 107–11.

———. "Cong Jianbo Yiji 'Wuxing' Tandao 'Daxue'" 李學勤 從簡帛佚籍《五行》談到《大學》. *Kongzi yanjiu* 孔子研究 March 1998.

———. "Guodian Chujian yu Rujia jingji" 郭店楚簡與儒家經籍. *Guodian Chujian Yanjiu. Zhongguo zhexue* 20 郭店楚簡研究《中國哲學》中國哲學第二十輯(1999): 18–21.

———. "Guodian jian yu Liji" 郭店簡與《禮記》. *Zhongguo zhexueshi* 中國哲學史4 (1998): 29–32.

———. "Jingmen Guodian Chujianzhong de Zisizi" 荊門郭店楚簡中的子思子*Wenwu tiandi* 文物天地 2 (1998). Reprinted in *Guodian Chujian yanjiu. Zhongguo zhexue* 20 (1999): 75–80. "The *Zisizi* in the Jingmen Guodian Chu Slips." *Contemporary Chinese Thought* 32.2 (2000–1): 61–67.

———. "Xianqin Rujia Zhuzuo De Zhongda Faxian" 先秦儒家著作的重大發現. *Jenmin Zhengxie Bao* 6 (1998): 8. Reprinted in *Guodian Chujian Yanjiu* 郭店楚簡研究. *Zhongguo zhexue* 20 《中國哲學》第二十輯(1999): 13–17.

Liang, Qichao 梁啟超. "Yinyang Wuxing Shuo Zhi Laili" 陰陽五行說之來歷 *Yinbingshi Wenji* 飲冰室文集. Vol. 7.36 卷三十六. Taipei: Chung Hwa Book Company, 1970. 47–64.

Liang, Tao梁濤. "Guodian Chujian yu 'Zhongyong'" 郭店楚簡與《中庸》*Gongan Taida Lishixuebao* 25 公案 台大歷史學報第二十五期，2000.

———. "Jianbo Wuxing xintan: Jianlun Wuxing zai sixiangshi zhong de diwei" 簡帛《五行》新探：兼論《五行》在思想史中的地位. *Kongzi yanjiu* 5 (2002): 39–51. Reprinted in Pang Pu et al., 191–217.

———. "Simeng Xuepai Kaoshu" 思孟學派考述 *Zhongguo zhexueshi* 3 中國哲學學史 (2002):27–34.

———. "Xunzi dui Simeng 'Wuxing shuo' de Pipan" 荀子對思孟"五行"說的批判. *Chinese Culture Research* 2001 (Summer): 40–46.

Liao,Mingchun廖名春.*GuodianChujianLaozijiaoshi*郭店楚簡老子校釋. Beijing: Qinghua Daxue, 2003.

———. "Guodian Chujian Rujia Zhuzuo Kao" 郭店楚簡儒家著作考. *Kongzi Yanjiu*孔子研究 3 (1998): 69–83.

———. "Guodian Chujian 'Wuxing' pian jiaoshi Chaji" 郭店楚簡《五行》篇校釋札記. *Zhongguo Zhexueshi* 中國哲學史 3 (2001): 27–34.

———. "Guodian Chujian yu Shijing" 郭店楚簡與《詩經》. In Yao Xiaoou et al., 81–101.

———. "Jingmen Guodian Chujian yu Xianqin Ruxue" 荊門郭店楚簡 與先秦儒學 *Guodian Chujian yanjiu*. *Zhongguo zhexue* 20 郭店楚簡 研究《中國哲學》中國哲學(1999): 36–74.

Liu, Feng 劉豐. "Cong Guodian Chujian Kan Xianqin Rujia De 'ren nei Yi Wai' Shuo" 從郭店楚簡看先秦儒家的"仁內義外"說. *Hunan Daxue Xuebao Sheke Ban* 湖南大學學報: 社科版2 (2001): 36–40.

Liu, Xinfang劉信芳. "Jianbo 'Wuxing' Shudu Jiqi Xiangguan Wenti" 簡 帛《五行》慎獨及其相關問題. *Hubei Shifan Xueyuan Xuebao: Zheshe Ban*. 湖北師範學院學報:哲社版2 (2001): 37–40.

———. "Jianbo 'Wuxing' Shulue" 簡帛《五行》述略. *Jianghan Kaogu* 江 漢考古1 (2001): 71–77.

Liu, Yameng. "Three Issues in the Argumentative Conception of Early Chinese Discourse." *Philosophy East and West* 46.1 (1996): 33–59.

Liu, Zeliang 劉澤亮. "Cong Guodian Chujian Kan Xianqin Dao Ru Guanxi De Yanbian" 從郭店楚簡看先秦道儒關係的演變. *Hubei Daxue Xuebao (Zhexue Shehui Kexue Ban)* 湖北大學學報 (哲學社 會科學版) 2 (1999): 9–10.

Liu, Zuxin. "An Overview of Tomb Number One at Jingmen Guodian." In Allan and Williams, 23–32.

Lo, Yunhuan 羅運環. "Guodian Chujian De Niandai, Yongtu Ji Yiyi" 郭店楚簡的年代、用途及意義. *Hubei Daxue Xuebao (Zhexue She-hui Kexue Ban)* 湖北大學學報 (哲學社會科學版) 2 (1999): 13.

Loewe, Michael, ed. *Early Chinese Texts: A Bibliographical Guide*. Berkeley: Society for the Study of Early China, 1993.

Loewe, Michael, and Edward L. Shaughnessy, eds. *The Cambridge History of Ancient China: From the Origins of Civilization to 221 B.C.* Cambridge: Cambridge University Press, 1999.

Ma, Yuliang 馬育良. "Xianqin Rujia Duiyu 'Qing' de Lilun Tansuo" 先秦儒家對于 "情" 的理論探索. *Anhui Daxue Xuebao: Zheshe ban* 安徽大學學報 (哲社版) 1 (2001): 30–37.

Maeder, Erik W. "Some Observations on the Composition of the 'Core Chapters' of the *Mozi*." *Early China* 17 (1992): 27–82.

Makeham, John. "The Earliest Extant Commentary on *Lunyu*: *Lunyu Zheng shi zhu*." *T'oung Pao* 83.4–5 (1997): 260–99.

———. "The Formation of *Lunyu* as a Book." *Monumenta Serica* 44 (1996): 1–24.

————. "The Legalist Concept of *Hsing-ming*: An Example of the Contribution of Archeological Evidence to the Re-interpretation of Transmitted Texts." *Monumenta Serica* 39 (1990–91): 87–114.

————. *Name and Actuality in Early Chinese Thought*. Albany: State University of New York Press, 1994.

Moline, Jon. "Aristotle, Eubulides and the Sorites." *Mind*, n.s., 78.311 (1969): 393–407.

Møllgard, Eske J. "Confucian Enlightenment." *Early China* 19 (1994): 145–60.

Munro, Donald J. *The Concept of Man in Early China*. Stanford, Calif.: Stanford University Press, 1969.

————, ed. *Individualism and Holism: Studies in Confucian and Taoist Values*. Ann Arbor: Center for Chinese Studies, University of Michigan, 1985.

Nivison, David S. "The Dates of Western Chou." *Harvard Journal of Asiatic Studies* 43.2 (1983): 481–580.

————. "Mengzi as Philosopher of History." In Alan K. L. Chan, *Mencius*, 282–304.

————. *The Ways of Confucianism: Investigations in Chinese Philosophy*. Ed. Bryan W. Van Norden. Chicago: Open Court, 1996.

Pan, Xiaohui 潘小慧. "'Wuxingpian' de Renxue Chutan" 《五行篇》的人學初探. In Chen Fubin et al., 1:79–98.

Pang, Pu 龐樸. *Boshu Wuxingpian Yanjiu* 帛書五行篇研究. Jinan: Qilu, 1980.

————. "Gumu xinzhi—Mandu Guodian Chujian" 古墓新知—漫讀郭店楚簡. *Guoji ruxue lianhehui jianbao* 國際儒學聯合會簡報 2 (1998). Reprinted in *Dushu* 讀書 9 (1998); *Guodian Chumu yanjiu, Zhongguo zhexue* 20 (1999): 7–12; Pang Pu et al., *Gumu xinzhi*, 1–6. Also as "Gumu xinzhi: Guodian Chujian de jiazhi" 古墓新知: 郭店楚簡的價值 in *Jingmen Zhiye Jishu Xueyuan xuebao* 2 (2003): 1–5. Also as "New Information from an Old Tomb: Reading the Guodian Bamboo Strips." *Contemporary Chinese Thought* 32.1 (2000): 43–49.

————. "Kong Meng zhijian—Guodian Chujian de sixiang shi diwei" 孔孟之間—郭店楚簡的思想史地位. *Zhongguo shehui kexue* 5 (1998): 88–95. Reprinted as "Kongmeng zhijian—Guodian Chujian zhong de rujia xinxing shuo" 孔孟之間—郭店楚簡中的儒家心性說 in *Guodian Chujian yanjiu. Zhongguo zhexue* 20 (1999): 22–35. Also as "From Confucius to Mencius: The Confucian

Theory of Mind and Nature in the Guodian Chu Slips." *Contemporary Chinese Thought* 32.2 (2000–2001): 39–54.

———. "Simeng Wuxing xinkao" 思孟五行新考. In *Zhubo Wuxing pian jiaozhu ji yanjiu*, 133–43.

———. "Zhubo 'Wuxing' Pian Bijiao" 竹帛《五行》篇比較 *Guodian Chumu yanjiu. Zhongguo zhexue* 20 郭店楚簡研究 《中國哲學》第二十輯中國哲學第二十輯 (1999): 221–27.

———. *Zhubo "Wuxing" pian jiaozhu ji yanjiu* 竹帛《五行》篇校注及研究. Chutu wenxian yizhu yanxi congshu P009. Taipei: Wanjuanlou, 2000.

Pang, Pu et al. *Gumu xinzhi* 古墓新知. Chutu sixiang wenwu yu wenxian yanjiu congshu 10. Taipei: Taiwan guji, 2002.

Peerenboom, R. P. "Confucian Justice: Achieving a Humane Society." *International Philosophical Quarterly* 30.1 (1990): 17–32.

———. *Law and Morality in Ancient China: The Silk Manuscripts of Huang-Lao*. Albany: State University of New York Press, 1993.

Peng, Hao. "Guodian yihao mu de niandai yu jianben Laozi de jiegou" 郭店一號墓的年代與簡本《老子》的結構. *Daojia Wenhua Yanjiu* 17 (1999): 13–21.

Peterson, Willard J. "Squares and Circles: Mapping the History of Chinese Thought." *Journal of the History of Ideas* 49.1 (1988): 47–60.

Pian, Yuqian 駢宇騫 and Duan Shuan 段書安. *Ben shiji yilai chutu jianbo gaishu* 本世紀以來出土簡帛概述. Taipei: Wanjuanlou, 1999.

Pines, Yuri. *Foundations of Confucian Thought: Intellectual Life in the Chunqiu Period, 722–453* B.C.E. Honolulu: University of Hawai'i Press, 2002.

Poo, Mu-chou. *In Search of Personal Welfare: A View of Ancient Chinese Religion*. Albany: State University of New York Press, 1998.

Puett, Michael. *The Ambivalence of Creation: Debates Concerning Innovation and Artifice in Early China*. Stanford, Calif: Stanford University Press, 2001.

———. "The Ethics of Responding Properly: The Notion of *Qíng* 情 in Early Chinese Thought." In Eifring, 37–68.

Pulleyblank, Edwin G. *Outline of Classical Chinese Grammar*. Vancouver: University of British Columbia Press, 1995.

Ri Jōri 李承律. "Kakuten Sobo chikukan *Ro Bokuko mon Shishi* yakuchū" 郭店楚墓竹簡《魯穆公問子思》譯注. *Kakuten Sokan no shisoshiteki kenkyū* 1 (1999): 10–18.

————. "Kakuten sokan 'Tō Gu no michi' yakuchū" 郭店楚簡『唐虞之道』譯注. *Kakuten sokan no Kenkyū* 郭店楚簡の思想史研究 (Tōkyō: Daitō Bunka Daigaku Daigakuin Jimukyoku, 1999–2004), 52–104.

Richards, I. A. *Mencius on the Mind: Experiments in Multiple Definition*. New York: Harcourt, Brace, 1932.

Riegel, Jeffrey. "Eros, Introversion, and the Beginnings of Shijing Commentary." *Harvard Journal of Asiatic Studies* 57.1 (1997): 143–77.

————. "Poetry and the Legend of Confucius's Exile." *Sinological Studies Dedicated to Edward H. Schafer*, ed. Paul W. Kroll. *Journal of the American Oriental Society* 106.1 (1986): 13–22.

Roberts, Moss, trans. *Dao De Jing: The Book of the Way*. Berkeley: University of California Press, 2001.

Roetz, Heiner. *Confucian Ethics of the Axial Age: A Reconstruction under the Aspect of the Breakthrough toward Postconventional Thinking*. Albany: State University of New York Press, 1993.

Rubin, Vitaly A. "Wu hsing and Yin-yang." *Journal of Chinese Philosophy* 19.2 (1982): 131–55.

Ryan, James A. "A Defence of Mencius' Ethical Naturalism." *Asian Philosophy* 7.1 (1997): 23–36.

————. "Moral Philosophy and Moral Psychology in Mencius." *Asian Philosophy* 8.1 (1998): 47–64.

Saussy, Haun. "Repetition, Rhyme, and Exchange in the *Book of Odes*." *Harvard Journal of Asiatic Studies* 57.2 (1997): 519–42.

Schofer, Jonathan W. "Virtues in Xunzi's Thought." *Journal of Religious Ethics* 21 (1993): 117–36.

Schrecker, John. "Filial Piety as a Basis for Human Rites in Confucius and Mencius." *Journal of Chinese Philosophy* 24.3 (1997): 401–12.

Schwartz, Benjamin. "The Thought of the *Tao-te-ching*." In Kohn and LaFargue, 189–210.

Shaughnessy, Edward L., trans. *I Ching: The Classic of Changes. The First English Translation of the Newly Discovered Second-Century B.C. Mawangdui Texts*. Classics of Ancient China. New York: Ballantine, 1996.

————. ed. *New Sources of Early Chinese History: An Introduction to the Reading of Inscriptions and Manuscripts*. Berkeley, Calif.: Institute of East Asian Studies, 1997.

————. *Rewriting Early Chinese Texts*. Albany: State University of New York Press, 2006.

Shun, Kwong-loi. "*Jen* and *Li* in the *Analects.*" *Philosophy East and West* 43.3 (1993): 457–79.

———. *Mencius and Early Chinese Thought.* Stanford, Calif.: Stanford University Press, 1997.

———. "Mencius on *Jen-hsing.*" *Philosophy East and West* 47.1 (1997): 1–20.

Slote, Walter H., and George A. De Vos, eds. *Confucianism and the Family.* Albany: State University of New York Press, 1998.

Smith, Kidder [Jr.]. "Sima Tan and the Invention of Daoism, 'Legalism,' *et cetera.*" *Journal of Asian Studies* 62.1 (2003): 129–56.

Soles, David E. "The Nature and Grounds of Xunzi's Disagreement with Mencius." *Asian Philosophy* 9.2 (1999): 123–34.

Sun, Kaitai 孫開泰. "Guodian Chumu Zhujian 'Wuxing' pian jiaoshi"《郭店楚墓竹簡·五行》篇校釋. *Jianbo Yanjiu* 簡帛研究 (2001): 137–48.

Sung, Qifa 宋啟發. "Cong Lunyu dao 'Wuxing'—Kongzi Yu Zisi De Jidian Sixiang Bijiao" 從《論語》到《五行》—孔子與子思的幾點思想比較. *Anhui Daxue Xuebao (Zheshe ban)* 安徽大學學報（哲社版）5 (1999): 40–42.

Tsien, Tsuen-hsuin. *Written on Bamboo and Silk: The Beginnings of Chinese Books and Inscriptions.* Chicago: University of Chicago Press, 1962.

Tu, Wei-ming [i.e., Du, Weiming, q.v.]. *Centrality and Commonality: An Essay on Confucian Religiousness* (A revised and enlarged edition of *Centrality and Commonality: An Essay on Chung-yung*), Albany: State University of New York Press, 1989.

———. "Probing the 'Three Bonds' and 'Five Relationships.'" In Slote and De Vos, 121–36.

Tye, Michael. "Sorites Paradoxes and the Semantics of Vagueness." *Philosophical Perspectives* 8 (1994): 189–206.

Van Norden, Bryan W., ed. *Confucius and the Analects: New Essays.* Oxford: Oxford University Press, 2000.

———. "Hansen on Hsün-Tzu." *Journal of Chinese Philosophy* 20.3 (1993): 365–82.

———. "Mencius on Courage." *Midwest Studies in Philosophy* 21 (1997): 237–56.

———. "Mengzi and Xunzi: Two Views of Human Agency." *International Philosophical Quarterly* 32.2 (1992): 161–84.

von Falkenhausen, Lothar. "The Concept of *Wen* in the Ancient Chinese Ancestral Cult." *Chinese Literature: Essays, Articles, Reviews* 18 (1996): 1–22.

Wang, Baoxuan 王葆玹. "Guodian Chujian De Shidai Jiqi Yu Zisi Xue-pai De Guanxi" 郭店楚簡的時代及其與子思學派的關係. *Guodian Chujian Guoji Xueshu Yantaohui Lunwenji* 郭店楚簡國際學術研討會論文集, 644–49.

Wang, Bo 王博. "Guodian chujian zhong suojian de Ru Dao zhi guanxi" 郭店竹簡中所見的儒道之關係. In *Jianbo sixiang wenxian lunji*, 185–207.

———. *Jianbo sixiang wenxian lunji* 簡帛思想文獻論集. Ed. Ding Yuanzhi. Chutu sixiang wenwu yu wenxian yanjiu congshu 5. Tai-pei: Taiwan guji, 2001.

———. "Jingmen Guodian Zhujian yu Xianqin Rujia Jingxue" 荊門郭店竹簡與先秦儒家經學. *Zhongguo Chuantong Zhexue Xinlun—Zhu Bokun Jiaoshou Qishiwu Shouchen Jinien Wenji* 中國傳統哲學新論—朱伯崑教授七十五壽辰紀念文集.

Wang, Deyu 王德裕. "Cong Guodian Chumu Zhujian Lun Zisi" 從《郭店楚墓竹簡》論子思. *Chongqing Shiyuan Xuebao: Zheshe Ban* 重慶師院學報：哲社版 3 (2000): 7–11.

Watson, Burton, trans. *Mo Tzu Basic Writings*. New York: Columbia University Press, 1966.

Wei, Qipeng 魏啟鵬. *Chujian Laozi jianshi* 楚簡《老子》柬釋. Chutu wenxian yizhu yanxi congshu P003. Taipei: Wanjuanlou, 1999.

———. "Jianbo 'Wuxing' Jianshi" 簡帛《五行》箋釋. Chutu wenxian yizhu yanxi congshu P010 出土文獻譯注研析叢書. Taipei: Wan-juanlou, 2000.

Wilhelm, Richard, trans. *The I Ching or Book of Changes*. Translated into English by Cary F. Baynes. Princeton, N.J.: Princeton University Press, 1990.

Wright, Arthur F., ed. *Studies in Chinese Thought*. Midway reprint. Chicago: University of Chicago Press, 1953.

Xi, Panlin 席盤林. "Lun Zisi de Chendao Sixiang" 論子思的臣道思想. *Kongzi Yanjiu* 孔子研究 1 (2001): 64–73.

Xiao, Han 曉菡. "Changsha Mawangdui Hanmuboshu Gaishu" 長沙馬王堆漢墓帛書概述 *Wenwu Bao* 9 文物報 (1974): 40–44.

Xing, Wen. "Lun Guobian *Laozi* yu jinben *Laozi* bu shu yixi—Chujian *Taiyi shengshui* ji qi yiyi" 論郭店《老子》與今本《老子》不屬一系—楚簡《太一生水》及其意義. *Guodian Chujian yanjiu Zhongguo zhexue* 20 (1999): 165–86.

——— 邢文. "Mengzi 'Wanzhang' yu Chujian 'Wuxing'" 《孟子 • 萬章》與楚簡《五行》. *Guodian Chujian Yanjiu. Zhongguo zhexue* 20 郭店楚簡研究《中國哲學》中國哲學第二十輯 (1999): 228–42.

———. "Scholarship on the Guodian Texts in China: A Review Article." In Allan and Williams, 243–57.

Xu, Shaohua 徐少華. "Chujian Yu Boshu 'Wuxing'pian zhang jiegou jiqi xiangguan wenti."楚簡與帛書《五行》篇章結構及其相關問題.*Zhongguo zhexuesshi* 中國哲學史3 (2001): 12–19.

Yang, Rubin 樣儒賓. "Zisi xuepai shitan" 子思學派試探. *Guodian Chujian Guoji Xueshu Yantaohui Lunwenji* 郭店楚簡國際學術研討會論文集, 606–24.

Yao, Xiaoou 姚小鷗et al., eds. *Chutu wenxian yu Zhongguo wenxue yanjiu* 出土文獻與中國文學研究. Beijing: Beijing Guangbo Xueyuan, 2000.

Yates, Robin D. S., trans. *Five Lost Classics: Tao, Huang-Lao, and Yin-Yang in Han China*. Classics of Ancient China. New York: Ballantine, 1997.

Yearley, Lee H. "Hsün Tzu on the Mind: His Attempted Synthesis of Confucianism and Taoism." *Journal of Asian Studies* 39.3 (1980): 465–80.

———. *Mencius and Aquinas: Theories of Virtue and Conceptions of Courage*. Albany: State University of New York Press, 1990.

Yu, Jiyuan. "Virtue: Confucius and Aristotle." *Philosophy East and West* 48.2 (1998): 323–47.

Yu, Ying-Shih. "'O Soul, Come Back!' A Study in the Changing Conceptions of the Soul and Afterlife in Pre-Buddhist China." *Harvard Journal of Asiatic Studies* 47.2 (1987): 363–95.

Zhang, Liwen 張立文. "Luelun Guodian Chujian de 'Jenyi' Sixiang" 略論郭店楚簡的 "仁義"思想. *Kongzi Yanjiu* 孔子研究 1 (1999): 56–69.

———. "Lun jianben Laozi yu Rujia sixiang de Hubu Huji" 論簡本《老子》與儒家思想的互補互濟. *Daojia Wenhua Yanjiu* 道家文化研究 17 (1999): 131–48.

Zhang, Weihong 張衛紅. "'Shilun Wuxing' de chengde jinlu" 試論《五行》的成德進路 *Shihezi Daxue Xuebao Zhexue Shehui Kexue Bao* 3.4 (2003): 22–30.

Transmitted Sources

Cheng, Shude程樹德 (1877–1944). *Lunyu jishi* 論語集釋. Beijing: Zhonghua, 1990.

Daxue 大學, in *Li ji zhengyi*.

*Hanshi Waizhu*an 韓詩外傳. In Sibu Congkan. vol. 4 四部叢刊初篇縮本 第四. Taibei: Shangwu, 1967.

Jiao, Xun 焦循 (1763–1820). *Mengzi zhengyi* 孟子正義. In *Zhuzi Jicheng* 諸子集成. Beijing: Zhonghua, 1996.

Liang, Shuren 梁叔任. *Xunzi yue zhu* 荀子約注. Taibei: Shijie, 1966.

Liu, Baonan 劉寶楠 (1791–1855). *Lunyu zhengyi* 論語正義. In *Zhuzi Jicheng* 諸子集成. Beijing: Zhonghua, 1996.

Ruan, Yuan 阮元 (1764–1849). *Chunqiu Zuozhuan zhengyi* 春秋左傳正義. In *Shisanjing Zhushu* 十三經注書. 1815. Reprint, Taipei: Yiwen, 1960.

———. *Li ji zhengyi* 禮記正義. In *Shisanjing Zhushu* 十三經注書. 1815. Reprint, Taipei: Yiwen, 1960.

———. *Mao shi zhengyi* 毛詩正義. In *Shisanjing Zhushu* 十三經注書. 1815. Reprint, Taipei: Yiwen, 1960.

———. *Shang shu zhengyi* 尚書正義. In *Shisanjing Zhushu* 十三經注書. 1815. Reprint, Taipei: Yiwen, 1960.

———. *Zhou yi zheng yi* 周易正義. In *Shisanjing Zhushu* 十三經注書. 1815. Reprint, Taipei: Yiwen, 1960.

Sun, Yirang 孫詒讓 (1848–1908). *Mozi Jiangu* 墨子閒詁. In *Zhuzi Jicheng* 諸子集成. Beijing: Zhonghua, 1996.

Wang, Xianqian 王先謙 (1842–1918). *Xunzi Jijie* 荀子集解. In *Zhuzi Jicheng* 諸子集成. Beijing: Zhonghua, 1996.

Wang, Xianshen 王先慎 (1859–1922). *Hanfeizi Jijie* 韓非子集解. In *Zhuzi Jicheng* 諸子集成. Beijing: Zhonghua, 1996.

Yang, Shuda 楊樹達 (1885-1956). *Lunyu shu zheng* 論語疏證. Beijing: Kexue, 1955.

Zhongyong 中庸 in *Li ji zhengyi*.

Index

foundations of Chinese
government and, 130
harmonization of aristocracy and
meritocracy, 105
ideal balance of individual and
familial concerns, 21, 103
Mawangdui text and, 43–45,
152n53, 161n53, 161n55
Mencius and, 29–31, 38
on the physical existence of
morals, 12
politics of, 11, 103, 105–106, 110,
168n80
relation of *Laozi* and Confucius
in, 81
relevancy of texts to the dead and
the living, 23
religious goal of, 10, 12, 14, 33,
78, 106
Guodian (tomb)
closed during state of Chu, 141n3
tomb occupant at, 5
Guo Qiyong, 41

Han Dynasty
Goudian texts as alternative view
of Chinese thought, 8
importance of *The Five Aspects of
Conduct* during, 40–41
jia (schools) in, 142n11
Mawangdui texts dated to, 40
school-centric interpretation of
Chinese thought, 5, 6–8, 41
Hanfeizi, 50
heaven. See *tian*
Horgan, Terence, 53
Hsiao Kung-chuan, 80, 165n35
human nature.*See* xing
humanity
double sorites and, 94–96
contextualized by lineage, 21
familial love and, 136
family relations, 96
general meaning of, 39
internal and social, 99
legal application of, 35
leniency and, 138
political method and, 109–110
righteousness and, 102, 106
self-cultivation and, 36
various attributes of, 39

Ikeda Tomohisa
The Five Aspects of Conduct,
43, 145n22, 147n22, 156n23,
164n25, 170n19
Wuxing and, 51
Xunzi, 156n23

jade
analogous to progression from
wisdom to sagacity, 73
as musical, 57
described in the *Li Ji,* 57
humane thoughts and, 133
ritual importance of, 34
jian (admonishment), 111, 137–138,
143n12
Jiang Guanghui, 47

keen hearing. See also rhetoric
absence from *Mencius,* 74
moral transformation through, 9
noble man and, 135
Kun Chunyu, 49

Laozi, 7, 10
Buddhist influence on
interpretations of, 84
shared conception of unity with
Taiyi shengshui, 12
shutting the senses in, 86
transmitted version of, 41
view of opposites in, 78, 81–88
view of unity in, 79, 81–88
Lau, D.C., 72, 159n15, 166n48
Lewis, Mark Edward, 129, 168n81
Li Xueqin
on different versions of *The Five
Aspects of Conduct,* 43
relation of *The Five Aspects of
Conduct* and Zisi, 48
Shizi identified as Shishuo, 48
Liang Qichao, 50
Liao Mingchun, 44, 49, 144n17
Li Yun. See *Book of Rites*
Liu De
equation of humanity and
righteousness to family and
state, 35
circles of morality, 36
grouping of the six classics and
the Warring States period, 42